The Japanese Television Cartel

STUDIES IN INTERNATIONAL TRADE POLICY

Studies in International Trade Policy includes works dealing with the theory, empirical analysis, political, economic, legal relations, and evaluations of international trade policies and institutions.

General Editor: Robert M. Stern

John H. Jackson and Edwin A. Vermulst, Editors. *Antidumping Law and Practice: A Comparative Study*

John Whalley, Editor. *Developing Countries and the Global Trading System.* Volumes 1 and 2

John Whalley, Coordinator. *The Uruguay Round and Beyond: The Final Report from the Ford Foundation Project on Developing Countries and the Global Trading System*

John S. Odell and Thomas D. Willett, Editors. *International Trade Policies: Gains from Exchange between Economics and Political Science*

Alan V. Deardorff and Robert M. Stern. *Computational Analysis of Global Trading Arrangements*

Jagdish Bhagwati and Hugh T. Patrick, Editors. *Aggressive Unilateralism: America's 301 Trade Policy and the World Trading System*

Ulrich Kohli. *Technology, Duality and Foreign Trade: The GNP Function Approach to Modeling Imports and Exports*

Robert M. Stern, Editor. *The Multilateral Trading System: Analysis and Options for Change*

J. Michael Finger, Editor. *Antidumping: How it Works and Who Gets Hurt*

Stephen V. Marks and Keith E. Maskus, Editors. *The Economics and Politics of World Sugar Prices*

Horst Herberg and Ngo Van Long, Editors. *Trade, Welfare, and Economic Policies: Essays in Honor of Murray C. Kemp*

Edwin Vermulst, Paul Waer, and Jacques Bourgeios, Editors. *Rules of Origin: A Comparative Study*

David Schwartzman. *The Japanese Television Cartel: A Study Based on* Matsushita v. Zenith

The Japanese Television Cartel

A Study Based on *Matsushita v. Zenith*

David Schwartzman

Ann Arbor

THE UNIVERSITY OF MICHIGAN PRESS

Copyright © by the University of Michigan 1993
Published in the United States of America by
The University of Michigan Press
Manufactured in the United States of America

1996   1995   1994   1993   4   3   2   1

A CIP catalogue record for this book is available from the British Library.

Library of Congress Cataloging-in-Publication Data

Schwartzman, David.
    The Japanese television cartel : a study based on Matsushita v.
Zenith / David Schwartzman.
        p.   cm. — (Studies in international trade policy)
    Includes bibliographical references and index.
    ISBN 0-472-10454-3 (alk. paper)
    1. Television supplies industry—Japan.   2. Television supplies
industry—United States.   3. Dumping (International trade)—Japan.
4. Import quotas—United States.   I. Title.   II. Series.
HD9696.T463J365   1993
338.4'7621388'0952—dc20   93-31954
                                                                    CIP

STUDIES IN INTERNATIONAL TRADE POLICY

For Elie and Ann

Acknowledgments

This book, which germinated from my consultancy to plaintiffs in *Matsushita Electric Industrial Co. et al. v. Zenith Radio Corp. et al.*, has grown out of an accumulation of debts. I learned much working with plaintiffs' lead counsel, the late Edwin P. Rome, and National Union Electric's General Counsel, the late Morton P. Rome, good men and fine lawyers. Too, the work has benefited from the masses of documents, many of which had to be translated from Japanese, gathered by the staff of Blank, Rome, Comisky and McCauley, amd more particularly from my discussions with William H. Roberts and Arnold I. Kalman.

While I was writing the book manuscript, Bill Roberts refreshed my memory on certain aspects of the case, and John Borst, Jr., General Counsel of Zenith, and Vito Brugliera, were generous with their memories.

Horace J. DePodwin and Marcio Teixeira shared with me the preparation of the study of the Japanese television industry that became known as the DePodwin Report, which supports parts of chapters 5 and 6, as footnotes acknowledge. Notes also acknowledge the reports by plaintiffs' consultants, Economic Consulting Services Inc., Kozo Yamamura, Gary Saxonhouse, and John O. Haley.

Eleanor Fox, William T. Lifland, and William A. Montgomery read early drafts and rescued me from embarrassing errors on matters of law. F. M. Scherer, red pen in hand, forced me to sharpen the economic analysis. The merit of the economics also owes something to my disputatious colleagues at the New School, in particular David M. Gordon and Anwar M. Shaikh. Another person who helped me to hone the analysis is Jeffrey L. Kessler, a member of Matsushita's legal team, who, at a meeting of one of Mike Scherer's classes at the Kennedy School, debated with me the proposition that the Japanese television manufacturers acted as a cartel in the United States. In addition, Michael O. Moore and Terence P. Stewart were kind enough to discuss with me evidence of the extent of Japanese dumping in the United States.

Persefoni Tsaliki, Francisco Grullon, and Togu Opposunggu provided excellent research assistance. Karen Ray and Julie Barnes were dependable, loyal secretaries.

My wife, Gertrude, as always, cheerfully and with good humor endured my long hours at the desk.

Contents

Abbreviations

AVC	Average variable cost
AC	Average cost
BIA	Best information available
BOJ	Bank of Japan
CEPs	Consumer electronic products
CVD	Countervailing duty
EIAJ	Electronic Industries Association of Japan
FILP	Fiscal Investment and Loan Program
FTC	Federal Trade Commission
FTCJ	Fair Trade Commission of Japan
GAO	General Accounting Office
GATT	General Agreement on Tariffs and Trade
ITA	International Trade Administration
ITC	International Trade Commission
JMEA	Japan Machinery Exporters Association
JEPAL	Japanese Electronic Products Antitrust Litigation
LTFV	Less than fair value
MC	Marginal cost
MEI	Matsushita Electric Industrial Co.
MELCO	Mitsubishi Electric Corp.
MITI	Ministry of International Trade and Industry
MOF	Ministry of Finance
NUE	National Union Electric Corp.
OECD	Organization for Economic Cooperation and Development
OMA	Orderly Marketing Agreement
SCAP	Supreme Commander for the Allied Powers
VER	Voluntary Export Restraint

CHAPTER 1

Introduction

The Antitrust Case

In December 1970 National Union Electric Corporation (NUE) filed suit under Sections 1 and 2 of the Sherman Act, alleging that Matsushita Electric Industrial Company Ltd. (MEI), Hitachi Ltd., Toshiba Corporation, Sony Corporation, Sanyo Electric Co., Ltd., Sharp Corporation, and Mitsubishi Electric Corporation (MELCO) had conspired to restrain competition among themselves in the U.S. markets for television receivers and other consumer electronic products (CEPs), including radios, tape equipment, phonographs, stereo and audio instruments, and certain components of the CEPs.[1] The focus was on TV receivers. The American defendants were Sears Roebuck and Company and Motorola.[2] NUE alleged that the defendants had conspired to reduce prices in the U.S. and to eliminate some competitors. Zenith Radio Corporation joined the suit in 1974. In the lower courts the case was known as the *Japanese Electronic Products Antitrust Litigation* (JEPAL). When it came before the Supreme Court in 1984 it became known as *Matsushita et al. v. Zenith Radio et al.*

Before setting out to discuss *Matsushita,* it behooves me to apprise readers of my connection with the case. Together with Horace DePodwin and Marcio Teixeira, of Horace J. DePodwin Associates, the present author was retained by plaintiffs to prepare a study of the Japanese television receiver manufacturing industry, which was submitted to the U.S. District Court of the

---

1. Capacitors; coils, deflection yokes, and transformers; resistors, varistors, and termistors; speakers; voltage triplers; electron discharge devices, including cathode ray tubes, diodes, and receiving tubes; semiconductor products, including diodes, transistors, and integrated circuits; tuners for VHF and UHF television channels; and tape decks. (In re Japanese Electronic Products Antitrust Litigation, Zenith Radio Corp. et al. v. Matsushita Electric Industrial Co. Ltd. et al., 513 F. Supp. 1100 [1981] at 1316.)

2. Sears Roebuck owned 25 percent of the shares of Warwick Electronics Inc. In 1976 a subsidiary of Sanyo Electric Company acquired Warwick. Sears retained its share of the ownership. Motorola Inc., a manufacturer of consumer electronic products sold its TV manufacturing business and its "Quasar" trademark to MEI in 1974. (In re Japanese Electronic Products Antitrust Litigation, Zenith Radio Corp. et al. v. Matsushita Electric Industrial Co. Ltd. et al., 723 F.2d 238 [1983] at 251–52.)

Eastern District of Pennsylvania in September 1979 and which is referred to in the courts' opinions as the DePodwin Report.[3] What follows reflects this author's views and not necessarily those of the other co-authors of the DePodwin Report. Concerning the objectivity of the DePodwin Report, I hope that it lived up to the expectation that experts present a professional, impartial analysis. In addition, in the thirteen years that have elapsed since the study was done any bias that I may have had should have vanished.

The plaintiffs alleged that through a cartel the defendants exercised monopoly power in the Japanese TV market and so obtained monopoly profits with which to subsidize dumping in the U.S. TV market over an extended period. The cartel members also entered into price and market-sharing agreements that restricted competition among themselves in the U.S. market. By means of dumping and the market-sharing agreements, the defendants depressed prices in and took a large share of the U.S. market. The conspiracy embracing both the home and export markets, which violated Section 1 of the Sherman Act, injured the plaintiffs by depressing the prices they received and taking sales away from them.

The district court granted the defendants' pretrial motion for summary judgment on several grounds. Judge Edward R. Becker decided that the minimum-price and market-sharing rules, which tended to raise prices, did not harm the plaintiffs and that, in any case, the defendants did not observe the market-sharing agreement. Moreover, the defendants independently set lower export than domestic prices; they did not collude to discriminate in price between the two markets.

The Court of Appeals for the Third Circuit decided that, since the record created a genuine issue of material fact with respect to the alleged conspiracy, the District Court had broken with the traditional standard for summary judgments by substituting its own interpretation of the record for a jury's. However, the Third Circuit affirmed the District Court's decision with respect to Sony and the American defendants, Sears Roebuck and Motorola.

In 1986 the Supreme Court reversed the Third Circuit's decision with respect to the Japanese defendants, excluding Sony. The five-member majority decided that neither the alleged home market cartel nor the minimum-price and market-sharing agreements restricting competition among the defendants in the U.S. market injured the plaintiffs. In the Court's view injury could only

---

3. Horace J. DePodwin, David Schwartzman, and Marcio Teixeira, *Economic Study of the Japanese Television Industry* (prepared for plaintiffs' counsel in the Japanese Electronic Products Antitrust Litigation, M.D.L. 189, Civil Action Nos. 74-2451 and 74-3247, in the U.S. District Court for the Eastern District of Pennsylvania, September 1979 [hereafter referred to as DePodwin Report]).

have been caused by a conspiracy to price "predatorily." The Court decided that to establish a genuine issue of material fact and so reach a jury the plaintiffs had to demonstrate a conspiracy to monopolize the U.S. market through predatory pricing. But, since the prospects of achieving a U.S. monopoly were poor, the defendants could not reasonably have expected to recoup the predatory losses and earn monopoly profits. The critical element in the decision was the view that the plaintiffs' allegation implied large predatory losses, which could not be recouped even if the defendants achieved a monopoly, which itself was highly unlikely. Thus, after sixteen years in the courts the case never came to trial.

My own view is that the Japanese TV manufacturers conspired to take a large share of the U.S. market. Although the evidence may be interpreted as pointing to the goal of a U.S. monopoly, this interpretation is less certain. The important elements of the story of the Japanese cartel supporting my more modest conclusion refer first to the home market. The large differences between the home market and export prices over the period from 1966 through 1977, and possibly longer, attest to the existence of a cartel having monopoly power in the home market. I emphasize the extent of the differences, as reported in chapter 6. Without the cartel it is highly unlikely that the firms would have succeeded in charging home market prices, which were much higher than the export prices over a long period. There is also the evidence, revealed by investigations by the Fair Trade Commission of Japan (FTCJ), of meetings of several groups of manufacturers' representatives, which set prices and output quotas and exchanged information on outputs, shipments, and inventories.

Second, the manufacturers invested their home market monopoly profits in building capacity to supply the United States. The capacity grew far beyond the needs of the home market, and the United States was the major export market.

Third, there is evidence that between 1967 and 1970 the export prices were below the average total costs. The evidence indicates that the goal of a large U.S. market share was important enough to warrant carrying losses over this four-year period, if not longer.

Fourth, the TV manufacturers agreed to and observed two market-sharing rules. The Five-company Rule limited each manufacturer's direct U.S. customers, and the Antiraiding Rule prohibited a manufacturer from taking a direct customer away from another manufacturer once that manufacturer had supplied the customer. By limiting the losses due to competition among themselves, the rules enhanced the incentive to undertake a campaign to take customers away from U.S. manufacturers. The manufacturers might not have undertaken the campaign had they not agreed to these restrictions on their competition.

Fifth, the conspiracy inflicted injury on the plaintiffs. Without the cartel in the home market and the restrictive export agreements it is unlikely that the dumping margins—the differences between the home market and export prices—would have been as large as they were. The margins were as large as was necessary for the defendants to take the share of the market they did. The defendants acquired a large share of the U.S. market and depressed the prices received by U.S. manufacturers, including the plaintiffs.

Sixth, the Supreme Court's interpretation of the alleged persistent large differences between the home market and the export prices as predatory losses was mistaken. The plaintiffs' experts provided evidence of below-cost pricing of exports over a shorter period than the period of dumping, and the estimated differences between the average costs and the export prices were smaller than the differences between the home market and export prices.

Seventh, the Court's views on the likelihood of predatory pricing were based on an inappropriate analysis of the likelihood of such pricing by a dominant firm having a large share of a domestic market and whose immediate predatory losses therefore would far exceed those of its victims. In the present case, because of their initial small share of the U.S. market, the immediate losses of the Japanese manufacturers were smaller than those of the U.S. manufacturers.

Unfortunately, *Matsushita* has robbed the Sherman Act of any effectiveness it may have had against foreign-based predators. Effective protection under the antitrust laws will require new legislation.

The Antidumping Case

The major focus of this book is on *Matsushita,* but I will also examine the related proceedings under the 1921 Antidumping Law. Before NUE filed the antitrust suit, the U.S. television industry complained to the Commissioner of Customs that the Japanese TV manufacturers were dumping in the United States. It took the administration twelve years to settle the case, and the penalties for the Japanese manufacturers were trivial. The hostility of the Nixon, Ford, and Carter administrations to dumping complaints, which they regarded as protectionist and, therefore, inconsistent with their trade liberalization policy, were responsible for the delays and the small size of the penalties. Reluctance to antagonize the Japanese government also contributed.

Although the United States has not adopted a policy directed specifically at predation by foreign monopolists, the Antidumping Law should provide adequate protection. But the law was ineffective against dumping by the Japanese TV manufacturers. They took advantage of the cumbersome process of assessing antidumping duties and of the administration's refusal to enforce the law vigorously. Although the Department of Commerce appears to be administering the law more effectively now than the Treasury Department did in the 1960s and 1970s, Japanese manufacturers continue to dump products in the United States.

Policy Proposals

If the TV case were the only instance of a Japanese cartel dumping its products in the United States, it would be unfortunate, but it would not call for a national policy. There are reasons to believe, however, that other Japanese industries have behaved similarly. Despite the frequently lavish praise of Japan's industrial prowess, its companies do not vaunt low domestic prices. Also, since the defendants were giant, multiproduct conglomerates, it is scarcely credible that the middle-level TV executives alone planned and carried out a scheme for taking a large share of the U.S. market, and there is evidence that the same companies applied much the same scheme earlier in the radio market. Moreover, the necessary conditions of a tight cartel in both home and export markets for persistent, large domestic-export price differences are present in many Japanese industries. Many cartels operate in Japan. The enforcement of the Antimonopoly Law, which has never commanded strong political support, has been weak, and cartels enjoy the encouragement of the Ministry of International Trade and Industry (MITI). In addition, export cartels, which are not illegal in Japan, are associated with domestic cartels in many industries. Also, the defendants in *Matsushita* said in their own defense that MITI forced the manufacturers of many products to restrict competition in the export market. Finally, a long list of U.S. antidumping orders for Japanese products also supports the conclusion that cartels discriminate in price between the home and export markets.

This evidence suggests that the success of other Japanese industries, as well as that of the TV manufacturers, has been due in part to the combination of a cartel possessing monopoly power in the home market, restricting competition among its members in the U.S., dumping in the U.S. market, and taking some losses in that market.

The much more popular view of the success of Japanese manufacturers ignores the contribution of cartel restrictions combined with dumping and export prices below costs. The emphasis has been on Japan's productivity. Some economists who are worried about the future of American manufacturing, including the Nobel laureate economist Robert M. Solow, say that the problem is that U.S. productivity growth has slowed while Japan has maintained a high rate of productivity growth. The U.S. must regain its productive edge.[4] Solow and his associates on the Massachusetts Institute of Technology (MIT) Commission on Industrial Productivity blame the poor competitiveness of the U.S. automobile, consumer electronics, machine tool, copier, and other industries on problems within these industries.[5] They ascribe the success of Japanese electronics companies to their longer time horizons. The U.S. firms did not want to devote the resources to develop low-cost, reliable videocassette recorders (VCRs). The lesson is that American firms should be less greedy; they should have been willing to act on the prospect of distant rewards. Unlike the Japanese, they refused to invest heavily in product and process development for more than two decades while returns were low and growing slowly.

The Commission faults U.S. managers as follows:

> In the immediate postwar years they were complacent; they held stubbornly to an outmoded mass-production model; they set inappropriate financial goals; they relegated product realization and production engineering to second-class status; and they failed to make the investments in plant, equipment, and skills necessary for timely product development and efficient manufacturing.[6]

The U.S. government also gets a share of the blame. According to the Commission, the government has neglected the commercial development and application of new technologies. The U.S. should have more actively promoted research and technology for economic development. The government also should have invested more in education. As the report says: "As a result of this high common level of competence, new entrants to the Japanese work force are generally literate, numerate, and prepared to learn. In the U.S. work force, in contrast, employers have discovered high rates of illiteracy and difficulty with basic mathematics and reading in workers with high school diplomas."[7]

These conclusions, which are based on a study of the performance of a

---

4. Michael L. Dertouzos, Richard K. Lester, and Robert M. Solow and the MIT Commission on Industrial Productivity, *Made in America: Regaining the Productive Edge* (Cambridge, Mass.: MIT Press, 1989).

5. Dertouzos et al. acknowledge that the Japanese consumer electronics industry engaged in deliberate dumping to drive out U.S. competition and that, although in the 1960s TV receivers were sold in the home market at twice the price at which they were sold in the U.S., American manufacturers could not gain entry to Japan. The market was closed to imports. Nevertheless, the analysis of the success of the Japanese industry emphasizes R&D expenditures and innovation. Thus, the analysis is incomplete. If innovation was so important, then dumping would have been unnecessary. Cf. Dertouzos et al., *Made in America,* 217–25.

6. Dertouzos et al., *Made in America,* 77.

7. Dertouzos et al., *Made in America,* 85.

sample of industries, agree with the popular view, which hails Japanese successes generally as miracles of industriousness, good management, good design, and, above all, great patience. Applauding Japan's executives for acting on distant objectives, Lester Thurow and Robert Reich hold them up as models to their impatient, greedy counterparts in this country. American managers' agitation about this quarter's earnings contrasts with Japanese executives' relaxed attitude toward the stock market's reaction to current profits.[8] Unlike U.S. businesses, those in Japan raise money from the banks, which take a more long-range view than the stock market. The Japanese have even become, in the eyes of economists, frugal puritans, who invest much of their income.

Thurow, Reich, and Solow and his associates urge policies to improve the productivity of U.S. manufacturing. They neither urge a change in the policy of trade liberalization nor more vigorous prosecution of the antidumping laws against Japanese exporters. Nor do they believe that Japanese cartels present a special problem for U.S. industries.

Success usually has several sources, and the gains in productivity of Japanese businesses cannot be denied. But in the TV manufacturing industry and possibly in other industries the story is more complex, and the sources of the triumph may have been less salutary than Japan's admirers believe. Moreover, if Japanese industries have dumped their products in the U.S., then superior productivity, low costs, and superior competitiveness cannot completely account for the growth of Japan's exports to the U.S. Dumping means that the Japanese could not gain as large a share of the U.S. markets as they did with export prices equal to their home market prices. As we will see, the differences between the home market and export prices have been large enough in the case of many industries to suggest that the story of their export success has been less salutary than their American admirers believe.

A change in national policy may have to await studies of other successful Japanese industries to determine the importance of dumping and cartel restrictions in the growth of their exports. If other Japanese industries' growth also was the result of preying on U.S. industries, then the U.S. should move to provide some protection. The Antidumping Law should be sufficient to protect U.S. industries against predation. Yet, as chapter 2 reports, Japanese manufacturers continue to dump their products in the U.S.

The Sherman Act might be another instrument. The threat of treble damage awards may be more effective than the antidumping duties. Because of *Matsushita*, however, effective protection under the antitrust laws will

8. Robert B. Reich, *The Next American Frontier: A Provocative Program for Economic Renewal* (New York: New York Times Books, 1983); Lester C. Thurow, *The Zero-Sum Solution: An Economic and Political Agenda for the 80s* (New York: Simon & Schuster, 1985).

require new legislation. This book advocates a special price standard. Foreign monopolists should be found to have violated the law if their export prices are persistently below their home market prices. The same standard that is used by the Department of Commerce in dumping cases should be applied by the courts in antitrust cases involving foreign monopolists. The law against predation generally is weak, partly because the Supreme Court in *Matsushita* deemed it to be rare and was afraid of dampening competition. The Court may be right about predation by dominant U.S. firms in their home markets. But the risk of predation by foreign monopolists, and more particularly by Japanese cartels, in the U.S. appears to be greater than the risk of predation generally. Thus, foreign monopolists should face a more severe standard for predatory pricing than U.S. firms. The proposal does not call for any foreign firm to be found in violation of the antitrust laws if it should export at prices below its home market prices. Plaintiffs would have to establish that the defendants, where there are several, have monopoly power in their home market and operate a cartel in the U.S. market as well as that the export prices are below the home market prices. Others who fear the spread of the power of Japanese cartels less than I do may prefer the less strict standard of average cost. A decision about the appropriate policy may have to await further study of the sources of Japan's export achievements.

CHAPTER 2

Market Conditions

Despite Japan's astonishingly speedy recovery from the war, completed as early as 1952, the development task remained huge. With a per capita GNP of only $188, compared to $2,181 in the U.S., $643 in West Germany, $870 in the U.K., $947 in France, and $359 in Italy, Japan was a less-developed country. Even Brazil, Malaysia, and Chile ranked ahead.[1] Undervaluation of the yen may account for part of the difference but not all of it. As in other less developed countries, the farm population was large and underemployed, and a backward technology and a small capital stock kept labor productivity in manufacturing far below that of the industrial West. By 1972 the Japanese surpassed the U.K. and Italy in per capita GNP, but in the early 1950s they had a long way to go.

MITI began to implement an industrial policy even before the end of the occupation in 1953 by subsidizing a few favored firms in selected industries and protecting them against imports. The favoritism, which concentrated output among a few firms, was critical for the emergence of the TV cartel. A few firms could more easily recognize and act on their mutual interest in maintaining high prices than many. Although it was central to the industrial policy, the practice of subsidizing a few selected firms was neither new nor invented by MITI. The policy of identifying the national interest with the objective of growth and therefore with the interests of particular enterprises began in the late nineteenth century. Japan has joined the rich nations' club, but the drive for growth continues. Before World War II the primary goal was military power, in the immediate postwar years it was recovery, and now growth itself appears to have become a permanent goal. Favoritism has been an aspect of the policy throughout.

Proponents of a U.S. industrial policy look to MITI as their model. While I do not pretend to have a complete explanation of the ministry's achievements, a clear, simple goal and the support of the Liberal Democratic party (LDP), not to mention that of the chosen industries, gave the ministry

---

1. Hugh Patrick and Henry Rosovsky, "Japan's Economic Performance: An Overview," in *Asia's New Giant: How the Japanese Economy Works,* ed. Hugh Patrick and Henry Rosovsky (Washington, D.C.: Brookings Institution, 1976), 4, 11.

great strength. Growth was virtually the sole objective; inequities or consumer interests gave little trouble. The unfavored firms opposed the policy, but they lacked power; firms that did not come into existence had none; and the opposition of consumers was both diffuse and sporadic. The pivotal part of the plan was to grant huge low-interest loans to the selected manufacturers while at the same time starving other companies of credit. It is hard to exaggerate the importance of the unique, unprecedented combination of selectivity and tight money, which was the foundation of the postwar economic policy and the source of many not obviously related industrial developments.

Monopoly power was one of the consequences. Without the discriminatory credit policy new entrants, attracted by the smell of high profits, would have destroyed any nascent monopoly, and the selectivity also ensured a high degree of concentration. Another consequence were the *keiretsu*. In the general credit crunch firms needed friendly connections with the city banks, the intermediaries between the central bank and the borrowers. The economy became a market for favors, the exchanges being made in the clubs of companies known as *keiretsu*, which were linked to a bank.

The *keiretsu* grew in the fertile soil of the long heritage of government favoritism. Refraining from directly managing enterprises, governments long had nurtured individual companies with indirect controls and subsidies. After the Meiji Restoration in 1868 government and business became closely entwined. Since industries furnished the essential underpinning of strong, modern armed forces, the government pioneered the development of railroads, communication facilities, mining, and shipbuilding. However, in 1880, surrendering direct control, the political leaders sold the public enterprises at bargain prices to their wealthy friends.

The bestowal of trained workers and low-cost, modern equipment provided a wonderful start for the financial and industrial empires, known as *zaibatsu*.[2] The *zaibatsu*—Mitsubishi and Mitsui are the familiar names of two of the earliest—usually were controlled by a family through a holding company. Viewed today, the *zaibatsu* were a strange feudal-capitalist mixture of familial authoritarianism and modern business practices. While employees pledged fealty to the *zaibatsu* family head, the groups employed the modern technique of acquiring companies through a holding company. They grew to enormous size in diverse markets. The Mitsubishi *zaibatsu* was prominent in heavy industry, shipbuilding, marine transportation, and plate glass and the Mitsui *zaibatsu* in the paper, coal, and synthetic dye industries.[3] However,

2. M. Y. Yoshino, *Japan's Managerial System: Tradition and Innovation* (Cambridge, Mass.: MIT Press, 1965), 20–21.

3. K. Bieda, *The Structure and Operation of the Japanese Economy* (Sydney: John Wiley and Sons, 1979), 208–9.

despite the privatization, the government's powerful influence endured. Eager for large government orders, big business was submissive to the political and military leadership.[4] This history was repeated after World War II, when similar favoritism contributed to the conception of the *keiretsu*, the successors of the *zaibatsu*.

Industrialization was accompanied by political struggles, which undermined the authoritarian government and the power of the *zaibatsu*. Along with large, wealthy firms came masses of not always happy factory workers in urban centers. There were many labor disputes, in the early 1920s new liberal movements arose, and in 1925 men won the vote. However, a strong, autocratic tradition persisted, and a conservative reaction inspired laws limiting speech and political action. Economic maladjustments fueled the reaction, augmenting the influence of the *zaibatsu*. In the early 1930s the government could not cope with the high unemployment induced by the worldwide depression. Allied to the reactionaries, military officers took power, and, despite mutual suspicion, the *zaibatsu* and the army cooperated. According to Edwin Reischauer, to guard the *zaibatsu* interests the army suppressed popular radicalism and the labor movement, and in return the *zaibatsu* tolerated the army's imperial ambitions. The imperialism was not entirely unwelcome, for the conquest of Manchuria presented the *zaibatsu* with great economic opportunities. For its part the army recognized that the *zaibatsu* were essential for the exploitation of Manchuria and the development of heavy industry. In the 1930s, as the government took more control over strategic industries, the ties between the *zaibatsu* and the state became even tighter.[5]

The close ties persisted into the postwar period. The government took an active part in determining the course of development, and, as in the prewar period, it favored the leading companies.

The Government's Growth Strategy

In 1952 production reached a level 15 percent above the 1934–36 level,[6] but rapid expansion continued. Some writers place the end of the high-growth period in the mid-1970s,[7] others at 1963.[8] The Korean War induced some

---

4. Yoshino, *Japan's Managerial System*, 21.

5. Edwin D. Reischauer, *The United States and Japan*, 3d ed. (New York: Viking Press, 1962), 178–204.

6. Edward F. Denison and William K. Chung, "Economic Growth and Its Sources," in Patrick and Rosovsky, *Asia's New Giant*, 73.

7. Koichi Hamada and Akiyoshi Horiuchi, "The Political Economy of the Financial Market," in *The Political Economy of Japan*, vol. 1: *The Domestic Transformation*, ed. Kozo Yamamura and Yasukichi Yasuba (Stanford, Calif.: Stanford University Press, 1987), 223.

8. Yoshino, *Japan's Managerial System*, 33.

expansion, but rapid growth did not stop with the war's end. Between 1956 and 1963 the average annual rate of increase of real GNP exceeded 10 percent, which was much higher than that for any other industrialized country. Between 1959 and 1961, when growth peaked, gross capital formation was 32.5 percent of the GNP, compared to 16.3 percent in the United States.[9]

Japan enjoyed the advantage over other less developed countries of a well-educated labor force, comparable to that of Western Europe. In 1950 the average number of years of schooling of employed males was 8.15, compared to 8.09 in France, 7.93 in Germany, and 9.16 in the U.K. The U.S. was somewhat ahead with an average of 9.68.[10] Japan also was rich in managerial, organizational, scientific, and engineering skills, ready to acquire advanced foreign technology.[11] However, partly because of the wartime destruction, its capital stock was small, and the technology was backward in most industries.[12]

The large, underutilized agricultural labor force provided a plentiful supply of labor for rapid industrial growth. The rise in wages and thus in prices was slowed. Agriculture's share of the labor force dropped from 41.9 percent in 1956 to 17.4 percent in 1971, while manufacturing's share increased from 17.7 percent to 27.2 percent.[13] Until 1972 wage increases did not exceed the growth of productivity.[14] The utilization of scale economies also enhanced growth. In 1971 manufacturing firms with one thousand or more workers employed 28.2 percent of the manufacturing labor force and produced 42.9 percent of the gross value added.[15] While part of the gain in productivity apparently due to size was based on capital equipment and labor quality, the gain from economies of scale may have been large.

We will assume that, being aware of Japan's economic strengths and weaknesses, MITI adopted the following growth plan, which may be close to the truth. The ministry did have a hand in directing government policies. Initially, the plan was to subsidize a few basic industries, including electric power, coal, steel, and shipping. In the second stage, beginning in 1955, industries that had grown in the industrialized West, including steel, machinery, electronics, synthetic fibers, chemicals, fertilizers, automobiles, and sew-

9. Yoshino, *Japan's Managerial System,* 32–33.

10. Denison and Chung, "Economic Growth and Its Sources," 110, table 2.15; Edward F. Denison, *Why Growth Rates Differ: Postwar Experience in Nine Western Countries* (Washington, D.C.: Brookings Institution, 1967), 107, table 8.12.

11. Patrick and Rosovsky, "Japan's Economic Performance," 12.

12. Patrick and Rosovsky, "Japan's Economic Performance," 11, 17.

13. Patrick and Rosovsky, "Japan's Economic Performance," 17, table 1.2; U.S. percentage estimated from *Historical Statistics of the United States,* pt. 1, ser. D 167, D 170.

14. Patrick and Rosovsky, "Japan's Economic Performance," 17.

15. Patrick and Rosovsky, "Japan's Economic Performance," 22.

ing machines, were to be favored. The list also included cotton spinning, cameras, textiles, and shipbuilding, in which Japan had been strong.[16] MITI also decided to promote the utilization of the economies of scale by supporting only a few firms in each industry.

MITI would make certain that the selected firms would get large low-interest loans, and to prevent inflation the total credit available would be restricted. Also, to encourage the utilization of scale economies MITI would keep imports small. Moreover, through its control over foreign exchange the ministry would allow the chosen companies to acquire licenses cheaply to foreign technology.

Giving consumers short shrift, MITI would tolerate collusion by manufacturers to maintain prices and market shares. The beneficiaries were expected to invest their monopoly profits in new machinery and to increase the scale of their plants. The profits would also finance sales efforts abroad and even more expansion.

Industrial policy proponents would promote those industries that employ skilled, highly paid workers and whose firms earn high profits, but these precepts did not guide the decision to nurture TV manufacturing. Neither the average skill of workers nor the level of profits of the U.S. industry was high. In 1966 the average hourly compensation of production workers in the electrical machinery, equipment, and supplies industry, which includes TV manufacturing, was $3.23 per hour,[17] compared to the not significantly different compensation of $3.30 for production workers in all manufacturing.[18] Another sign that the workers were not highly skilled was the decision by the Japanese companies to shift manufacturing to Taiwan and Mexico. Concerning profitability, in the late 1960s, when the Japanese industry expanded its capacity greatly to supply the U.S., profits in the U.S. industry were low. Of the fourteen TV manufacturers that submitted profit-and-loss information to the U.S. Tariff Commission for 1966–70, six sustained operating losses in 1967, nine in 1968, six in 1969, and ten in 1970.[19]

The industry probably was a prime candidate, because the technology was already developed, and MITI expected both the home and export sales to grow rapidly. In addition, low wages gave the Japanese TV manufacturers an advantage over their U.S. competitors. The Bureau of Labor Statistics esti-

16. International Trade Commission (ITC), *Foreign Industrial Targeting and Its Effect on U.S. Industries, Phase 1: Japan*, ITC Publication No. 1437, October 1983, 51.

17. U.S. Tariff Commission, *Television Receivers and Certain Parts Thereof*, TC Publication No. 436, November 1971, A-75, table 26.

18. Bureau of Labor Statistics, *Handbook of Labor Statistics, 1975—Reference Edition*, Bulletin No. 1865, 309, table 119.

19. U.S. Tariff Commission, *Television Receivers*, A-37.

mated that the average hourly compensation in Japan in 1966 was $0.51 per hour,[20] compared to $3.23 in the U.S. MITI may not have known at the outset that, as chapter 6 shows, the low-wage advantage was insufficient to allow the industry to take a large part of the U.S. market without selling at prices below cost.

Monetary Policy

The two-pronged monetary policy included a credit crunch and supplying the available credit to promising companies. The policy, which did not bloom suddenly from an inventive mind, developed during the Korean War boom, when manufacturers were scrounging for funds to finance new plants to supply the burgeoning American demand. The Bank of Japan (BOJ), which controlled the money supply and charged the commercial banks a much lower interest rate than other sources of funds, could and did force the banks to keep their deposit rates at artificially low levels. Because other financial instruments were unavailable, the policy effectively imposed a tax on depositors. The BOJ also had legal authority to control interest rates under the Temporary Interest Rate Adjustment Law of 1947, requiring banks to set the short-term prime rate at a fixed margin above the official discount rate.

In 1954 the BOJ began to share its authority with the Ministry of Finance (MOF) and MITI. These agencies worked closely with the major banks, whose policies they regulated, and also with the large borrowers. The large private firms were not simply regulated subjects but took part in implementing the policy. There was no pretense of consulting with representatives of all businesses; those consulted were a select group. Together with this group, the agencies decided the life-and-death issue for businesses of who would get credit. Representatives of the agencies and the private companies met in the Bond Issue Committee, the Financial Institutions Council, and MITI's Industrial Finance Committee. This last committee's important function was to approve major industries' investment and related finance plans.[21] Not until 1979 was the regulation of financial markets eased, and foreign capital controls were relaxed as late as the following year. Only after that year did the formerly favored companies have to pay market-determined interest rates. Credit to other firms is no longer severely restricted. The BOJ, however, can still apply pressure through the banks.[22]

As with any effective price ceiling, because the demand exceeded the supply, the interest rate ceiling entailed selecting buyers—in this case

---

20. U.S. Tariff Commission, *Television Receivers,* A-75, table 26.

21. Hamada and Horiuchi, "The Political Economy of the Financial Market," 236.

22. ITC, *Foreign Industrial Targeting,* 80, 82–83.

borrowers—from among an eager queue. Many potential borrowers, including thousands of retailers, whose inventories the banks traditionally financed, and who would gladly have paid higher interest rates, were left stranded. On the other hand, the banks accumulated huge negative balances with the BOJ, and their clients' debts mounted to very high levels.[23]

Blocking access to foreign capital more directly, the Law Concerning Foreign Investment limited foreign ownership of any company to 49 percent. After 1973 foreigners were permitted to take complete ownership, but the government took care to exclude them from specific industries. Foreign investment remained small.[24]

As a result, businesses received the bulk of their funds for investment from the large city banks. Between 1958 and 1962 these institutions supplied an annual average of 70.1 percent of credit to nonfinancial corporations. Equity financing supplied 16.6 percent, bonds 5.6 percent, foreign loans 1.9 percent, and government funds, which included those obtained from postal savings accounts, 7.8 percent.[25] In later years equity financing's share declined by more than half, and that of government funds increased. City banks continued to supply by far the major portion of financing.

The government assisted the preferred companies' investments in R&D and in the acquisition of foreign technology with direct grants and long-term, low-interest loans.[26] The funds came from the postal savings system through the Fiscal Investment and Loan Program (FILP).[27] In addition, in 1957 the Provisional Measures Law Concerning the Promotion of the Electronic Industry, which was effective until 1969, provided tax exemptions for the costs of developing overseas markets, permitted depreciation allowances for increased exports, and provided financial assistance for investment to develop selected products.[28]

The restrictions gave the favored companies monopoly power. With low-cost loans unavailable little-known companies could not sell their bonds and equity shares. When deprived businesses protested bitterly through members of the Diet, the head of MITI, Ikeda Hayato, forcefully recognized the costs in 1952: "It makes no difference to me if five or ten small businessmen are

---

23. Chalmers Johnson, *MITI and the Japanese Miracle: The Growth of Industrial Policy, 1925–1975* (Stanford, Calif.: Stanford University Press, 1982), 198–203.

24. Lawrence B. Krause and Sueo Sekiguchi, "Japan and the World Economy," in Patrick and Rosovsky, *Asia's New Giant*, 444–46.

25. Hamada and Horiuchi, "The Political Economy of the Financial Market," 239, table 8.

26. James E. Millstein, "Decline in an Expanding Industry: Japanese Competition in Color Television," in *American Industry in International Competition: Government Policies and Corporate Strategies,* ed. John Zysman and Laura Tyson (Ithaca, N.Y.: Cornell University Press, 1983), 113.

27. Ytaka Kosai, "The Politics of Economic Management," in Yamamura and Yasuba, *Political Economy of Japan,* vol. 1: *Domestic Transformation,* 584–85.

28. Millstein, "Decline in an Expanding Industry," 113.

forced to commit suicide." His frankness cost Ikeda his job, but the government remained firm.[29]

The discriminatory credit policy may have fostered high concentration, thereby encouraging collusion, more than technological scale economies.[30] The high debt-equity ratios resulting from the monetary policy also promoted collusion by increasing the beneficiaries' aversion to risks, including those of competition. Collusion was less risky than competition.[31] According to Gary Saxonhouse, the average debt-equity ratio of large Japanese manufacturing corporations in 1974 was 4.6 compared to 0.88 in the U.S.[32] More specifically, Saxonhouse reported that the Japanese TV manufacturers had much higher debt-equity ratios than Zenith Radio. Between 1960 and 1970 the average debt-equity ratio of MEI, Sanyo, Sony, Hitachi, Toshiba, MELCO, and Sharp was almost 2.2, or more than three times the average for Zenith.[33]

Another source of high fixed costs in large corporations, and thus of the proclivity to collude, is the large companies' system of permanent employment. After a probationary period an employee cannot be discharged or even laid off in periods of low demand or because of poor performance. Retirement at the age of fifty-five is mandatory for most workers in large corporations.[34] Sources of cost flexibility are limited. Wages and even bonuses appear to be independent of changes in sales. In some industries, when they have more orders than their own employees can fill, firms turn to smaller subcontractors, which have less rigid costs. Reducing orders to subcontractors at other times, however, raises the large firms' average costs, since their own workers are paid higher wages.[35]

High fixed costs also may influence international competitive behavior. Chapter 4 shows that to eliminate competitors in export markets a cartel may reduce its export prices below their average variable costs (*AVC*). The variable costs are those costs that vary with output, including raw materials, fuel, and power. In the U.S. it usually includes at least part of the cost of labor, since firms may lay off or fire employees when they reduce output. In Japan the high debt-equity ratio results in fixed costs accounting for a large proportion of

29. Johnson, *MITI and the Japanese Miracle,* 202.

30. Richard E. Caves and Masu Uekusa, *Industrial Organization in Japan* (Washington, D.C.: Brookings Institution, 1976), 40.

31. Caves and Uekusa, *Industrial Organization in Japan,* 40.

32. Gary R. Saxonhouse, "The Impact of Japanese Financial and Employment Practices on Japanese Production, Marketing, and Price Behavior" (prepared for plaintiffs in Japanese Electronic Products Antitrust Litigation, M.D.L. 189, September 1979, 15, app. table 1 [hereafter referred to as Saxonhouse Report]). Saxonhouse cites the Mitsubishi Research Institute, *Analysis of Enterprise Performance* (Kigyo keiei no bunseki).

33. Saxonhouse Report, 4, app. table 4.

34. Walter Galenson and Konosuke Odaka, "The Japanese Labor Market," in Patrick and Rosovsky, *Asia's New Giant,* 614–15.

35. Caves and Uekusa, *Industrial Organization in Japan,* 41.

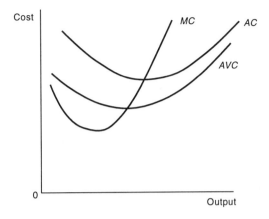

Fig. 2.1. The cost curves

total costs. The permanent employment system has the same effect. Owing to high fixed costs, the cartel members' *AVC* (fig. 2.1), including transportation costs, may be less than the prey's *AVC*, while their average costs (*AC*) are no lower.[36] The monetary policy may have influenced the Japanese TV manufacturers' prices by raising their fixed costs and thus reducing the ratio of variable to total costs.

The *Keiretsu*

Like the earlier *zaibatsu*, the *keiretsu* included banks, other financial intermediaries (such as insurance companies), and general trading companies, as well as manufacturing, mining, and other goods producers. In the early stages of each industry, the *keiretsu* entered, organizing and assembling large quantities of capital and other resources. Their *keiretsu* attachments facilitated the major companies' efforts to organize cartels and gain monopoly power. Without such links potential entrants had even less access to capital than the monetary stringency alone caused.

---

36. Average variable cost equals total variable cost divided by output. Total cost is the sum of total fixed and total variable cost, and average cost is total cost divided by output. Marginal cost (*MC*) equals the change in total cost resulting from a unit change in output. Since fixed costs do not change with output, *MC* equals the change in total variable cost resulting from a unit change in output. At low levels of output increases bring about a reduction in *AVC*, and at higher levels *AVC* rises with output. The shape of *AC* is similar, but, because it includes fixed costs, the minimum is reached at a higher output than the minimum for *AVC*. At low levels of output *MC* also descends as output increases and then increases at a faster rate than *AVC*. At high outputs *MC* exceeds *AVC*. Moreover, the difference between *AC* and *AVC* at any output will increase with the size of fixed costs.

Bank connections being vital, companies courted the banks. By relaxing market discipline and thus adding to buyers' and sellers' discretionary power, the credit policy lay the seeds for the *keiretsu*, just as government subsidies had for the *zaibatsu*. The *keiretsu* facilitated exchanges of favors by limiting the circle of traders, and the long-term relationships fostered by the *keiretsu* reduced the banks' costs of assessing credit worthiness and monitoring performance. On the borrowers' side the credit crunch made the *keiretsu* connections essential.

Some *keiretsu* were simply reconstituted *zaibatsu*. Seeking to impose a competitive economy, the Supreme Commander for the Allied Powers (SCAP) ordered the dissolution of the *zaibatsu* and the banning of holding companies. Also, they had sinned by supporting the militarist government that had invaded China and attacked Pearl Harbor. With the return of self-government the *zaibatsu*, now called *keiretsu*, were resurrected in modified form, and new ones were founded.

The *keiretsu* are not controlled by a family, and the holding company remains illegal. Since common directors, mutual ownership of shares, and presidents' clubs expedite agreement on joint policies, the loss of the holding company is no great hardship. The presidents' clubs have actively protected individual *keiretsu* members, as when the Mitsui club blocked a takeover of the Mitsui Mining Company. In the early 1970s the Sumitomo *keiretsu* saved Mazda from bankruptcy when the company had trouble with its rotary engine. The linked banks provided funds, and other *keiretsu* members employed its laid-off workers; they bought Mazda's products, and they sold supplies to the company on favorable terms.[37] An example of intervention in individual companies' affairs is the Sumitomo *keiretsu*'s taking control of Japan Sheet Glass to improve its performance.[38] When a large company dominates a *keiretsu*, a presidents' club is unnecessary. Toshiba's operations department helps manage the related firms.[39] In some groups a bank and a trading company, which buys supplies for the members and sells their products, are the central institutions.[40]

37. Clyde V. Prestowitz, Jr., *Trading Places: How We Are Giving Our Future to Japan and How to Reclaim It* (New York: Basic Books, 1989), 298.

38. Misonou Hitoshi et al., *Kokumin no dokusen hakusho: Kigyo shudan* (People's White Paper on Monopolies: Economic Groups (Tokyo: Ochanomizu Shobo, 1978), 45. Cited by Kozo Yamamura, "The Pervasive Use of Collusive and Company Group (Keiretsu) Activities in Achieving the Rapid Increase in Japanese Exports of Television Receivers to the United States" (prepared for plaintiffs in Japanese Electronic Products Antitrust Litigation, M.D.L. 189, 44 [hereafter referred to as Yamamura, "Pervasive Use"]).

39. Tokyo Shibaura Electric Co., *Toshiba Hyakunenshi* (A Hundred-Year History of Toshiba) (Tokyo: Diamond Publishing Co., 1977), 122. Cited by Yamamura, "Pervasive Use," 45–46.

40. Bieda, *The Structure and Operation of the Japanese Economy,* 208–9.

Large intercompany shareholdings provide additional assurance of a cohesive policy. In 1974 the average percent of shares of members of the Mitsubishi, Mitsui, Sumitomo, Fuyo, Daiichi Kangyo Bank, and Sanwa *keiretsu* owned by other members was 22.6. Ownership by a single company of a large proportion of the shares of members assures unity even more. Hitachi owned between 20 and 60 percent of the shares of the thirty-five or so key members of its *keiretsu*, and for MEI the percentage usually was between 30 and 75.[41] Sanyo, Sharp, and Sony usually owned all the shares of their *keiretsu* members.[42]

The *keiretsu* members could raise the required sums of capital for risky large investments, and, according to the FTCJ, each *keiretsu* sought to enter each major industry.[43] The tendency to build such a set of companies has become well enough recognized to be labeled "one-setism." Between 1955 and 1965 several *keiretsu* entered the nuclear energy and petrochemical industries, and between 1967 and 1975 several entered the housing, leisure activity, and information industries.[44] The Mitsui, Mitsubishi, and Sumitomo *keiretsu* formed three of the four early petrochemical complexes. Twenty-three major Mitsubishi industrial and financial firms jointly established Mitsubishi Atomic Energy Industries Ltd., thirty-seven Mitsui-related companies together formed Nippon Atomic Energy Industry Ltd., and seventeen Sumitomo *keiretsu* firms established an atomic energy enterprise.[45]

Another source of *keiretsu* strength is the market power of the trading companies, which also comes from access to funds. Not only do they act as the members' purchasing and sales agents, but they also supply credit to the small businesses. Dependent for credit on the large trading companies, all of which belong to *keiretsu*, the small raw-material suppliers and distributors do not dare deal with competitors. The Mitsubishi, Mitsui, and Sumitomo trading companies are members of the *keiretsu* of the same name, the Marubeni trading company is a member of the Fuyo *keiretsu*, C. Itoh and Kanematsu-Gosho belong to the Daiichi Kangyo Bank *keiretsu*, and Nissho-Iwai to the Sanwa *keiretsu*.[46] The leading trading companies are very large. Mitsubishi Shoji employs thousands of people in over one hundred branches throughout the world, and Mitsui Busan is about the same size. In part, the prosperity of the

---

41. Misonou et al., *People's White Paper*, 187–91. Cited by Yamamura, "Pervasive Use," 48.

42. Nihon Keizai Shimbun, *Kaisha Nenkan* (Companies' annual reports, 1978 ed.), 881–953. Cited by Yamamura, "Pervasive Use," 48.

43. Fair Trade Commission of Japan (FTCJ), *The Second Survey*, 15–16. Cited by Yamamura, "Pervasive Use," 53.

44. FTCJ, *Second Survey*, 15–16. Cited by Yamamura, "Pervasive Use," 53.

45. Yoshino, *Japan's Managerial System*, 131–32.

46. Yamamura, "Pervasive Use," 69.

largest trading companies is the product of an explicit, direct national policy of favoring them with tax write-offs, rather than of inherent economic advantages or of the monetary policy. As a result, the number of trading companies dropped from two thousand immediately after the occupation to about twenty, each of which was linked to a *keiretsu* or a cartel of smaller producers.[47]

The trading companies have protected their *keiretsu* members from competition against imports. According to the *Oriental Economist* in February 1983, as cited by Clyde Prestowitz, "As a rule, the trading companies refrain from dealings in imports of steel materials because of the pressure from blast-furnace steel makers, particularly Nippon Steel Corporation." Prestowitz also cites the Japanese journal *Technocrat* as follows: "Sogo Sosha (general trading company) is one of the most powerful agents against any unwanted competitors. It functions as the umbrella company for business groups, by guarding their marketing channels, supplying raw materials, and providing necessary financing."[48] The trading companies may no longer protect the members of their *keiretsu* against imports, but they did so during the 1960s and 1970s.

Returning to the TV industry, the major manufacturers belong to *keiretsu*. Toshiba, which heads its own, also is a member of the Mitsui presidents' club, and it borrows from the Bank of Mitsui.[49] Hitachi heads its own *keiretsu*, and it is a member of the presidents' clubs of the Fuyo, Daiichi Kangyo, and Sanwa *keiretsu*. MEI leads its own group of about one hundred companies. Sanyo belongs to the Sumitomo financial *keiretsu*. Sharp's largest shareholders are the Sumitomo Life Insurance Company and the Sumitomo Bank, and it is a member of the Sansui Kai, the presidents' club of the Sanwa *keiretsu*. Considered by some students to lead its own *keiretsu*, Sony also belongs to the Mitsui *keiretsu*, its major creditors being the Mitsui Bank, Mitsui Credit, and Mitsui Life Insurance Company.

Competition in Distribution

Historically, small retailers and wholesalers have been prevalent in Japan in part because of the high population density, the lack of space, and the immobility of consumers. Neither the consumer nor the merchant has much space for storage, and the automobile in the period under investigation still was a luxury. Since small retailers and wholesalers, which made the vast majority of sales of electrical appliances, were financed by their suppliers, few could take advantage of new and foreign companies' lower prices. A study by MITI

---

47. Johnson, *MITI and the Japanese Miracle*, 206.
48. Prestowitz, *Trading Places*, 300.
49. This discussion of the *keiretsu* affiliations of television manufacturers is based on Yamamura, "Pervasive Use," 41–43.

reported that in 1970 the total sales of color TV receivers were divided among small retailers with 85 percent; mass retailers, similar to Sears Roebuck and J.C. Penney, with 10 percent; and department stores, supermarkets, cooperatives, and other stores with the remaining 5 percent. Beginning in the early 1950s, consumer products manufacturers made concerted efforts to expand control over existing marketing channels. They have used various means to induce retailers to join a network of affiliated establishments to handle their products exclusively. To prevent the mass retailers, which purchased receivers directly from manufacturers and sold them under their own label, from challenging the system of resale price controls, the manufacturers did not allow their share of total sales to grow any more. In 1976 the share was the same as in 1970.[50]

The credit stringency shifted the dominance of distribution from wholesalers and large trading companies to the manufacturers. In a few industries, including sewing machines and European-style beds, the manufacturers entered into wholesale and retail distribution with fully owned outlets. In other industries, including gasoline, automobiles, and confectionery, the refiners or manufacturers granted franchises. Other manufacturers, including those of cosmetics and electrical goods, organized affiliated groups of wholesalers and retailers.

To discourage aligned distributors from buying even unrelated merchandise from competitors the manufacturers greatly extended their product lines and gave affiliates rebates at progressive rates, which increased with the manufacturer's share of total sales of all product lines and with the increase in total sales.[51] The combination of progressive rebates and long product lines discouraged distributors from buying from manufacturers with short product lines. The result was that in the mid-1950s exclusive dealerships proliferated. The manufacturers classified their affiliated dealers into groups based on their sales dependence. "Toshiba stores," which had the highest degree of dependence among four groups, obtained 80 percent or more of their supplies from Toshiba and received the highest rebate rate. Matsushita and Hitachi established similar classifications.[52] By the mid-1960s about two-thirds of all consumer electric appliance retailers had become affiliated with a single manufacturer.[53] In the late 1970s, MEI had over forty thousand outlets; Toshiba and Hitachi each had about twenty thousand; MELCO, Sharp, and Sanyo had from

50. Economic Consulting Services, Inc., *Economic Analysis of Evidence relating to Japanese Electronic Products Antitrust Litigation* (prepared for Zenith Radio Corp., Civil Action Nos. 74-2451 and 74-3247, in the U.S. District Court for Eastern Pennsylvania, September 11, 1979, vol. 1: III-20. [hereafter referred to as Nehmer Report]).

51. Caves and Uekusa, *Industrial Organization in Japan,* 51.

52. Nehmer Report, vol. 1: III-18-19.

53. Yoshino, *Japan's Managerial System,* 115.

four to five thousand each.[54] In 1983, of the seven thousand retailers selling consumer electronic goods, about five thousand were integrated into the exclusive distribution system of particular manufacturers.[55]

In the recession of the early 1960s, accumulating stocks of obsolete models provoked desperate wholesalers to offer rebates and relax terms of payment. Because the immature cartel did not limit output sufficiently to maintain the suggested wholesale prices, the wholesalers cut prices to cash-paying discounters to get rid of unwanted stocks. To impose greater discipline, after 1965 the companies assigned only a single sales company to each area. In addition, the manufacturers acquired larger ownership shares of their wholesalers, so that by the 1970s, they owned a majority interest of nearly all the wholesalers.[56] Nourishing them with credit and service support, MEI gave two hundred sales subsidiaries exclusive territories and so gained control over resale prices and trade discounts. For the same purpose Sony shipped on consignment.[57]

Other Barriers to Entry

The credit stringency and the grip on distribution apparently provided insufficient protection, for the government provided specific protection against imports, perhaps because high monopoly profits made entry especially attractive. Until 1967 the Law Concerning Foreign Investment prohibited foreign companies from establishing more than ten wholly controlled outlets,[58] and the Foreign Exchange and Foreign Trade Control Law barred imports of many products. Since then government approval of manufacturing or sales facilities has been required.[59] Tariff rates on TV receivers were high through 1968, when they were between 20 and 30 percent, but between that year and 1973 the Kennedy Round reduced the rates to 4 percent.[60] There were other barriers. Through the late 1960s importers were required to deposit 5 percent of the value of foreign TV receivers prior to their receipt,[61] and the govern-

---

54. Kawagoe, *Ryutsu keirtsuka no jittai*. Cited by John O. Haley, "Vertical Restraints by Japanese Television Manufacturers: Anticompetitive Effects" (MS., University of Washington, n.d.)

55. Hugh T. Patrick and Thomas P. Rohlen, "Small-Scale Family Enterprises," in Yamamura and Yasuba, *Political Economy of Japan*, vol. 1: *Domestic Transformation*, 350.

56. Nehmer Report, vol. 1: III-17-18.

57. Caves and Uekusa, *Industrial Organization in Japan*, 51.

58. Cabinet decision, April 27, 1973. Cited by John O. Haley, *Report: Prospective Testimony by John O. Haley* (prepared for plaintiffs in Japanese Electronic Products Antitrust Litigation, M.D.L. 189, June 1, 1979, 30 (hereafter referred to as Haley, "Report for Plaintiffs").

59. Haley, "Report for Plaintiffs," 29.

60. Nehmer Report, table IV-1.

61. Kiyoshi Kojima, *Non-Tariff Barriers in Japan's Trade*, Japanese Research Center, Center Paper No. 16, December 1971, 34. Cited in Nehmer Report, vol. 1: IV-6.

ment continued to require imports to be paid for within four months of the receipt of the bill of lading.[62] Over and above these barriers MITI used its control of foreign exchange to enforce quantitative import restrictions.[63] In addition, MITI required imported electrical equipment to meet specified tests by an authorized laboratory. The U.S. embassy said that the design requirement for imports of color receivers violated the international standards code.[64] According to Chalmers Johnson, MITI made every effort to suppress imports of finished goods, particularly those that competed with domestic products.[65]

In addition, efforts by foreign manufacturers to distribute their products through a trading company were blocked. We have already noted that no foreign manufacturer was permitted to wholly own more than ten retail stores.[66] In 1962 Zenith's efforts to distribute TV receivers through C. Itoh failed. A letter to Zenith from the trading company said that, owing to the popularity of Zenith's products, MITI refused to allocate the needed foreign exchange.[67] A later similar effort through Nichimen also failed. A letter from Nichimen to Zenith reported that it had withdrawn from the import program because of pressure on the government and on leading chain and department stores by the Japanese Electronic Industry Association. The letter also reported pressure on Nichimen itself to refrain from aggressively distributing the products.[68]

Antitrust Laws and Their Enforcement

The Antimonopoly Law of 1947 prohibited cartels, but the law, which lacked support because it violated the tradition of tolerance of cartels and was an American intrusion, was not enforced.[69] From the 1920s through World War II the government did more than just tolerate cartel agreements: it enforced them. The Export Society Law and the Major Export Commodities Industry Law of 1925 required the government to enforce agreements fixing prices,

---

62. U.S. Tariff Commission, *Report to Senate Finance Committee, April 1974*, 5: 272. Order concerning Standard Method of Settlement, Ministry of Finance Order No. 62, 1962. Cited in Nehmer Report, vol. 1: IV-7.

63. Nehmer Report, vol. 1: IV-8; table IV-8.

64. Nehmer Report, vol. 1: IV-10.

65. Johnson, *MITI and the Japanese Miracle*, 194, 217.

66. Nehmer Report, vol. 1: IV-11.

67. Letter from I. Kobayashi, C. Itoh and Co., Ltd. of Japan to Y. Tamiya of C. Itoh and Co. (America), Inc., July 24, 1962. Cited by Nehmer Report, vol. 1: IV-15.

68. Letter from Dan M. Andre, general sales manager for Nichimen Co., Inc., Chicago, to John Miguel, Jr., vice president–export, Zenith Radio Corp., May 16, 1963. Cited by Nehmer Report, vol. 1: IV-16.

69. Caves and Uekusa, *Industrial Organization in Japan*, 47–58; Yoshino, *Japan's Managerial System*, 169–77; Eleanor M. Hadley, *Antitrust in Japan* (Princeton, N.J.: Princeton University Press, 1970), 370–89.

output quotas, and market shares. The laws even mandated the concerned minister to order uncooperative firms to comply. In the 1930s, because the cartels were useful for mobilizing war resources, the militarists went to the greater extreme of forcing cartels on unwilling producers. After 1932 cartels legally could control an entire industry, despite the opposition of up to half the members, but to enforce an agreement the Minister of Commerce and Industry still needed the approval of two-thirds of the producers. Eager to accommodate the cartels, which were learning what success required, the Diet made other important changes. Since information on their operations exposes cheaters, in 1933 the Diet ordered cartel members to exchange information on production, shipments, and prices. In addition, since cartels fail without limits on production, the Diet authorized the Minister of Commerce to license capacity expansion. The cartelization campaign accelerated in 1938, when legislation decreed cartels in industries over the resistance of producers. Under the National General Mobilization Law, which ordered industrywide cartels in nearly all industries, the government was to enforce agreements regardless of the number of recalcitrant members. After the war started cartels proliferated even faster. One important law permitted cartels to regulate parts of industries.[70]

Defeat not having converted the Japanese to the virtues of competition, General Douglas MacArthur imposed the Antimonopoly Law. Closely resembling the Sherman Act, the law banned monopolization, unreasonable restraints of trade, conspiracies to set prices, and, more generally, restraints on competition. Going beyond the Sherman Act, the law proscribed holding companies and unfair methods of competition, it attempted to limit disparities in bargaining power, and it regulated intercorporate directorates and stockholdings.[71] SCAP's lawyers evidently enjoyed designing what they considered to be the ideal law. SCAP's response to opponents within the government was that the laws should recognize the public interest in competition.[72] Not surprisingly, in view of the opposition, the law prescribed inadequate penalties, and once SCAP was gone the Diet quickly moved to weaken it further.

MITI could not wait for the end of the occupation to begin to restrict competition. In 1952 the fall in American procurements intensified competition, and the newly formed ministry went into action. Using its power to deny foreign exchange, MITI "advised" cotton, rubber, and steel manufacturers to organize cartels. The FTCJ protested, but, according to the ministry, the Antimonopoly Law did not apply to informal government advice.[73] Further,

---

70. Hadley, *Antitrust in Japan*, 364–66.

71. Johnson, *MITI and the Japanese Miracle*, 222.

72. Supreme commander of the Allied Powers, Monograph No. 26, "Promotion of Fair Trade Practices," 95, 101. Cited by Johnson, *MITI and the Japanese Miracle*, 221.

73. Johnson, *MITI and the Japanese Miracle*, 224–25.

calling for the legalization of cartels in industries in recession and the implementation of plans for rationalization, MITI said that the Antimonopoly Law had caused small firms to proliferate and had discouraged the investment necessary for increasing exports. In addition, MITI asked for power to permit companies to share technologies, limit product lines, use warehouses jointly, and consult with one another on investment plans.[74]

The Diet responded quickly. In 1953 the legislature deleted from the Antimonopoly Law the section dealing with disparities in bargaining power, weakened the prohibition of unfair methods of competition, and allowed resale price maintenance. More important, reverting to the pre-occupation pro-cartel policy, the Diet authorized MITI to organize cartels in depressed industries, and it permitted production and price agreements in those industries. The act also allowed rationalization cartels to improve technology, to use or buy products, to share transportation facilities, and to improve efficiency.[75] The cartels had to receive the approval of the FTCJ,[76] but the courts severely restricted the commission's power.

MITI's "advice" cartels were not explicitly allowed by law, but, because the ministry's administrative guidance was to individual firms, the FTCJ could not prohibit them. Thus, through its administrative guidance MITI gave colluding firms immunity from the law. Moreover, a MITI advice cartel disciplined firms more effectively than a voluntary agreement, and official approval protected the colluding firms against unfavorable publicity. Later recessions prompted the growth of more advice cartels.[77]

Despite growing opposition in the Diet, MITI continued to gain power. The opposition prevented passage of the Special Measures for Strengthening the International Competitive Ability of Designated Industries, which, to raise some industries' competitiveness, would have firms cooperate, exempting them from the Antimonopoly Law. Despite the failure of this legislation to pass, in 1974, acting under its residual powers of administrative guidance, MITI established cooperation discussion groups in synthetic textiles and petrochemicals, and it announced that it might do the same in other industries.[78]

Before 1977 weak sanctions and remedies reduced the Antimonopoly Law's effectiveness. The law did not specify criminal sanctions, and the fines were small. Moreover, although the law allowed cease and desist orders, the commission required specific authority for its orders, and, despite its language, the commission could order companies to desist only from those

---

74. Johnson, *MITI and the Japanese Miracle,* 225.

75. Hadley, *Antitrust in Japan,* 197–201.

76. "Trustbusting in Japan: Cartels and Government-Business Cooperation," *Harvard Law Review* 94 (1981): 1070.

77. Yoshino, *Japan's Managerial System,* 170–71.

78. Johnson, *MITI and the Japanese Miracle,* 258–60, 264–69.

violations specified in the immediate case. The second, third, and subsequent agreements were separate violations.[79] Companies could enter into agreements despite repeated prosecutions. Moreover, the FTCJ lacked broad subpoena powers, which meant that it had to identify and demand specific documents. Worse, since neither the commission nor the courts possessed contempt power, it lacked an enforcement weapon. A respondent took no risk by refusing to produce documents. To secure documents the FTCJ resorted to raids on respondents' offices, which were inefficient and usually ineffective.[80]

Further, surrendering to pressure by business and by MITI, the FTCJ refrained from vigorously enforcing the law. The average annual number of prosecutions under the Antimonopoly Law fell from twenty-seven during the occupation to six between 1952 and 1959. In response to consumer protests the number of prosecutions picked up and reached sixty-four in 1973.[81]

In the late 1960s the FTCJ began to win more support. A consumer movement protested against price cartels, and academics began to advocate procompetitive policies.[82] In 1973 the FTCJ began to expose many cartels, and roughly half the cases in which the commission found a violation involved second offenses. In 1973–74 one company received seven warnings, and two others were warned six times. Companies repeatedly revived the cartels in the paper, chemical, petroleum, cement, and plate glass industries. Immediately following the FTCJ's advice to break up, the ethyl acetate cartel began preparing its own revival. After the oil industry was advised to abandon a price-fixing agreement but before the FTCJ could issue a formal decree, the industry concluded five price reduction agreements.[83]

The big rise in the price of oil in 1973 triggered public protests against the domestic oil cartel,[84] which MITI had encouraged to limit its output and set prices. The FTCJ took action, and early in 1974 the petroleum producers accepted its recommendation ordering them to halt their price-fixing activities. At the same time, in the first criminal prosecution under the Antimonopoly Law, the Tokyo High Court found the oil companies guilty of price fixing.[85] Rejecting the defense that the companies were implementing government policy, the Court ruled that their joint decision to reduce production was a violation. Although MITI had used the conduct to implement its policy, as well as approved it, this did not change the private decision into a government

79. Haley, "Report for Plaintiffs," 18.
80. Haley, "Report for Plaintiffs," 18.
81. Masu Uekusa, "Industrial Organization: The 1970s to the Present," in Yamamura and Yasuba, *Political Economy of Japan,* vol. 1: *Domestic Transformation,* 477–79.
82. Uekusa, "Industrial Organization," 477–78.
83. Yamamura Report, app. A, 23.
84. "Trustbusting in Japan," 1074–75.
85. "Trustbusting in Japan," 1076–78.

decision. When the government delegated decisions to private parties or when the conduct was in cooperation with a government policy, it was immune from the law, but the Petroleum Association could not be excused on either ground. The proof of criminal intent necessary for criminal liability, however, was absent.[86]

Despite the FTCJ's victory, the effect of MITI's approval on the legality of collusion remained an unsettled issue. According to the Court, while actions by businesses that were individually instructed by MITI did not violate the law, it might find a violation if each company agreed to the administrative guidance on the assumption that competitors also agreed.[87]

A strengthening amendment, which came in 1977, included the prohibition of "states of monopoly" and new remedial powers for the FTCJ to ensure competition, including the authority to order divestiture. The amendment also supplied a series of definitions of monopoly power based on market structure or on conduct. Thus, monopolistic conditions existed in an industry when the value of a product exceeded ¥ 50 billion and a firm's market share exceeded 50 percent or when two firms had more than 75 percent of the market. The second definition specified difficult entry. The third definition said that monopolistic conditions existed when over a considerable period there was evidence of the absence of competition, such as a remarkable increase in prices, no change in prices when changes were to be expected, high profits, or high administrative expenses. In addition, to deprive cartel operations of profits the FTCJ was required to levy a surcharge on illegal cartel profits. Further, the maximum penalty for certain violations was ¥ 5 million, which, although a small amount, was ten times the previous level. More significant, the amendments empowered the FTCJ to give parallel price increases adverse publicity without requiring the agency to show communication between the alleged conspirators. Another provision limited the number of shares that a large corporation could hold in other corporations.[88]

But conflicting measures were passed. In May 1983 the Diet passed the Specified Industry Structural Improvement Temporary Measures Law, granting MITI authority to design and implement plans for the aluminum, chemical textile, chemical fertilizer, and petrochemical industries. Under the ministry's supervision manufacturers could engage in the joint sale of products, merge

86. Mitsuo Matsushita, "The Legal Framework of Trade and Investment in Japan," *Harvard International Law Journal* 27, special issue (1986): 380–82.

87. "Trustbusting in Japan," 1079–80; Matsushita, "Legal Framework of Trade and Investment in Japan," 381; Seichi Yoshikawa, "Fair Trade Commission vs. MITI: History of the Conflicts between the Antimonopoly Policy and the Industrial Policy in the Post War Period of Japan," *Case Western Reserve Journal of International Law* 15 (Summer 1983): 499–502.

88. "Trustbusting in Japan," 1081–82; Yoshikawa, "Fair Trade Commission vs. MITI," 500–502.

plants, jointly develop technology, and assign production to other companies. The FTCJ agreed to resolve antitrust problems by consultation with MITI. Also, government leaders began to move to reduce the Antimonopoly Law's severity.[89]

Returning to the TV cartel, the commission was ineffective. The FTCJ 1957 decision in the "Case against Home Electric Appliance Market Stabilization Council" described the anticompetitive activities of the Japanese TV manufacturers in the home market. The commission found that the manufacturers had fixed their own prices and the resale prices of distributors, and the respondents assented to the finding.[90] The FTCJ's Recommendation Decision prohibited the respondents from carrying out their agreement and to cease resale price maintenance. The order, however, applied only to the agreement, dated prior to the order, not to a subsequent agreement.

In the Six-Company Case of 1966 the FTCJ trial examiners decided in 1970 that Sanyo, Toshiba, Sharp, Hitachi, MELCO, and MEI had violated the Antimonopoly Law, but they also decided that the violations had ceased.[91] Yet, as chapter 5 demonstrates, the cartel continued to operate after 1970.

Number of Sellers

A single seller, a monopoly, is likely to set a high price, and a few sellers, an oligopoly, are more likely to collude to set a high price than many sellers, a polypoly. Oligopolists readily recognize their mutual interest. Competition does not become a pleasure when there are many sellers, but without state intervention it is difficult for them to avoid. They will not be equally sanguine about future sales; some will be more desperate than others to gain sales, and some will produce more efficiently or pay lower wages or design their products more attractively than others. Moreover, a price agreement is difficult to maintain without output restrictions, which firms are reluctant to accept. Since a price-cutter who is one among many sellers will ring up large sales before competitors follow, the incentive to stick to a price agreement is weak. What is more, cheaters are less easily discovered among the many than among the few. When an oligopolist cuts prices individual rivals suffer large losses, and they can easily discover the cheater. The potential price-cutter also knows

89. Yoshikawa, "Fair Trade Commission vs. MITI," 503–4.

90. Brief of Appellants, Zenith Radio Corp. and National Union Electric Corp., in the U.S. Court of Appeals for the Third Circuit. In re Japanese Electronic Products Antitrust Litigation, 189 M.D.L., December 1, 1981, 35.

91. DePodwin Report, vol. 1, app. exhibit 2. Office of the Fair Trade Commission of Japan, Case No. 6, "Initial Decision," June 9, 1970.

that its rivals have a strong incentive to retaliate. The common interest is more obvious and compelling for firms that have few competitors.[92]

After 1965 the average level of seller concentration in manufacturing increased. Firms built large plants and, to ensure supplies, integrated backward. Moreover, as the large firms gained control of their distribution, entry became more difficult.[93]

Cartels became more prevalent. According to M. Y. Yoshino's estimate, by 1963 over one thousand cartels were operating in Japan, and their activities influenced the behavior of industries producing more than 28 percent of the output of the country's manufacturing industries.[94] A 1975 study by Sanekata Kenji and his associates reported the existence of numerous, deeply rooted cartels, and in the authors' judgment businesses could not function without them.[95] Following the imposition of inflation controls in 1973, cartelization accelerated.[96] In Masu Uekusa's judgment, while competition intensified when demand stagnated in the late 1970s, the large manufacturing firms continue to have considerable monopoly power.[97]

Exercising its control over foreign exchange and to refuse technology import licenses, MITI reduced competition through "administrative guidance." Richard Caves and Masu Uekusa said that MITI sought to have plants of efficient size built and to prevent excess capacity and resulting price competition. The ministry strove to control investment rather than set minimum prices.[98]

The TV manufacturing industry was an oligopoly, with the top six producers—Matsushita, Toshiba, Hitachi, Sanyo, Mitsubishi, and Sharp—accounting for 73 percent of monochrome and 93 percent of color TV receivers produced in 1965.[99] They had every incentive to avoid competition, but their control of the industry's output may have been insufficient to maintain high prices. A cartel consisting of only the leaders might have been vulnerable to price cuts by the smaller competitors, who might have expanded their market share. Fortunately from the industry's standpoint, the smaller producers were willing to enter and observe the agreements, which, as we will

---

92. George J. Stigler, "A Theory of Oligopoly," *Journal of Political Economy* 72 (February 1964): 44–61.

93. Uekusa, "Industrial Organization," 479–81.

94. Yoshino, *Japan's Managerial System,* 169.

95. See Yamamura, "Pervasive Use," app. A, for translation of relevant sections of the study.

96. Uekusa, "Industrial Organization," 479–81.

97. Uekusa, "Industrial Organization," 481.

98. Caves and Uekusa, *Industrial Organization in Japan,* 54–56.

99. Nehmer Report, vol. 2: VII-4.

see, specified prices, restricted output, and provided for the exchange of information on outputs and shipments.

Export Cartels

The Antimonopoly Law explicitly allows export cartel agreements,[100] and in the 1950s and 1960s, through trade associations, firms in a large number of industries entered into cartel agreements.[101] Agreements covering both home and export markets required MITI's express authorization, and, since agreements set prices in the home markets for many of the products covered by the export agreements, the ministry did not present any problems. According to an FTCJ report for the years 1967–72, cartel agreements regulated both the home and export markets for the following products: rayon thread, rayon staple, polyester staple, acrylic staple, nylon, cellophane, aluminum ingot, hot rolled steel, wire rod, tin plate, stainless steel, cement, paints, caustic soda, acetic acid, auto tires and tubes, acid glutamate, phthallic anhydride, polypropylene. Many of these products were produced by members of highly concentrated industries.[102] Since the list includes only those domestic cartels that were reported to the FTCJ, there were probably other monopolistic industries. A large number of cartels may not have reported, because they did not qualify as lawful rationalization or depression cartels.

The Japan Machinery Exporters Association (JMEA) sponsored the export agreements for TV receivers, the first one of which was entered into in 1963. In 1958 the trade association had sponsored the export agreements for radios.[103] The JMEA also sponsored export agreements for the following other products in the years shown: binoculars (1960), photographic cameras (1958, 1962, 1964), radio broadcast receivers with transistors (1961), batteries (1963), digital tabletype electronic computers (1968), electronic machinery

---

100. Organization for Economic Cooperation and Development (OECD), *Export Cartels* (Paris: OECD, 1974).

101. Japan Cotton Textile Exporters Assoc., Japan Wool and Linen Textiles Exporters Assoc., Japan Textile Products Exporters Assoc., Japan Sewing Machines, Japan Machinery Exporters Assoc., Japan Bicycle Exporters Assoc., Japan Electric Wire, Japan General Merchandise Exporters Assoc., Japan Glass Products Exporters Assoc., Japan Pottery Exporters Assoc., Japan Paper Exporters' Assoc., Japan Land and Sea Products Exporters Assoc., Japan Pearl Exporters' Assoc., Japan Artificial Pearls and Glass Products Assoc., Japan Canned Foods Exporters Assoc., Japan Chemical Exporters Assoc., Japan Pharmaceutical Medical and Dental Supply Exporters' Assoc.

102. Cited by Alexis Jacquemin, Tsuruhiko Nambu, Isabelle Dewez, "A Dynamic Analysis of Export Cartels: The Japanese Case," *Economic Journal* 91 (September 1981): 685–96, table 2.

103. See chapter 6 for details.

and apparatus (1969), parts and accessories of motor cars (1962), machine tools (1967), and wooden screws (1968).[104] As chapter 6 reports, the TV receiver agreements were very similar to those for radios, so it is reasonable to infer that the JMEA agreements for the other products also were similar. Since MITI participated in the discussions leading to the agreements sponsored by other associations, as well as those sponsored by the JMEA, all the agreements may have contained similar restrictions on competition.

Dumping in the United States

Chapter 3 argues that noncolluding firms will not export at substantially lower prices than they can receive abroad, but, as we have seen, cartels are widespread in Japan. Chapter 3 also argues that export cartels minimize the cost to the participants of predatory attacks on manufacturers in export markets, and we have seen that there are many Japanese export cartels.

These domestic and export cartels have facilitated dumping by Japanese manufacturers of many products. The International Trade Administration (ITA) of the Department of Commerce has issued a long list of antidumping orders for Japanese products, indicating that the manufacturers have dumped persistently. Since the cumbersome procedures alone ensure that sporadic, short-term dumping does not provoke an order, the orders reflect some persistence. The ITA publishes an antidumping order when it decides that the price at which a product is exported to the U.S. is less than the home market price and the International Trade Commission (ITC) finds that the imports have caused material injury to a U.S. industry, and after it has assessed the difference between the home market price and the export price expressed as a percentage of the export price, which is known as the dumping margin.[105] To satisfy the ITC the complainants must show that their sales, employment, and profits have been reduced over a long period.

Currently the U.S. Customs Service is implementing antidumping orders against Japanese manufacturers of fifty-five products,[106] and, as Table 2.1 shows, many of the dumping margins have been large. Robert Baldwin and Michael Moore estimate that the average dumping margin for Japanese prod-

---

104. OECD, *Export Cartels.*

105. The domestic price is the usual standard. When this price is difficult to determine the standard may be the average cost of production or the export price to a third country. See chapter 6 for more details.

106. International Trade Administration (ITA), Import Administration, Office of Compliance, *Antidumping and Countervailing Duty Orders, Findings, and Suspension Agreements Currently in Effect,* May 1, 1991.

TABLE 2.1. Dumping Margins against Japanese Products by Products and Companies

Product and Company	Margin	Federal Register Reference			
		Volume	Number	Date	Page
Spun acrylic yarn	48.05	45	69	4/8/80	23685
Portable electric typewriters					
Nakajima	4.36	45	92	5/9/80	30619
Silver Seiko	36.53				
Brother	48.70				
Other	37.12				
Portable electric typewriters					
Brother	62.79	56	213	11/4/91	56400
Silver Seiko	88.85				
Canon	88.85				
TWT high power Microwave amplifiers	25.40	47	139	7/20/82	31413
Klystrom high power Micro-wave amplifiers	41.10	47	139	7/20/82	31413
High capacity pagers					
Matsushita Communications	109.06	48	259	8/16/83	37059
Nippon Electric	70.35				
Other	89.97				
Titanium sponge					
Osaka Titanium	15.09	49	232	11/30/84	47054
Toho Titanium	34.25				
Nippon Soda	56.27				
Others	28.47				
Cellular mobile telephones					
MELCO	87.83	50	244	12/19/85	51725
NEC	95.57				
Matsushita Communications	106.60				
OKI	9.72				
Hitachi	2.99				
Toshiba (excluded)	0.00				
Other	67.81				
64K DRAMs					
NEC	22.76	51	115	6/16/86	21782
Hitachi	11.87				
OKI	35.34				
Mitsubishi	13.43				
Other	20.75				
Tapered roller bearings > 4 inches					
Koyo Seiko	70.44	52	193	10/6/87	37353
NTN Toyo Bearing	47.05				
Others	47.57				

TABLE 2.1.

Product and Company	Margin	Federal Register Reference			
		Volume	Number	Date	Page
Butt-Weld pipe fittings					
Awaji Sangyo	30.83	52	27	2/10/87	4167
Nippon Benkan Kogyo	65.81				
Others	62.79				
Amorphous silica filament fabric					
All exporters	193.94	52	184	9/23/87	35750
Malleable cast iron pipe fittings					
Hitachi Metals	57.39	52	128	7/6/87	25282
Others	57.39				
Granular Polytetrafluoroethylene Resin					
Dalkin	103.00	53	164	8/24/88	32267
Asahi Fluoropolymers	51.45				
Others	91.74				
Nitrile Rubber					
Nippon Zeon	146.50	53	116	6/16/88	22553
Others	146.50				
Brass sheet and strip					
Nippon Mining	57.98	53	156	8/12/88	30455
Sambo Copper	13.30				
Mitsubishi Shindo	57.98				
Kobe Steel	57.98				
Others	45.72				
Forklift trucks					
Toyota Motor	17.29	53	109	6/7/88	20883
Nissan Motor	51.33				
Komatsu Forklift	47.50				
Sumitomo-Yale	51.33				
Toyo Umpanki	51.33				
Sanki	13.65				
Kasagi Forklift	56.81				
Others	39.45				
Color picture tubes					
Mitsubishi	1.05	53	4	1/7/88	431
Hitachi	22.29				
Matsushita	27.46				
Toshiba	33.50				
Others	27.93				
Brother	58.71	56	167	8/28/91	42595
Kyushu Matsushita	58.71				
Other	58.71				

(*continued*)

TABLE 2.1.— *Continued*

Product and Company	Margin	Federal Register Reference			
		Volume	Number	Date	Page
Drafting machines					
Mutoh Industries	90.87	54	249	12/29/89	53871
Others	90.87				
Electrolytic manganese dioxide					
Mitsui Mining	77.43	54	72	4/17/89	15244
Tosoh	71.91				
Others	73.30				
3.5-inch microdisks					
Sony	51.00	54	62	4/3/89	13407
Hitachi Maxell	27.73				
Fuji Photo	50.52				
Others	42.95				
Ball bearings					
Koyo	73.55	54	92	5/15/89	20905
Minebea	106.61				
Nachi	48.69				
NSK	42.99				
NTN	21.36				
Others	45.83				
Spherical plain bearings					
Minebea	84.26	54	92	5/15/89	20905
NTN	92.000				
Others	84.33				
Industrial belts					
Bando Chemical	93.16	54	113	6/14/89	25315
Others	93.16				
Small-business telephone systems					
Toshiba	136.77	54	236	12/11/89	50790
Matsushita	178.93				
Others	157.85				
Light scattering instruments					
Otsuka Electronics	129.71	55	223	11/19/90	48145
Others	129.71				
Industrial nitrocellulose					
Asahi Chemical	66.00	55	132	7/10/90	28268
Others	66.00				
Active matrix liquid crystal flat panel displays					
Hosiden	62.67	56	171	9/4/91	43742
Others	62.67				

TABLE 2.1.

| Product and Company | Margin | Federal Register Reference | | | |
		Volume	Number	Date	Page
Benzyl paraben					
Ueno Fine Chemicals	126.00	56	30	2/13/91	496
Others	126.00				
Television receivers					
Fujitsu General	35.40	56	28	2/11/91	5401
Matsushita	35.40				
NEC	35.40				
Toshiba	35.40				
Victor	35.40				

ucts reaching the final determination stage in antidumping proceedings between 1980 and 1989 was 43.5 percent.[107]

Critics of the administration of the dumping law say that the procedure for computing dumping margins necessarily results in a positive estimate when home market prices are the same as those in the export market. The individual export transaction prices at the factory are compared to the average factory price of corresponding products sold in the home market over a six-month period. Since transaction prices differ, dumping will be found to have occurred when the average export price equals the average home market price. The procedure is justified by ITA's desire to prevent "spot" dumping.[108] The ITA fears that exporters will systematically eliminate individual U.S. manufacturers one by one by selective dumping.

The procedure results in an upward bias in the computed dumping margins, and when the margins are small the exporters may not have been dumping. While a small estimated margin may be due entirely to the bias, errors are unlikely to account for high dumping margins. According to Tracy Murray, simulations indicate that the estimated margin of dumping will not exceed the true margin by more than 10 percent where the true margin is large. If the true margin is 20 percent, the ITA methodology will on average yield an estimated dumping margin not exceeding 22 percent.[109]

---

107. Letter from Michael O. Moore, January 28, 1992. Cf. Robert E. Baldwin and Michael O. Moore, "Political Aspects of the Administration of the Trade Remedy Laws," in *Down in the Dumps: Administration of the Unfair Trade Laws*, ed. Richard Boltuck and Robert E. Litan (Washington, D.C.: Brookings Institution, 1991), 273–77.

108. Richard Boltuck and Robert E. Litan, "America's 'Unfair' Trade Laws," in Boltuck and Litan, *Down in the Dumps*, 14.

109. Tracy Murray, "The Administration of the Antidumping Duty Law by the Department of Commerce," in Boltuck and Litan, *Down in the Dumps*, 37.

The other criticism of the ITA assessments of dumping margins concerns the reliance on "best information available" (BIA). When the ITA receives incomplete or no information from the exporters in an antidumping investigation it may make a BIA estimate, which may rely on the information supplied by the complaining industry. The dumping margins based on BIA estimates, which are higher than those based on information supplied by the respondents, may be biassed upward.[110] When respondents do not supply the requested information, however, they presumably have decided that such information will not reduce the assessment.

Thus, the errors are unlikely to invalidate the general conclusion that Japanese manufacturers dumped many products between 1980 and 1990 and that the average dumping margin has been high.

Conclusion

The major instrument of MITI's industrial policy over most of the postwar period was the combination of generally tight credit with generous loans to favored firms in selected industries. This combination fostered the TV and other cartels by encouraging concentration and by depriving potential entrants of access to capital. The monetary policy also encouraged the formation of *keiretsu*, and it resulted in closing off distribution channels to potential entrants. The monetary policy increased the fixed costs of large Japanese corporations, inducing them to attempt to escape the uncertainties of competition by entering into cartel agreements. In addition, the government blocked the entry of foreign manufacturers by high tariffs on imports, and MITI used its control over foreign exchange to further its industrial policy. The weak Antimonopoly Act was no hindrance to the TV cartel's restriction of competition. MITI fought the vigorous enforcement of the act against cartels, but the weak enforcement was due also to the FTCJ's lack of strong political support. Many cartels operated in both the home and export markets, and many manufacturers participating in the cartels exported at much lower prices than they received in the home market.

---

110. N. David Palmeter, "The Antidumping Law: A Legal and Administrative Nontariff Barrier," in Boltuck and Litan, *Down in the Dumps*, 65.

CHAPTER 3

The Economics and Law of Dumping

The *Matsushita* plaintiffs supported their main charge of a conspiracy to restrict competition and to depress prices in the United States with evidence of dumping. While they produced other evidence of a conspiracy, the charge raised the question of whether the defendants were likely to have engaged independently in dumping. This chapter investigates the economics of dumping.

Inasmuch as the U.S. TV industry filed a complaint under the Antidumping Act of 1921, this chapter also discusses the law relating to dumping. It does not discuss predatory dumping, which is dumping undertaken for the purpose of destroying competitors. The antidumping law, which says nothing about intent, prohibits any dumping that causes injury to a U.S. industry. It is the Sherman Act that applies to predatory dumping, so this subject is left to be discussed in chapter 4, which examines the antitrust issues raised in *Matsushita*.

The Economics of Dumping

Jacob Viner's definition of dumping, proposed as far back as 1923, was simply price discrimination between national markets.[1] The definition included sporadic dumping, which Viner said should not disturb governments of importing countries. Title VII of the Trade Agreements Act of 1979 defines dumping similarly as the sale of foreign merchandise at less than the home market price. The General Agreement on Tariffs and Trade's (GATT) definition is also the same. According to Article VI, dumping is the export of a product at a price below "normal" value, which usually means the home market price.

Both the Trade Agreements Act and GATT, however, provide an alternative definition. Without information on home market prices fair value may be the cost of the merchandise plus an allowance for profit. If the exporter's

---

1. Jacob Viner, *Dumping: A Problem in International Trade* (New York: Augustus M. Kelley, 1966), 3.

prices are below costs, an antidumping order may be issued even if these prices exceed those in the home market. GATT contains a similar provision.

Price Discrimination between the Home and Export Markets

We turn to an analysis of the conditions under which firms will discriminate in price between the home and export markets. This section attempts to explain simply the economics of price discrimination between national markets. For those readers who do not wish to work through what may appear to be an abstruse analysis I summarize it in nontechnical language.

Under highly competitive conditions a firm will increase its sales by reducing its price slightly, even if it sells a branded product that commands some consumer loyalty. A firm then will not export if to do so it must accept a price that is much lower than its home market price.

By contrast, a profit-maximizing monopolist in the home market, which competes with other sellers in the export market, may set an export price that is much less than its home market price. The export price may be high enough to be profitable. The monopolist will not choose the option of substantially increasing the quantity that it offers in the home market, because to do so would entail reducing its home market price significantly and therefore its profits. If the firm has a monopoly in both national markets, it will set a higher price in the market with the more favorable conditions, such as the one with higher incomes of buyers and the unavailability of close substitutes. The analysis is the same for a cartel having monopoly power in the home market. If it competes with many sellers in the export market, the export price will be lower. If it also has monopoly power in the export market, the export price may be higher or lower than its domestic price. However, a monopolist or members of a monopolistic cartel will not build capacity for export at prices that do not cover total costs. If, because the monopolist has overestimated home market demand, it has excess capacity, then it may export at prices that do not cover total costs but which do cover the incremental costs of the exports.

Suppose the cartel members, who together have a monopoly of the home market, compete independently in the export market. Their export prices will be less than their home market prices. Again, they will not build capacity to supply the export market at prices that are less than total unit costs. The cartel members may decide to collude in the export market to raise their export prices. Combined for the purpose of competing in the export market, they may enhance their market power.

Matsushita raised the issue of whether dumping implied that the Japanese TV manufacturers colluded in the home market. We assume that the oligopolists competed independently in both the home and export markets. This issue is difficult to resolve without resorting to a technical analysis. Briefly, the oligopolists are unlikely to sell at prices that are substantially above the competitive level in the home market when their market shares in that market are modest, say less than 20 percent. If they cannot sell at supracompetitive prices in the home market, then their export prices will not be substantially less than their home market prices. On the other hand, a dominant firm, which has a large share of the domestic market, say 60 percent, may have considerable home market monopoly power. In this case the firm may export at prices well below its home market prices.

The more technical analysis follows. A seller in a perfectly competitive home market will not export at a lower price than the one that it receives in the home market. If the price in the export market is $2.25 and the transportation cost, including insurance, import duties, and freight, is $0.50, then the export price is $1.75. If the home market price is any higher than this price, the firm will not export. The firm need not export to increase its sales, and it can get a higher price in the home market. It will get rid of surplus merchandise at distress prices as much in the home as in the export market.

Figure 3.1, in which the vertical axis represents price or cost and the horizontal axis represents the quantity of output (Q), depicts a competitive firm's output decision. The firm sells at the market price (P), and the horizontal demand curve (D) indicates that the firm can increase its sales at that price. The firm decides to produce Q, at the point at which marginal cost equals price, $MC = P$; Q is the maximum-profit output. At that output the increment in revenue from an additional unit of output, or marginal revenue (MR), equals the increment in cost. The increment in revenue is the price, while the increment in cost is MC. At a lower output the firm will increase its profits (total revenue − total cost) by increasing output; at a higher output it will do so by reducing output.

Before turning to price discrimination between two markets by a monopolist, consider the price decision of a profit-maximizing monopolist selling in only a single market. The vertical axis of figure 3.2 represents the price (P), the horizontal axis the quantity produced and sold (Q). The demand curve (D) shows the quantities that will be sold at different prices; as the price falls, the quantity sold increases. The marginal revenue (MR) curve shows the increments to total revenue resulting from an increase of one unit in the quantity sold. It falls at a faster rate than D, because to increase the quantity sold by one unit the seller must reduce the price not only for that unit but also for all the units that would otherwise be sold at higher prices. The marginal cost (MC) curve shows the increment to total cost resulting from an increase in output of one unit. To maximize its profit the firm will set the price where $MC = MR$. An additional unit produced will increase the cost more than it does

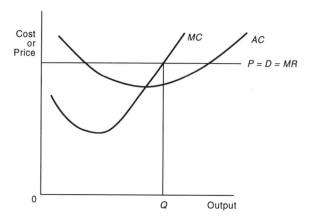

Fig. 3.1. The competitive firm's output

the revenue. A reduction in output will result in a loss of revenue that exceeds the reduction in cost. We introduce another element, e, representing the elasticity of demand. An elasticity of 2 signifies that a 1 percent reduction in price will yield an increase of 2 percent in the quantity sold. Since

$$MR = P(1 - 1/e) \qquad (3.1)$$

the profit-maximizing price varies inversely with the demand elasticity. In other words, the monopolist's power to raise price without suffering a large decline in sales is measured by e. If e is large, then the monopolist's power is small.

Suppose we have two geographically separate markets and that the buyers in one cannot resell to buyers in the other, so the monopolist's prices can differ in the two markets. To maximize its profits the monopolist will set prices so that its combined MC equals the MR in each of them. In other words,

$$MC = MR_1 = MR_2 \qquad (3.2)$$

The subscripts refer to the separate markets. The price in the market with the higher elasticity of demand will tend to be the lower one. We saw earlier that a monopolist's price will vary inversely with e. Following equations 3.1 and 3.2, we see that

$$MC = P_1(1 - 1/e_1) = P_2(1 - 1/e_2) \qquad (3.3)$$

Suppose that it is market 1 in which the firm is a monopolist, while market 2 is highly competitive. Assume that the firm's elasticity of demand in market 1

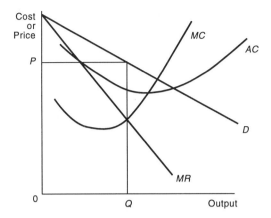

Fig. 3.2. The monopolist's output

equals 2. To estimate its elasticity of demand for market 2 we proceed as follows. In any market the firm's elasticity will be given by:[2]

$$e_i = e^d/S_i + e^s_j(1 - S_i)/S_i \qquad (3.4)$$

e_i = the elasticity of demand of firm i

e^d = the market elasticity of demand

S_i = firm i's market share

e^s_j = the elasticity of supply by other firms.

Suppose that the market elasticity of demand in market 2 is 1,[3] the firm's market share there is 10 percent, and the supply elasticity of other firms is 2. If the other firms have excess capacity, then their output will increase sharply when the price rises. They can increase their output without a significant increase in *MC*. In that case their supply elasticity will greatly exceed 2. Assuming that their supply elasticity is 2, firm i's elasticity of demand in market 2 is 28. If other firms' supply elasticity exceeds 2, then firm i's demand elasticity will exceed 28. We retain this figure, which for the present

2. For a discussion of equation 3.4 see William M. Landes and Richard A. Posner, "Market Power in Antitrust Cases," *Harvard Law Review* 94 (March 1981): 945.

3. The market elasticity of demand at a monopoly price will exceed 1. Here I assume a competitive market.

purpose is very high. We also assume that the firm's combined MC = $2.00. Then, substituting these numbers in equation 3.3, we get

$$2 = P_1(1 - 0.5) = P_2(1 - 0.04) \tag{3.5}$$

Thus, P_1 = $4.00, and P_2 = $2.07.

If brand names have some appeal in market 2, the elasticity of demand facing the exporter may be less than 28. We can substitute other values for e_2 in equation 3.3. As long as they are higher than the elasticity faced by the monopolist in market 1, the price in market 2 will be lower. Figure 3.3 shows graphically the pricing decision by the price-discriminating monopolist. Prices P_1 and P_2 are set at points on the demand curves, D_1 and D_2, corresponding to quantities sold, Q_1 and Q_2, where MR_1 and MR_2 are equal to MC. We see that the seller's elasticity of demand in market 1, where it has a monopoly, is less than the elasticity it faces in market 2.

The analysis is the same for a seller that is a monopolist in both markets. Because the number of competing sellers is not the only determinant of a firm's demand elasticity, having a monopoly in two markets does not entail the same elasticity in both. The monopolist's price in the market with the lower elasticity will exceed its price in the other market.

The same analysis would apply to a cartel that has a monopoly in its home market and maximizes the joint profits of its members. If the cartel members compete as a cartel against other sellers in the export market, then it will discriminate in the same way as the single-firm monopolist.

We can also see that the cartel members will dump in the export market even if they compete independently there. We retain the assumption of a tight cartel with monopoly power in the home market. Then the home market elasticity facing each firm is the same as that for the cartel as a whole. In the export market the firms compete independently. Each firm's demand elasticity in the export market will exceed its demand elasticity at home. Hence, each firm will dump in the export market.

If, however, a firm's profit-maximizing export price is less than its average cost, then it will not dump persistently. It will not build capacity to sell in the export market if the price there does not cover its average cost. The price that the firm could get as a member of an export cartel would be higher than its independently competitive price. It is possible that, as a cartel, the firms will dump, and, as independent competitors, they will not export at all.

The members of the home market cartel might be able to narrow the difference between their home market and export prices by colluding in the export market. Suppose that the cartel had a complete monopoly in the home market and that the market elasticity of demand was 2. Its share of market 2 is 40 percent, the market elasticity of demand in that market is 1, and the

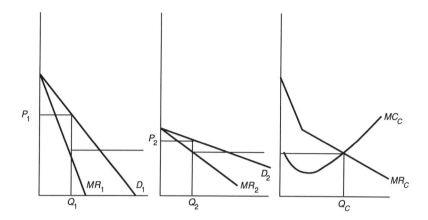

Fig. 3.3. The price-discriminating monopolist

elasticity of supply of other sellers there is 2. Given the assumed *MC* of $2.00, the price in market 1, as before, would be $4.00. The price in market 2 would be $2.44. Were they competing independently, each with a small share of the export market, the export price would be close to the estimate obtained for the monopoly with a 2 percent share of the export market, which is $2.02.

Does dumping by oligopolists imply that they collude in the home market? Let us suppose that they compete independently in both markets. Again, a seller will ask a higher price in the market in which its elasticity of demand is lower. The home market elasticity of demand facing seller *i* competing with other sellers is given by equation 3.4. Assume that seller *i*'s market share (S_i) is 20 percent, the market elasticity of demand (e^d) is 1, and the elasticity of supply (e^s) is 1. Then the seller's elasticity of demand in market 1 equals 9. As we see, the independently competing oligopolist that has a market share of 20 percent will have a high elasticity of demand, even when the supply elasticity of other sellers is assumed to be as low as 1 and the market elasticity of demand is also assumed to have the low value of 1. The assumed supply elasticity will err on the low side when the other sellers have excess capacity, which enables them individually to produce more without an increase in their marginal cost. Even as a group, their supply elasticity will exceed 1 if they have excess capacity and wages and prices of materials purchased do not rise as they hire more labor and purchase more materials. Under conditions of excess capacity and an abundant supply of labor, the supply elasticity may greatly exceed 1. Raising the supply elasticity to 3 has the effect of raising firm *i*'s demand elasticity to 17.

As we saw earlier, a firm will set a lower price in the market in which its demand elasticity is higher. Let us estimate the elasticity of demand facing the firm in the export market, where its share is 5 percent, the market demand elasticity is 1, and the elasticity of supply of other sellers also is 1. Substituting these numbers in equation 3.4, we obtain an estimate of the firm's elasticity of demand in the export market of 39. To see what effect this difference in elasticities will have on prices in the two markets, substitute the values 9 and 39 for e_1 and e_2, respectively, in equation 3.3. I retain 2 as the value for MC. P_1 then is equal to \$2.25, and P_2 is equal to \$2.05. The difference is equal to 9 percent of the home market price. For the present purpose of analyzing the pricing decisions of the Japanese TV manufacturers, I consider this difference to be small. As chapter 7 reports, the actual differences were much larger.

For a dominant firm with a large share of its home market, however, the margin between the prices in the two markets may be much greater. If we were to assume that the firm in question is a dominant firm in its home market, with a share of say 60 percent, then a market elasticity of demand of 1 and a supply elasticity of other firms of 3 would result in the firm's elasticity of demand being 3. A dominant firm with so large a market share may have considerable monopoly power, even when the supply elasticity of other firms is as high as 3. If we substitute 3 for e_1 and, as before, 39 for e_2 in equation 3.3, then P_1 becomes \$3.00, while P_2 remains at \$2.05. The margin is 32 percent of the home market price, which is large.

The assumption concerning the market demand elasticity probably errs a little on the low side for TV receivers. H. S. Houthakker and Lester Taylor estimated for the U.S. the short-run relative price elasticity of demand for radio and TV receivers, records, and musical instruments to be 1.19 and the long-run elasticity to be 1.27.[4] The market share assumption errs on the high side for each of the manufacturers other than the largest, Matsushita Electric Industrial Co. Chapter 6 reports their market shares. It also discusses the conditions affecting the manufacturers' supply elasticity, assuming independent output decisions.

Thus, a firm that has a monopoly in the home market or a cartel that has such a monopoly will set lower prices in the export market, where it must compete with other sellers. A dominant firm that has a large share of its home market is also likely to discriminate in price between its home and export markets. The case is similar for a cartel that is dominant and has a large home market share. Independently competing oligopolists, not one of which has a dominant share, may also discriminate in price, but the margin between the market prices will be much smaller than in the case of a dominant firm or cartel.

---

4. H. S. Houthakker and Lester D. Taylor, *Consumer Demand in the United States, 1929–1970: Analyses and Projections* (Cambridge, Mass.: Harvard University Press, 1966), 130.

Selling below Cost

A firm's price need not cover its total cost per unit of output. A competitive firm's average total cost may exceed the market price; it cannot avoid losses. Even a monopoly may be unable to set a price that yields a profit; demand may be less than the firm anticipated when the plant was constructed, and the price may not cover the fixed as well as the variable costs. Under the U.S. antidumping laws the firm may be found to be dumping even though the export price and home market price are the same. Figure 3.4 describes the case of a profit-maximizing monopolist that sets a price that is less than average cost. This is the profit-maximizing price, inasmuch as, at the quantity produced, $MR = MC$. The firm will not continue to produce at this price indefinitely. It will not build capacity or maintain its current capacity if it expects the price to remain at the same level. Average cost, it should be noted, includes a reasonable return on investment. What is a reasonable return will depend on alternative investment opportunities.

We should note, following the earlier analysis, that the competitive firm will sell at the same price in both its domestic and export markets. If it is suffering losses in its export market, the same will be true in its domestic market.

The monopolist may experience losses in the export market while earning profits in the home market. The profit-maximizing price in the export market may entail losses, while the profit-maximizing price in the home market may be sufficiently high to be profitable.

Possible motives for loss pricing of exports by a monopolist include the expectation of gains from scale and learning economies. Paul Krugman's analysis of the gains from trade due to scale economies argues that, in the absence of trade, market size limits product variety. Accordingly, countries will trade in goods, the production of which requires similar factor proportions. The monopolists in the two countries will specialize in different goods. Each monopolist will expect to gain economies as its output grows and it moves down the cost curve. Krugman also suggests that a protected home market may enable an exporter to realize scale economies and deny them to foreign competitors.[5]

Krugman's argument is easily extended to include the case of monopolists deliberately accepting losses on exports to gain scale economies. It is necessary to assume some monopoly power, since a perfectly competitive firm can increase its sales without significantly reducing prices. Anticipating scale economies, the firm may build a larger plant than it needs immediately.

---

5. Paul Krugman, *Rethinking International Trade* (Cambridge, Mass.: MIT Press, 1990), 38–52, 185–92.

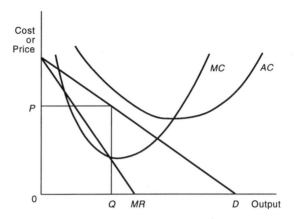

Fig. 3.4. The monopolist suffers a loss

The firm may recoup the resulting immediate losses as output and capacity utilization rise. Figure 3.5 shows the early period demand curve (D_1) below the AC curve and P, the price, resulting in losses. The firm's demand curve moves to D_2 as competitors are eliminated, so output grows, and AC falls. At the higher output and lower AC, P yields a profit. To maximize profits the firm will raise its price above P, but even at P it will earn profits. Figure 3.5 does not show the gain in price due to the rise in the firm's demand curve resulting from the elimination of competitors, because the focus here is on the profits due to the exploitation of scale economies.

Krugman and others, who are sometimes referred to as strategic trade theorists, assume that oligopolists selling differentiated products can achieve the economies of scale in a protected market and maintain lower export than domestic prices.[6] The model that the strategic theorists use, however, specifies only a single seller in the home market facing a single seller in the export market. The argument, which is based on the Cournot duopoly model, assumes that these rivals anticipate each other's output. The protected seller gains the scale economies, which are denied to the rival. The Cournot model is inappropriate, however, for markets consisting of independently competing oligopolists. It may describe the behavior of a tightly regulated cartel possessing monopoly power in the home market facing a similar cartel or single-firm

6. James A. Brander, "Intra-industry Trade in Identical Commodities," *Journal of International Economics* 11 (1981): 1–14; James A. Brander and Barbara J. Spencer, "Tariffs and the Extraction of Foreign Monopoly Rents under Potential Entry," *Canadian Journal of Economics* 14 (1981): 371–89; James A. Brander and Paul R. Krugman, "A 'Reciprocal Dumping' Model of International Trade," *Journal of International Economics* 15 (1983): 313–21; A. K. Dixit, "International Trade Policy for Oligopolistic Industries," *Economic Journal*, supp. (1984): 1–16; E. Helpman, "International Trade in the Presence of Product Differentiation, Economies of Scale,

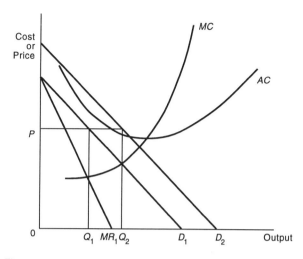

**Fig. 3.5. The monopolist's below-cost price results in the exit
of other firms and an increase in the monopolist's demand**

monopolist in the export market. It may also describe the behavior of dominant firms in the two markets, each of which has a large share of its market.
Yet, these are special cases. The essential feature of these cases is that the
seller, or cartel of sellers, possesses sufficient monopoly power in its home
market to sell in the export market at substantially lower prices than in the
home market. As we have seen, independent oligopolists, each having consid-
erably less than a major share of the home market, will not have the required
monopoly power.

An independent oligopolist, which is willing to accept losses, may set a
higher margin between its home market and export price. It also has the
option, however, of reducing its home market price. If such action triggers a
round of price-cutting by other sellers, then it would not achieve the goal of
increasing the firm's home market share. But if this anticipation leads it to
confine its price cutting to the export market, then the firm is joining in
collusion with the other sellers in the home market to restrict competition
there.

Krugman also models the effect of learning economies on trade. A monopolist may set its output on the basis of its expected *MC* at a future date, the

---

and Monopolistic Competition: A Chamberlinian-Heckscher-Ohlin Approach," *Journal of Inter-
national Economics* 11 (1981): 305–40; Paul R. Krugman, "Scale Economies, Product Differen-
tiation, and the Pattern of Trade," *American Economic Review* 70 (1980): 950–59; Paul R.
Krugman, ed., *Strategic Trade Policy and the New International Economics* (Cambridge, Mass.:
MIT Press, 1986); Paul R. Krugman, *Rethinking International Trade* (Cambridge, Mass.: MIT
Press, 1990).

MC declining as the cumulative output grows between the present and that future date. If learning economies reduce the *MC* over time, then the output in the intervening period will exceed that which the firm would have produced had it based its decision on the actual current *MC*.[7] Again, Krugman relies on a Cournot model, which is appropriate for the special cases already referred to in connection with scale economies. It is inappropriate for independent oligopolists, none of which has a large market share.

The Law of Dumping

The antidumping laws have expressed a general policy of protecting U.S. industries against "unfair" foreign competition. "Unfair" in this context has referred to export prices that are below either costs or home market prices. The first such legislation came as early as 1897 when Congress required the secretary of the Treasury to impose a special duty, a countervailing duty (CVD) to offset an export subsidy by a foreign government.[8]

In 1921 Congress passed the Antidumping Law, under which in 1968 the U.S. TV industry filed a complaint against Japanese dumping. The Antidumping Act of 1916, which extended the provisions of the Sherman Act to imports, was not intended to stop dumping generally. The 1916 act was explicitly aimed at predatory dumping, which is to say dumping motivated by the intention to destroy a U.S. industry or to prevent its growth. The 1921 legislation applied to dumping generally. Nevertheless, it was prompted by the fear that German cartels would seek to enter and take a large share of U.S. markets by dumping. This act gave the president the power to impose special duties against goods found to have been dumped by the administering authority and the Tariff Commission, the International Trade Commission's predecessor, found to have caused material injury to a U.S. industry. The Tariff Commission might recommend the imposition of special duties, but the president might not accept the recommendation.

The administrative authority was the Treasury. To decide whether goods were dumped, the Treasury determined whether the exports were at less-than-fair-value (LTFV) prices. The export price at the factory was compared to the home market price also at the factory at the time of exportation, allowances being made for warranties and other differences in the circumstances of sale.[9] When small home market sales or other reasons made accurate comparisons

---

7. Krugman, *Rethinking International Trade,* 195–97.

8. I. M. Destler, *American Trade Politics: System under Stress* (Washington, D.C.: Institute for International Economics, 1986), 20, 111.

9. Leslie W. Jacobs and Randall A. Hove, "Remedies for Unfair Import Competition in the United States," *Cornell International Law Journal* 13 (1980): 6.

difficult, the criterion might be the export price to other countries. Another standard was a "constructed value," based on the cost of production. Following the LTFV determination, the Tariff Commission decided whether the LTFV imports inflicted "material injury" on a domestic industry. It considered the volume of imports or the increase in the volume either absolutely or relatively to production in the U.S., whether the prices of competitive U.S. products had been depressed either absolutely or relative to production in the U.S., whether the prices of competitive U.S. products had been depressed significantly, and the effects of the dumping on the output, sales, market share, profits, productivity, return on investments, utilization of capacity, cash flow, inventories, employment, wages, growth, ability to raise capital, and investment of the domestic industry.[10] Prior to 1980 a finding of injury resulted in the Customs Service determining the dumping margin, the difference between the fair value and the export price. Since 1980 the ITA has made the determination. The merchandise, then, is subject to special dumping duties equal to the dumping margin.[11]

GATT provides a similar definition. Article VI defines dumping as the export of a product at a price below normal value, which usually means the home market price. GATT also provides the alternative definitions based on prices of exports to third countries and the exporter's cost of production. Further, when dumping causes or threatens injury to domestic firms GATT permits governments to take action against it.[12]

From the mid-1930s, when the Roosevelt administration began to negotiate trade agreements with other countries, many members of Congress became apprehensive about the effects on some industries. In addition, they contended that the administration was not vigorously enforcing the unfair trade laws. During the 1950s and 1960s U.S. petitioners for either antidumping duties or CVDs won few cases. Out of 371 antidumping cases processed from 1955 through 1968, only 12 concluded with findings of dumping. But 89 other cases resulted in a revision in the price or termination of exports.[13] The results for CVD petitions were similar. In addition, the antidumping case arising from the TV industry's petition in 1968 had not been decided by the time Congress passed the Trade Act of 1974. The long delay may have influenced the legislation.

The 1974 act dealt with other areas as well as with antidumping duties,

10. Jacobs and Hove, "Remedies for Unfair Import Competition," 8.

11. Sandra E. Lorimer, "Effective Judicial Review of Antidumping Determinations," *Cornell International Law Journal* 12 (1979): 272.

12. Hoekman and Leidy, "Dumping, Antidumping, and Emergency Protection," 30.

13. "Report of the Secretary of the Treasury," *Annual Report of the Department of the Treasury* (Washington, D.C.: GPO, 1968), 416. Cited by Destler, *American Trade Politics,* 113 n. 6.

but here I will confine my discussion to these duties. Congress intended to limit the president's discretion in unfair competition proceedings. To signify the importance of the change the act renamed the commission, the International Trade Commission. The act required the president to provide import relief, "unless he determines that provision of such relief is not in the national economic interest of the United States."[14] Prior to 1974 the Tariff Commission conducted the investigation and then reported its findings to the president, who could reject the report. The act strengthened the commission's authority. Not only did the act require the president to provide relief unless he or she decided that it was not in the national interest to do so, but it also specified several criteria for his or her decision: the effect on the prices paid by consumers, the effect on U.S. international economic interests, the effect on other U.S. industries, the effectiveness of the antidumping duty for promoting adjustment, and the costs to taxpayers, communities, and workers of the refusal to grant relief.[15] In addition, the president was required to act within sixty days of the recommendation. If he or she did not grant the relief, Congress could implement the recommendation by a majority vote of both houses.[16]

To further limit the president's power in this area the act gave the commission greater independence by increasing the term of its members from six to nine years, stipulating that they could not be reappointed. In addition, the president lost control over the commission's budget, which was now to be set only by Congress.[17]

Despite the act, the number of antidumping cases did not increase significantly. In general, the changes in the administration of import relief were benefiting the injured industries only slightly. In 1979 the U.S. House Ways and Means Committee said that the countervailing duty and antidumping duty laws were being inadequately enforced.[18]

In 1979 Congress had to approve the agreements under the Tokyo Round of multilateral trade negotiations. This round, unlike the previous ones, focused on nontariff barriers to trade rather than on tariff cuts. Congress thus had another opportunity to enact legislation. The changes set time limits for antidumping and CVD investigations and the assessment of penalties. It es-

---

14. Quoted by Robert E. Baldwin, *The Political Economy of U.S. Import Policy* (Cambridge, Mass.: MIT Press, 1985), 129.

15. Baldwin, *Political Economy of U.S. Import Policy,* 129.

16. Destler, *American Trade Politics,* 115.

17. Baldwin, *Political Economy of U.S. Import Policy,* 88–89.

18. U.S. Congress, House, Committee on Ways and Means, Trade Agreements Act of 1979, 96th Cong., 1st Sess., July 3, 1979, H.R. 96-317. Cited by Destler, *American Trade Politics,* 120.

tablished a system of customs valuation that would use the actual export price paid.[19]

The Congress also forced the executive branch to transfer responsibility for the administration of the unfair trade remedy laws from the Treasury to the Commerce Department. This was not part of the act, but the Senate Finance Committee made the transfer a condition of its approval.[20] The Commerce Department was much more sympathetic to the interests of U.S. industries competing with imports than the Treasury Department, which, along with the State Department, placed a higher priority on promoting trade. The Treasury Department regarded the import relief laws as essentially protectionist.

---

19. *Trade: U.S. Policy since 1945* (Washington, D.C.: Congressional Quarterly Inc., 1984), 89.

20. Destler, *American Trade Politics*, 122–23.

CHAPTER 4

Some Rudiments of Antitrust Law and Economics

Although *Matsushita* primarily was a Sherman Act Section 1 case, the plaintiffs also invoked Section 2, and they brought charges under the Wilson Tariff Act and the 1916 Antidumping Act. To help direct this book's inquiry, I will review some rudiments of antitrust law, but, before doing so, I comment briefly on the latter two acts. In 1894 the Wilson Tariff Act extended the scope of the Sherman Act to imports. Judge Edward R. Becker ruled that the provisions of the Wilson Tariff Act were substantively the same as those of the Sherman Act.[1]

To guard U.S. industries against predatory, foreign cartels, in 1916 Congress outlawed predatory dumping by passing the Antidumping Act, which usually is referred to as the 1916 Antidumping Act to distinguish it from the 1921 Antidumping Act. Unlike the 1921 act, which was intended to stop dumping generally, the 1916 act was antitrust legislation. The 1916 act outlawed: "such act or acts be done with the intent of destroying or injuring an industry in the United States, or of preventing the establishment of an industry in the United States, or of restraining or monopolizing any part of trade and commerce in such articles in the United States."[2] Difficulties in proving predatory intent, obtaining jurisdiction over foreign manufacturers, and uncertainty whether it required price comparisons between identical articles sold in the home market and in the U.S. rendered the act ineffective.[3]

In *Matsushita* the principal charge was that the defendants had conspired to expand their share of the U.S. TV market. The plaintiffs alleged that the Japanese TV manufacturers had injured them by depressing prices and by taking a large share of the market. The Section 2 charge was that the defendants had attempted and conspired to monopolize the U.S. market.

I will review elements of the law relating to conspiracy, injury to plaintiffs, summary judgments, and attempts to monopolize. Under the last head-

---

1. 513 F. Supp. 1100 (1981), at 1162–64.

2. U.S.C. §72 (1976).

3. Barry S. Fisher, "The Antidumping Law of the United States: A Legal and Economic Analysis," *Law and Policy in International Business* 5 (1973): 93; *Columbia Journal of Transnational Law* 20 (1981): 139.

ing I will discuss the *Matsushita* Supreme Court's chief concern: the definition of predatory pricing. The case is a landmark in the related law.[4]

Agreements in Restraint of Trade

Addyston (1899) established that price-fixing and market-sharing agreements are per se violations of Section 1.[5] The six leading producers of iron pipe had agreed to divide the market into territories and to fix prices in each. The defendants offered the justification that the agreement protected them against destroying themselves and that, in any case, the agreed prices were reasonable. But neither defense was valid, according to Judge (later Chief Justice) William Howard Taft's opinion in the appeals court, which the Supreme Court endorsed.[6] The prohibition covers market-sharing as well as price agreements. Lawrence Sullivan says: "A *per se* rule applies to market division arrangements regardless of whether they are linked to price fixing or other restraints, and apparently without need for a specific showing of significant power or discernible competitive effects."[7] Mentioning exclusive territories, exclusive customers, and exclusive products, Sullivan insists that all forms of market division are unlawful.

Legal questions arising in *Matsushita* concerned the sufficiency of proof of conspiracy, whether the alleged conspirators acted independently, and the proof of injury inflicted on the plaintiffs by the alleged conspiracy. On the first question the specific issue was whether written price and market-sharing agreements were sufficient proof of a conspiracy. Did the plaintiffs have to show that the agreements were effective? The main text of *Socony-Vacuum* (1940) answers yes, when it says that a combination formed for the purpose and with the effect of fixing a price is illegal.[8] An important footnote contra-

---

4. Wesley J. Liebeler, "Whither Predatory Pricing? From Areeda and Turner to *Matsushita*," *Notre Dame Law Review* 61 (1986): 1052–98; Kenneth G. Elzinga, "The New International Economics Applied: Japanese Televisions and U.S. Consumers," *Chicago-Kent Law Review* 64 (1988): 941–67; James F. Ponsoldt and Marc J. Lewyn, "Judicial Activism, Economic Theory and the Role of Summary Judgment in Sherman Act Conspiracy Cases: The Illogic of *Matsushita*," *Antitrust Bulletin* (Fall 1988): 575–613; Franklin M. Fisher, "*Matsushita:* Myth v. Analysis in the Economics of Predation," *Chicago-Kent Law Review* 64 (1988): 969–77; Kenneth L. Elzinga, "Collusive Predation: *Matsushita v. Zenith (1986)*, in *The Antitrust Revolution*, ed. John E. Kwoka, Jr., Lawrence J. White (Glenview, Ill: Scott, Foresman, 1989), 241–62; F. M. Scherer and David Ross, *Industrial Market Structure and Economic Performance*, 3d ed. (Boston: Houghton Mifflin, 1990), 469–71.

5. Addyston Pipe and Steel Co. v. U.S., 175 U.S. 211 (1899).

6. In *BMI* (1979) the Supreme Court ruled that a price-fixing agreement is lawful when it enhances economic efficiency and renders markets more competitive (441 U.S. 1, at 19–20).

7. Lawrence Anthony Sullivan, *Handbook of the Law of Antitrust* (St. Paul, Minn.: West Publishing Co., 1977), 217.

8. Sullivan, *Handbook of the Law of Antitrust*, 213.

dicts this statement, however, by saying that Section 1 strikes down conspiracies in restraint of trade, whether or not they are "wholly nascent or abortive on the one hand, or successful on the other."[9]

Logically prior to the issue of the effectiveness of an agreement is whether one exists. Whether there was an agreement is not an issue when the plaintiffs produce direct evidence, which is to say they produce documents, such as written agreements, or the testimony of participants at meetings. It becomes an issue when the plaintiffs can offer only circumstantial evidence, which refers to secondary facts, such as simultaneous or nearly simultaneous price changes. Defendants may deny that the alleged meetings took place, but, once it is established that they did and that their representatives agreed on prices, there is no problem of inference. The direct evidence establishes the existence of a conspiracy. A case based on circumstantial evidence may present a problem of inference. The defendants may have determined that costs had risen and decided independently to raise their prices simultaneously and by the same amount. Moreover, once one of them raises its price each of the others may independently decide to ask the same price.

An important case on permissible inferences is *Interstate Circuit* (1939),[10] for which the facts are as follows. In many cities the defendant film exhibitor Interstate Circuit, and one other exhibitor had a monopoly or dominated the market. The defendant wrote identical letters to eight movie distributors, asking each to stop distributing first-run movies to exhibitors whose admission prices were below those in the specified schedule or who showed such movies as part of a double feature. Each letter referred to the other letter recipients, the distributors adhered to the restrictions, and there was no evidence of communication among the distributors. The Supreme Court decided that, since it was unlikely that the distributors would have changed their policies without an understanding that all were doing so, one could reasonably infer a conspiracy. No direct evidence was needed. Competitors' adherence to a plan that was not in their independent self-interest justified the inference of conspiracy.

In *Theatre Enterprises* (1954),[11] which developed this line of reasoning,

---

9. 310 U.S. 150 (1940), at 224–26 n. 59. The footnote reads, in part:

But that does not mean that both a purpose and a power to fix prices are necessary for the establishment of a conspiracy under §1 of the Sherman Act. That would be true if power or ability to commit an offense was necessary in order to convict a person of conspiring to commit it. But it is well established that a person "may be guilty of conspiring although incapable of committing the objective offense." And it is likewise well settled that conspiracies under the Sherman Act are not dependent on any overt act other than the act of conspiring. It is the "contract, combination . . . or conspiracy in restraint of trade or commerce" which §1 of the Act strikes down, whether the concerted activity be wholly nascent or abortive on the one hand, or successful on the other. (References omitted.)

10. Interstate Circuit v. United States, 306 U.S. 208 (1939).

11. Theatre Enterprises v. Paramount Film Distributing, 346 U.S. 537 (1954).

the plaintiff film exhibitor complained of a boycott by all film distributors in the Baltimore area. They had refused to allow Theatre Enterprises to show first-run films in the suburbs. According to the distributors, it was in the interest of each of them independently to allow first-run films to be shown only in downtown theaters. The jury found for the defendants. The Supreme Court affirmed, saying: "'conscious parallelism' has not yet read conspiracy out of the Sherman Act entirely."[12] By pointing to the independent interest of each defendant, the Court imposed a stricter standard on plaintiffs than in *Interstate Circuit*.

Moving on to another issue, according to the footnote in *Socony-Vacuum*, which I have mentioned, plaintiffs need not prove the effectiveness of a conspiracy. Nevertheless, private plaintiffs in private suits must show that they have been harmed to gain standing to sue, and ineffective agreements are harmless. A bystander cannot sue sellers conspiring to set prices. As a private action, *Matsushita* was brought under Section 4 of the Clayton Act, which provides a treble damage remedy for antitrust violations.[13] If a jury had found for the plaintiffs, then Zenith and NUE would have presented their claims for damages, and the District Court would have decided what was fair and awarded treble that amount. The Supreme Court established the standing requirements in *Brunswick* (1977.)[14] In that case the Court decided that a plaintiff had to show that an antitrust violation had driven it out of business, reduced the prices at which it was able to sell its goods, or reduced its sales. Had the Department of Justice sued, it would only have had to prove a violation, which it could have done by producing the agreements.

Standard for Summary Judgments

Federal Rule of Civil Procedure 56(c) provides that a court grant summary judgment when "there is no genuine issue as to any material fact." When there is such an issue the judge must allow a trial. In deciding on a motion for summary judgment, a judge must determine whether a reasonable jury could decide in the plaintiff's favor. The judge rules on issues of law and on which issues are factual. Thus, the law has given plaintiffs the benefit of the doubt on such motions, and antitrust cases are not an exception. As in other cases, juries are expected to decide factual issues after hearing and appraising the testimony from both sides.

The appropriate scope of judicial discretion depends in part on the kind of evidence to be heard by the jury. If the evidence is to be circumstantial,

---

12. 346 U.S. 537 (1954), at 541.
13. 15 U.S.C. §15 (1973).
14. 429 U.S. 477 (1977).

then the judge may not allow a trial, because he or she decides that the inference of a conspiracy is too implausible to persuade a reasonable jury. Direct evidence eliminates this discretion, but the judge decides whether the evidence is direct. Defendants may deny the truthfulness of the direct evidence, but the judge may not decide the issue. It must be left up to the jury.

In *Poller* (1962) the Supreme Court took a strong pro-plaintiff stand. The Court ruled that to win summary judgment the defendant had to rebut conclusively the plaintiff's case, thus strengthening the force of circumstantial evidence. The Court forcefully asserted:

> We believe that summary procedures should be used sparingly in complex antitrust litigation where motive and intent play leading roles, the proof is largely in the hands of the alleged conspirators, and hostile witnesses thicken the plot. It is only when the witnesses are present and subject to cross-examination that their credibility and the weight to be given to their testimony can be appraised. Trial by affidavit is no substitute for trial by jury which so long has been the hallmark of "even handed justice."[15]

I summarize the facts of *Poller*. The plaintiff operated the TV channel, WCAN, a CBS affiliate. CBS persuaded another party to purchase WOKY, a competitor of WCAN, agreeing to buy this station subsequently, which it did. Later CBS refused to renew WCAN's network affiliation. No longer able to compete, the channel ceased operations. The major issue of material fact was whether CBS conspired with others to eliminate WCAN.

The Supreme Court said that the support for a motion for summary judgment had to be conclusive.[16] Although the Court conceded that the plaintiff might not prevail at trial, the charge was not mere "fantasy." The evidence showed that the complaint raised a genuine issue of material fact.[17]

In *Cities Service* (1968), swinging to the defendant's side, the Court decided that a plausible case was not enough for a plaintiff to survive a summary judgment motion. The plaintiff's theory had to be more plausible than an alternative, innocent explanation of defendant's conduct. According to the Court, the inference that Cities Service's conduct was due to causes other than a conspiracy "was at least equal to the inference that it was due to conspiracy."[18] While the Court suggested that the rival theory had more credibility than the plaintiff's, it required only equal plausibility to deny the

---

15. Poller v. Columbia Broadcasting System, 368 U.S. 464 (1962), at 473.

16. Poller, 368 U.S., at 465–73.

17. 368 U.S., at 472.

18. First National Bank of Arizona v. Cities Service Co., 391 U.S. 253 (1968), at 280.

plaintiff a trial. In this case, as in the subsequent ones that are reviewed here, the Court appears to have become an active fact finder.

The facts are as follows. The plaintiff had agreed to purchase oil from the National Iranian Oil Company (NIOC) and to resell this oil to Cities Service. NIOC was the successor to the Anglo-Iranian Oil Company, which the Iranian government had expropriated. According to the plaintiff, Anglo-Iranian organized a boycott against companies reselling oil purchased from NIOC. Cities Service therefore canceled its agreement with the plaintiff and purchased oil from Kuwait, after being invited to do so by Anglo-Iranian.[19]

To decide in the defendant's favor the Court appears to have appropriated the jury's job of assessing the facts and to have abandoned the precedent of giving the plaintiff the benefit of the doubt.[20] Attempting to reconcile the decision with *Poller,* the Court said that in that case the defendants had a common interest in concerted action. In *Cities Service* this critical element was absent.

The next important case was *Norfolk Monument* (1969), in which the Court, veering the other way, reversed the grant of summary judgment. The plaintiff had alleged that a manufacturer of bronze grave markers and five cemetery operators had conspired by jointly adopting certain restrictions to prevent the sale of its markers.[21] The district court granted summary judgment, and the Fourth Circuit affirmed, because the parallel practices were justified on business grounds. The Supreme Court reversed, because the reasonableness of the rules was a question of material fact, which the jury, not the judge, had to decide. For the summary judgment to stand the alleged conspiracy had to be disproved by pretrial discovery. The Court quoted its opinion in *Poller* that summary procedures should be used sparingly in complex antitrust litigation.[22]

I also comment on *Monsanto* (1984), on which the Supreme Court relied heavily in *Matsushita.* In *Monsanto* the plaintiff survived a motion for a directed verdict, the jury decided in favor of the plaintiff, and the Seventh Circuit and the Supreme Court affirmed.[23] In spite of the decision, *Monsanto* departed from *Norfolk* and raised the hurdle for plaintiffs above the one in *Cities Service* by requiring evidence excluding the possibility of independent action by the alleged conspirators.[24]

The facts are as follows. Between 1957 and 1968 the plaintiff, Spray-Rite, sold Monsanto's herbicides at discount prices. In 1968 Monsanto termi-

---

19. First National Bank of Arizona v. Cities Service Co., 391 U.S. 253 (1968), at 260–78.
20. 391 U.S., at 280.
21. Norfolk Monument Co. v. Woodlawn Memorial Gardens, Inc., 394 U.S. 700 (1969).
22. Norfolk Monument, 394 U.S., at 704 (quoting Poller v. Columbia Broadcasting System, 368 U.S., at 473).
23. Spray-Rite Service v. Monsanto Co., 465 U.S., 752 (1984).
24. 465 U.S., at 768.

nated the plaintiff's distributorship, and four years later Spray-Rite went out of business. The complaint alleged that Monsanto had conspired with some distributors to fix retail prices. Monsanto replied that Spray-Rite had been terminated because it had failed to fulfill the requirements of the new distributor policy announced in 1967 by neither promoting sales to retailers nor hiring trained sales personnel. Spray-Rite contended that the true explanation was in the complaints by distributors about its pricing.[25] The jury found for the plaintiff, and the Seventh Circuit and the Supreme Court affirmed.

The Supreme Court opinion declared that, while a manufacturer, acting independently, has the right to refuse to deal with a distributor, it was unlawful for the manufacturer to agree with its distributors to fix resale prices.[26] According to the Court, the direct evidence included testimony by a Monsanto district manager that, after terminating Spray-Rite, the company threatened to reduce its shipments to other discount distributors. Also, Monsanto complained to a price-cutting subsidiary's parent, which then instructed its subsidiary to comply, and compliance followed. In addition, a newsletter from a distributor to a customer assured readers that Monsanto-owned outlets would not undercut the suggested retail price. Also, a defendant's former employee testified that the company had repeatedly asked Spray-Rite to maintain prices, and the latter's president reported that Monsanto had threatened termination unless prices were maintained. Moreover, Monsanto never complained to Spray-Rite about the purported failure to meet distributorship requirements.[27] According to the Court, a reasonable fact finder could infer a price agreement between distributors and retailers, which Monsanto would enforce.

The Court toughened the requirement for plaintiffs, however, by emphasizing that the direct evidence excluded the possibility of independent action by the manufacturer and tended to prove that the manufacturer and the distributors had joined in a common scheme. The Court rejected the appeals court's conclusion that evidence of distributors' complaints followed by the termination of a price-cutting distributor was a sufficient ground for dismissing a directed verdict motion.[28] A plaintiff had to show more than this sequence of events. But all the direct evidence taken together warranted the jury's decision.

Attempts to Monopolize

In *Matsushita* the Section 2 complaint of attempting and conspiring to monopolize the sale of TV receivers raised the related issues of the specific intent to

---

25. 465 U.S., at 755–63.
26. 465 U.S., at 761.
27. 465 U.S., at 765–67.
28. 465 U.S. 752 (1984), at 759.

monopolize the market, the probability of success, and the definition of predatory pricing. Following *Swift* (1905) fact finders in "attempt" cases must
determine the "specific intent" behind the defendants' actions.[29] Antitrust law
inherited the requirement from criminal law. A fired gun shows specific intent, but not the purchase of a weapon nor the expression of murderous
intentions. Finding the fired gun may be difficult for antitrust plaintiffs.

Justice Holmes's majority opinion in *Swift* required as well that the
defendant's behavior have a dangerous probability of success. The Ninth
Circuit's notable opinion in *Inglis* (1981) examined this requirement.[30] Inglis,
a wholesale baker in the northern California-Nevada area, claimed that ITT
Continental Baking Company and two other companies had attempted to
monopolize the white bread market in that area by charging discriminatory
and less-than-cost prices over a period of about ten years. Inglis went out of
business in 1976. The Court held that the law recognized three elements of an
attempt claim:

> (1) specific intent to control prices or destroy competition in some part of
> commerce; (2) predatory or anticompetitive conduct directed to accom-
> plishing the unlawful purpose; and (3) a dangerous probability of suc-
> cess.[31]

The opinion did not say that plaintiffs had to prove a dangerous probability of
success but only that proof would help the fact finder to gauge intent. A
defendant would not be foolish enough to make an attempt, if there was no or
little chance of succeeding. According to the Court:

> Thus, if market conditions are such that a course of conduct described by
> the plaintiff would be unlikely to succeed in monopolizing the market, it
> is less likely that the defendant actually attempted to monopolize the
> market. Conversely, a firm with substantial market power may find it
> more rational to engage in a monopolistic course of conduct than would a
> smaller firm in a less concentrated market.

As the Ninth Circuit recognized, however, a small probability of success need
not exclude the possibility of an attempt. Although a defective gun cannot

---

29. Swift & Co. v. United States, 196 U.S. 375, at 396; Richard A. Posner and Frank H.
Easterbrook, *Antitrust: Cases, Economic Notes, and Other Materials*, 2d ed. (St. Paul, Minn.:
1980), 616.
30. William Inglis & Sons Baking Co. v. ITT Continental Baking Co., 668 F.2d 1014 (9th
Cir. 1981).
31. William Inglis, 668 F.2d, at 1027.

kill, the criminal may manifest the specific intent by trying to fire one. Thus, the Ninth Circuit recognized that a reasonable jury might infer the intent to monopolize from the conduct, despite a slight chance of achieving the goal:

> But, in general, conduct that will support a claim of attempted monopolization must be such that its anticipated benefits were dependent upon its tendency to discipline or eliminate competition and thereby enhance the firm's long-term ability to reap the benefits of monopoly power. Such conduct is not truly competition; it makes sense only because it eliminates competition. It does not enhance the quality or attractiveness of the product, reduce its cost, or alter the demand function that all competitors confront. Its purpose is to create a monopoly by means other than fair competition.[32]

The Court insisted only on a showing of the motive to eliminate competition; the evidence of intent may be ample without the firm having a high probability of success. A demonstration that the defendant sought to eliminate competitors was an adequate proof of an attempt.

Predatory Pricing by a Domestic Firm

Turning to the law on predatory pricing, in some of the cases the charge was monopolization, and in others it was attempted monopolization. The antitrust cases involving predatory pricing prior to *Matsushita* and the debate in the journals on appropriate criteria revolved around a dominant firm in a domestic market. Despite its apparent inappropriateness, this section discusses domestic predation for three reasons. First, it was the basis for the Supreme Court's decision in *Matsushita*. Second, most of the literature on predatory pricing examines only domestic predation. Third, it is the basis for my suggested standard for international predation. This section concerns the antitrust cases involving predatory pricing and the debate in the journals. I will leave the case of a foreign-based predator to the next section.

The famous monopolization cases of 1911, *Standard Oil* and *American Tobacco*, have remained classics, despite the Supreme Court's failure to establish a standard for distinguishing predatory from competitive behavior. Ample evidence of intent relieved the Court of the need to set a rule. With predatory prices being only part of the Department of Justice's narrative, the weight of all the facts in *Standard Oil* convinced the Court that the defendant sought monopoly power. In addition to acquiring nearly all the oil refineries in the Cleveland area and many others outside the area, Standard Oil had gained

---

32. 668 F.2d, at 1030–31 (nn. omitted).

control of pipelines, had refused to supply competitors from its pipelines, and had obtained preferential rates and rebates from the railroads, forcing smaller companies to join it or leave the business. The Department of Justice also had argued that to force competitors to accept its takeover bids the company had cut prices deeply in particular regions.[33] The Court found it hard to excuse the behavior as merely aggressively competitive, innocent of the alleged predatory intent.

In the same eventful year for antitrust law a similarly long record of predatory behavior convinced the Supreme Court of American Tobacco's monopolization of the cigarette industry.[34] American Tobacco had engrossed supplies of leaf tobacco, bought out many former rivals, and sold some brands in its competitors' local markets at prices less than cost. On one occasion the effective after-tax price was zero. Not surprisingly, competitors sold out to American Tobacco at distress prices. The Court found it especially interesting that the company had closed many of the purchased plants. Refraining from depending exclusively on a single, simple rule, the Court attached no great significance to the comparison between costs and prices in the evidence.

But if judges were to compel plaintiffs to tell dramatic tales, they would debilitate Section 2. Predators may not have become extinct with the passing of John D. Rockefeller and James B. Duke. Moreover, a law that intervenes only after the victim has died accomplishes little, yet it was the death of the prey that made the stories so persuasive. Finally, by refusing to announce a rule, the Court has imposed on plaintiffs the laborious task of narrating long histories and on courts that of establishing their validity.

To lighten the burden, Phillip Areeda and Donald H. Turner offered a cost-based definition of predatory pricing.[35] Their paradigmatic, hypothetical villain was a powerfully entrenched firm with a large market share destroying its present competitors and blocking the entry of potential competitors. The authors specified two goals: to provide the courts with a badly needed definition of predatory pricing and to dispel the widespread, exaggerated fear of predators.[36]

The adoption of a clear, correct definition would ease the courts' task by eliminating those cases based on a false definition. With intent the chief issue the problem was to identify pricing behavior aimed at monopoly power.

---

33. U.S. v. Standard Oil Co. of New Jersey et al., 173 Fed. 177 (1909), 221 U.S. 1 (1911).

34. U.S. v. American Tobacco Co., 221 U.S. 106 (1911).

35. Phillip Areeda and Donald H. Turner, "Predatory Pricing and Related Practices under Section 2 of the Sherman Act," *Harvard Law Review* 88 (1975): 697–733.

36. Areeda and Turner, "Predatory Pricing," 698.

Areeda and Turner took on the task of drawing the line between behavior that was so motivated and vigorously competitive behavior.

The participants in the debate in the journals, triggered by Areeda and Turner's article, disagreed about the appropriate criterion. Where the line should be drawn is not obvious. Suppose that a brash, new firm tries to break into a market by undercutting the dominant firm's price. Instead of quietly suffering sales losses, the dominant firm retaliates by quoting an even lower price. How large must the cut be for the dominant firm to be a predator? Suggested criteria include average cost (AC), average variable cost (AVC), and marginal cost (MC). AC, which would prevent retaliation against firms taking losses, may be too severe a standard. Also, prices may drop for other reasons. Demand may fall, and not every entrant comes in at the right time. Another problem is that AC is not always easily measured. An accountant's estimate, based on the irrelevant book value of an old and obsolete plant, may exceed the true AC, which is based on the cost of the required plant utilizing the current technology, which may not be known.

The key problem in the debate over the appropriate standard for predatory pricing is the probability of the behavior, disagreement spawning different proposed pricing standards.[37] Those who believe that it is highly improbable advocate a lenient standard to avoid deterring competitive behavior by large firms. Others believe that predatory pricing is a problem and advocate a severe standard to deter the practice. The participants in the debate have agreed that the criteria should include some measure of cost, but which measure remains an issue. Acceptance of the AVC standard is predicated on the assumed rarity of predatory pricing. Its defenders say that the severe standard would do more harm than good by inhibiting the competitive price cuts of large firms. The alternative standard is AC.

---

37. John S. McGee, "Predatory Price Cutting: The Standard Oil (N.J.) Case," *Journal of Law and Economics* 1 (October 1958): 137–69; and "Predatory Pricing Revisited," *Journal of Law and Economics* 23 (October 1980): 289–330; Areeda and Turner, "Predatory Pricing," 697–733; Oliver E. Williamson, "Predatory Pricing: A Strategic and Welfare Analysis," *Yale Law Journal* 87 (December 1977): 284–340; William J. Baumol, "Quasi-Permanence of Price Reductions: A Policy for Preventing Predatory Pricing," *Yale Law Journal* 89 (November 1979): 1–26; Paul L. Joskow and Alvin K. Klevorick, "A Framework for Analyzing Predatory Pricing Policy," *Yale Law Journal* 89 (December 1979): 213–70; F. M. Scherer, "Predatory Pricing and the Sherman Act: A Comment," *Harvard Law Review* 89 (March 1976): 883–88; Janusz A. Ordover and Robert D. Willig, "An Economic Definition of Predation: Pricing and Product Innovation," *Yale Law Journal* 91 (1981): 8–53; Roland H. Kollar II, "The Myth of Predatory Pricing: An Empirical Study," *Antitrust Law and Economics Review* 4 (1971): 105–23; Frank H. Easterbrook, "Predatory Strategies and Counterstrategies," *University of Chicago Law Review* 48 (1981): 263–337.

Areeda and Turner based their standard for predatory pricing on the following considerations:

1. A monopolist should not be permitted to set prices that are sufficiently low to drive efficient firms out of business or to keep out efficient entrants.
2. Prices should be consistent with optimum resource allocation.
3. Prices should be consistent with competition on the merits.

According to Areeda and Turner, the prospect of future high profits may induce monopolists or potential monopolists to prey on efficient but vulnerable firms. Because efficient firms, those with low average costs, survive under competition, as distinguished from oligopoly or monopoly, Areeda and Turner based their standards on the competitive pricing model.

Areeda and Turner also referred to optimum resource allocation as a goal. When shifts in resources between plants cannot increase total output they are optimally allocated, which tends to be so under competition. Under competition the price tends to equal MC. If the price exceeds MC, buyers are willing to pay more for an additional unit of output than what that unit costs. Therefore, an increase in output would add to total welfare. If MC exceeds the price, then buyers are unwilling to pay the cost of an additional unit, and the output should be reduced. Cutting output and raising the price would release labor, materials, and other resources to produce other goods. This was the argument Areeda and Turner advanced in behalf of an MC standard. Nevertheless, for practical reasons the authors ultimately recommend the AVC test.

Competing on the merits means competing on the basis of costs. The "fairness" criterion sets low costs, based on competitive market prices of the resources used, as the goal. Fair advantages, which stem from efficiency and the availability of resources, include low wages, low prices of materials, large scale, a superior technology, and an abundance of superior skills. No real cost benefits come from unfair advantages, which include superior financial resources, collusive arrangements, and political advantages. Accordingly, the competitive price is the reference point.

Although, strictly speaking, the predator that has a competitor to destroy is not a monopolist, to analyze its behavior Areeda and Turner employed the monopoly model. The model may be appropriate, for the predator is assumed to command a large market share. It may also be appropriate for colluding oligopolists, which together have a large market share and which jointly set prices to maximize their total profits. In contrast to a competitive model, in the monopoly model the market does not determine the price; the monopolist sets it. Figure 3.2 depicts the monopolist's price-output decision.

Areeda and Turner's predator was a monopolist deliberately setting a price low enough to destroy a competitor or to exclude a new competitor from the market. Areeda and Turner were unwilling to adopt the monopolist's profit-maximizing price, which exceeds the socially optimal price, as the floor below which a price is deemed predatory. Resources would be better employed at a lower price and larger output.[38] Accordingly, Areeda and Turner deemed any price above AC nonpredatory. They did not select an intermediate floor, such as MC, perhaps because, as they said later in their discussion, usually MC is not known.

Nor did Areeda and Turner select AC as the minimum. They suggested that the demand curve may lie below AC (see fig. 3.4), which is to say, the monopolist may suffer losses at any price. No sales may be possible at any profitable price; the profit-maximizing price is the loss-minimizing price. The price at which losses are the smallest corresponds to the output at which MC = MR. Moreover, requiring prices to exceed AC would reduce output below the socially optimal level, where $P = MC$.[39] The lowest allowable price, according to Areeda and Turner, is MC. At any lower price the monopolist would be suffering losses on the use of its variable inputs.

Nevertheless, to relieve the courts of the difficult task of estimating MC, the authors chose AVC as the standard. Firms do not keep accounts to compute MC, while AVC is more readily known. And, in fact, AVC may equal MC. Although conventionally drawn AVC diagrams show a single-value minimum and smoothly descending and ascending curves, actual AVC curves may be constant over some output ranges, and over these ranges $MC = AVC$. But at high outputs, when MC exceeds AVC, the AVC standard is more permissive than the MC standard. Also, AVC, which excludes fixed costs, is more permissive than the AC standard, particularly in periods of depressed demand, when capacity utilization is low and fixed costs are a large part of total costs. For the same reason the AVC standard is especially permissive for dominant firms in industries in which fixed costs are high even in prosperity. In such industries, however, even nonpredators may cut prices far below AC when demand falls.[40] The bottom price is AVC. Unless it has a predatory goal, a firm will not reduce its price below AVC.

Perhaps the courts should reserve the more lenient AVC standard for depressed periods and insist on the AC standard for other periods. Areeda and Turner, however, made no exceptions. As they said:

---

38. Areeda and Turner, "Predatory Pricing," 703.

39. Areeda and Turner, "Predatory Pricing," 711.

40. For an extended analysis of the effect of fixed costs on the change in prices associated with a fall in demand, see Scherer and Ross, *Industrial Market Structure and Economic Performance,* 286–88.

Recognizing that marginal cost data are typically unavailable, we conclude that: (a) A price at or above reasonably anticipated average variable cost should be conclusively presumed lawful. (b) A price below reasonably anticipated average variable cost should be conclusively presumed unlawful.[41]

Even though, as Areeda and Turner conceded, below-*AC* prices menace competition by eliminating or blocking the entry of efficient competitors, they refused to urge an *AC* standard.[42] In a brief defense Areeda and Turner said that, since only less efficient competitors will suffer larger losses per unit of output than the monopolist, equally efficient firms would survive. Presumably, they would add that equally efficient competitors will have as much access to capital. Areeda and Turner were willing to tolerate the long-run threat to competition because the prohibition of prices below *AC* would protect less efficient competitors as well as equally efficient ones.[43]

Evidently, the protection of equally efficient competitors was not a high-priority goal. Although it was not listed as one of their objectives, Areeda and Turner may have wanted to preserve the freedom of large companies to respond to smaller firms' price cuts with matching or greater price cuts. Moreover, as we saw earlier, because they judged predatory pricing to be rare, Areeda and Turner were unwilling to have an *AC* standard inhibiting the behavior of large firms.[44]

Other less sanguine writers urged greater strictness. Accepting the same social goals as Areeda and Turner, they judged the *AVC* standard to be an inadequate shield for efficient firms. F. M. Scherer said that it would allow a monopolist to exclude efficient entrants that would have to cover their *AC*.[45] A price below *AC* would increase entrants' uncertainty about their potential profits. Indeed, according to Scherer, since the available scale economies might require a firm to supply a large part of the market to survive, even a price exceeding *AC* might be predatory. Its output added to that of the dominant and other firms might push the price below *AC*. Scherer concluded that a court should undertake an extensive analysis of the relative costs of the monopolist and other firms, the minimum efficient scale of plant, and other conditions. Scherer also urged courts to determine whether fringe firms have been driven out or merely suppressed temporarily. In addition, they should determine whether, after its rivals withdrew, the monopolist expanded output or restricted output again. Having achieved its goal, a predator would restrict

---

41. Areeda and Turner, "Predatory Pricing," 733.
42. Areeda and Turner, "Predatory Pricing," 705–6.
43. Areeda and Turner, "Predatory Pricing," 711.
44. Areeda and Turner, "Predatory Pricing," 699.
45. Scherer, "Predatory Pricing and the Sherman Act," 869–903.

output and raise its price back to the monopoly level. In short, Scherer doubted that the courts can avoid an extensive analysis.

Another contributor, Judge (then professor) R. A. Posner, urged the *AC* test. He argued that the *AVC* rule would permit a monopolist to exclude efficient rivals, which must cover their full cost.[46]

Paul Joskow and Alvin Klevorick argued that the decision rules should vary between types of markets with the probability of predatory pricing.[47] Although Joskow and Klevorick did not address the probability question directly, they obviously believed that the likelihood is high enough in monopolistic markets to warrant a trial on the issue of predatory pricing, once it is established that a market is of this type. Suggesting that the courts undertake a two-tier inquiry, Joskow and Klevorick proposed that the first stage investigate the monopoly power of the alleged predator. The evidence of monopoly would include difficult entry, high concentration, and high profits. Monopoly power would be considered absent in a market to which entry is easy, which is unconcentrated, and when the defendant's profits have been low. Where no monopoly problem exists the court should dismiss the action.[48] Although the decision whether to go ahead will not always be easy, Joskow and Klevorick believed that the two-tier approach will reduce litigation costs. Having established that a defendant has monopoly power, a court should apply the *AVC* standard. A positive finding would decide the predatory issue. If, however, the price covers *AVC* but not *AC*, then the burden of proof should be on the defendant to show that it maximizes short-run profits. Joskow and Klevorick suggested that this defense will pass muster only when the industry has substantial excess capacity, and even then not if the excess is part of a dominant firm's strategy to deter entry. Following Oliver Williamson, Joskow and Klevorick proposed that this defense not be acceptable when the dominant firm has increased its output after entry.[49] Finally, they suggested, following William Baumol, that to be acceptable a price cut even to a level above *AC* should be maintained for a period of, say, two years.[50]

John McGee, who did address the probability question directly, concluded that predatory pricing is highly improbable, because the predator's losses will exceed the prey's.[51] McGee assumed that the predator is larger

46. R. A. Posner, *Antitrust Law: An Economic Perspective* (Chicago: University of Chicago Press, 1976), 184ff.

47. Joskow and Klevorick, "A Framework," 213–70.

48. Joskow and Klevorick, "A Framework," 246–48.

49. Joskow and Klevorick, "A Framework," 250–54. Joskow and Klevorick cite Williamson, "Predatory Pricing," 307–10.

50. Joskow and Klevorick, "A Framework," 255. Joskow and Klevorick cite Baumol, "Quasi-Permanence of Price Reductions," 4–6.

51. McGee, "Predatory Pricing Revisited," 289–330.

than the prey, has the same minimum AC, and the predatory price is below AC. Because its output is larger, the predator's loss will exceed the prey's. The target company will not simply go out of business. Expecting the dominant company to cease its predatory campaign and return to its original prices, the putative victim will resist. If it needs capital to match the predator's prices, then it will borrow. Anticipating this response, the dominant firm will decide to buy the small firm out and not take the predatory losses. The purchase would entail a smaller cost than reducing prices to loss levels. The basic reason the dominant firm will not prey is that its large size entails larger losses than those its potential victims will have to bear.

Another reason the dominant firm will not prey is that when it raises its price the victim may reenter and others may enter for the first time. McGee's reply to the argument that predators have deep pockets was that liquid reserves are costly and victims also can acquire reserves. Also, for the present value of future profits to equal the immediate losses, the nondiscounted future profits must be much larger than the losses.[52] Further, if the present value of the monopolist's future profits exceeds its predatory losses, then the present value of the prey's future profits should also exceed the losses resulting from the monopolist's assault. In short, if it pays the monopolist to prey, then it will pay the victim to hold out.

A more important argument was that it is cheaper for a dominant firm to buy out a competitor than to prey. McGee reasoned as follows. The dominant firm could buy the competitor's assets at a price equal to or a little more than the present value of its expected future income stream. If a firm holds out, then the dominant firm will be willing to pay any price up to the present value of the future monopoly profits resulting from the acquisition. This transaction is more attractive for the dominant firm than a predatory attack, since it then enjoys the monopoly profits immediately and does not suffer predatory losses. The competitor would gladly accept the maximum price that the dominant firm would pay. This price would exceed the present value of its future stream of earnings given the current state of competition in the market.[53]

This analysis depends critically on the assumption that the predator, as the dominant firm, has a larger market share than the victim. The conclusion follows that the predator's losses will exceed the victim's and, therefore, that the dominant firm will buy out its smaller competitors. But, suppose, as in *Matsushita,* the putative predator is not the dominant firm but has a small market share initially. Dealing with this possibility, McGee said that to depress the price below the competitive level the predator must be prepared to

52. McGee, "Predatory Pricing Revisited," 296–97.
53. McGee, "Predatory Price Cutting," 139–40.

sell increasing quantities. Therefore, the predator will be in the position of selling more and therefore losing more than its competitors.[54]

Yet, the predator that begins from a small market share need not supply a large part of the market at a loss price to drive out its competitors. Figure 4.1 shows the market demand curve (D) and the supply curve (S_D) at different prices. The competitive equilibrium price is P_C, and the output is Q_C. Enter the predator, which offers the product at the predatory price (P_P), which is below the other firms' AC but above their AVC. They now supply Q_1, and the predator supplies $Q_2 - Q_1$. Figure 4.1 shows $Q_2 - Q_1$ to be much smaller than Q_1. The predator's losses are much smaller than those of the other firms. Their demand is highly elastic, because the predator's supply is elastic. The other firms meet the predator's price, because they are unwilling to lose market share to the predator. They may prefer to maintain their prices at the cost of market share, expecting the predator not to maintain the low price as it gains sales. But, as long as they supply a large part of the market and match the predator's price, their losses will exceed the predator's. As long as the predator supplies a small part of the market, it can at small cost to itself impose large losses on the other firms. The losses may result in the elimination of these firms. If the predator maintains the same price as the other firms leave the market, its losses will grow. To keep its losses small, however, the predator may raise its price as they leave.

The market situation for the predator with a small market share is the converse of that which McGee envisaged. McGee's dominant firm will not prey because its immediate losses are larger than those of its small competitors, and its future profits, which must be discounted, must be very large to offset its losses. The competitors' small immediate losses do not require the prospect of large future profits to induce them to hold out. But a predator's immediate losses are small when its market share is small, and the competitors' immediate losses are large.

McGee also argued that a firm will not prey on competitors because when it raises its price entry will occur. Yet, even if entry is easy, the predator may deter entry by constructing sufficient capacity to supply all or a large part of the market at a price at or below the AC of potential competitors.[55] A history of loss pricing to eliminate competitors also may deter entrants.

Also, entry may not be easy. McGee assumed that entry will be rapid

54. McGee, "Predatory Price Cutting," 140.

55. See Stephen C. Salop, "Strategic Entry Deterrence," *American Economic Review, Papers and Proceedings* 69 (May 1979): 335–38; Richard L. Schmalensee, "Entry Deterrence in the Ready-to-Eat Breakfast Cereal Industry," *Bell Journal of Economics* 9 (Autumn 1978): 305–27; A. Michael Spence, "Entry, Capacity, Investment, and Oligopoly Pricing," *Bell Journal of Economics* 8 (Autumn 1977): 534–44.

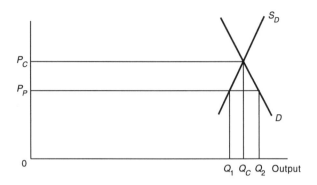

Fig. 4.1. The predator supplies a small part of the market

when the price exceeds the competitive level. He did not consider a more complex model in which entry is moderately difficult. McGee examined only the payoff to the strategy of setting and for a period maintaining a price below the profit-maximizing level and then returning to the original level. Darius Gaskins presented a model in which the dominant firm's strategy varies depending on the difficulty of entry and its cost advantage over potential competitors.[56] The predator may set a price that permits some entry and still obtain excess profits. It may manipulate the price over time to maximize the present value of a stream of profits. The predator need not reduce the price all at once and by the full amount needed to destroy all competitors, and it need not wait until it has destroyed all its competitors to raise its price. The price decisions will depend on how quickly entry will occur. If rapid entry is likely, then it will delay raising its price. If entry is likely to be quick in response to a rise in price, then the dominant firm will raise its price more slowly and take losses over a longer period. Moreover, excess profits may be consistent with conceding a substantial market share to fringe firms. The goal of the predatory campaign may be a large enough market share to dominate the market rather than a complete monopoly. Profitable predation does not require an absolute barrier to entry. Moderately difficult entry may permit monopoly profits.

In Gaskins's model the output growth rate of small firms and entrants increases with the dominant firm's price, and it varies inversely with the height of entry barriers, including the minimum efficient size of a firm relative to the market and the fraction of the market already supplied by the dominant firm. For the dominant firm the optimal strategy to maximize the present value

56. Darius W. Gaskins, Jr., "Dynamic Limit Pricing: Optimal Pricing under Threat of Entry," *Journal of Economic Theory* 3 (September 1971): 306–22.

of the expected stream of profits may call for eliminating fringe output by setting a price under the fringe firms' minimum *AC*. The likelihood of this strategy increases with the dominant firm's cost advantage over the fringe firms. Moreover, to reduce predatory costs the dominant firm may raise its price before the fringe output disappears. The cost may be smaller than McGee suggested, and the present value of the profits from a predatory campaign may be positive.

Neither Gaskins nor McGee considered the effect of uncertainty. Under uncertainty, the probability of predatory pricing is greater than when firms are informed about each other's costs and have other pertinent information. Taking advantage of this ignorance, the dominant firm may attempt to eliminate the fringe firms. It will refrain from announcing its intentions, and fringe firms may believe that the dominant firm's price reflects low costs. Moreover, predation may deter potential competitors from entering after the price returns to the monopoly level. The payoff from signaling potential entrants to expect a costly battle may exceed that from preying on a single victim. In short, some dominant firms may prey, and some competitors may yield quickly.

Also, the capital market may be imperfect. Citing George Stigler's general dismissal of this argument, McGee rejected it.[57] In an uncertain world, however, a deep pocket is an advantage. Potential lenders and investors may not be informed about the predator's intentions and thus about the prospects of later high profits.

Thus, predatory pricing cannot be ruled out. Evaluating the relevant literature, F. M. Scherer and David Ross have written:

> The evidence is persuasive, although it is not completely clear whether this reflects the rarity of hard-core predation or the barrenness of historical records. Certainly, other cases have been identified in which an inference of predation, even under the strictest definition of the term, appears indisputable.[58]

An inconclusive theoretical analysis is the basis for the view that predatory pricing is improbable and for the *AVC* standard. We leave the discussion of predatory pricing by a domestic firm with this negative conclusion. This meager result would be unfortunate were the present study's subject domestic predatory pricing. Yet there is more to say about our subject, which is foreign-based predation.

---

57. McGee, "Predatory Pricing Revisited," 297; George J. Stigler, "Imperfections in the Capital Market," in Stigler, *The Organization of Industry* (Homewood, Ill.: Richard D. Irwin, 1968), 113ff.

58. Scherer and Ross, *Industrial Market Structure and Economic Performance*, 390.

Foreign-Based Predation

We return to the problem of appropriate standards for predatory pricing, with attention to foreign-based predation. Not alarmed by geographic discrimination, Areeda and Turner proposed that their general *AVC* rule be applied.[59] One of their instances of harmless dumping referred to an export market dominated by a monopolist. Yet this case probably is less common than the alternative, in which the export market is competitive. Another of Areeda and Turner's tolerable instances is one in which the alleged predator's small sales fail to reduce the price significantly, and the discrimination displaces only one or two of an "ample" number of competitors.[60] But tolerance under Areeda and Turner's supposed conditions is immaterial, since plaintiffs are unlikely to emerge when only one or two of many competitors are displaced. Areeda and Turner presumably would be less permissive when the defendant's market share is large or growing. Another broader reason for a permissive policy, according to Areeda and Turner, is that monopoly does not threaten when entry is easy, which they take to be the general case. In short, a strong law is unnecessary because foreign-based predation is rare and does not harm consumers in the export market. The possibility of a foreign monopolist driving American companies out of the U.S. market did not worry Areeda and Turner. As we observed earlier, the protection of efficient firms did not have a high priority.

Areeda and Turner's list of objectives provides an acceptable basis for a definition of international predation, but the objectives can be made more specific, as follows:

1. A foreign-based monopolist should not be permitted to utilize its excess profits to extend its monopoly power to the U.S.
2. A foreign-based monopolist should not be permitted to set prices that are sufficiently low to drive efficient U.S. firms out of business or to keep efficient entrants out of a U.S. market.
3. Prices should be consistent with optimum resource allocation among countries as well as within countries.

A well financed, foreign-based monopolist may be able to eliminate efficient U.S. firms. The third objective is consistent with the long-standing U.S. policy of trade liberalization. The U.S. has supported the GATT rounds of tariff reductions, because trade benefits the trading countries. Predatory prices, however, which are inconsistent with optimum international allocation, deprive the argument of much of its force.

---

59. Areeda and Turner, "Predatory Pricing," 724–25.
60. Areeda and Turner, "Predatory Pricing," 725.

To choose a standard for predatory export pricing we need some idea of its probability. As the present analysis indicates, in the cases of a home market monopolist and a cartel having monopoly power at home the probability may be high enough to warrant a strict standard. Moreover, the enormous growth of Japanese exports may have been partly due to a home market monopoly combined with predatory pricing. As chapter 2 shows, many Japanese markets are controlled by cartels, and there is considerable evidence of Japanese dumping. That the probability of predatory export pricing by Japanese cartels is high cannot be dismissed out of hand.

I propose the home market price as the standard for predatory export pricing under the antitrust laws. It already is the standard for dumping under the Trade Agreements Act. I propose that the export price be ruled predatory when it is less than the home market price and the exporter has monopoly power in its home market. It is important to protect efficient U.S. firms against predation, and the proposed standard is consistent with international optimum resource allocation, which requires that a product be sold at the same price in different geographic regions after allowing for transportation costs. In addition, it conforms to the requirement that relative efficiency govern success in business; monopoly profits should not confer an advantage. Perhaps the most important argument favoring a strict standard is that monopoly in other countries may spread to the U.S.

The adoption of the home market price standard would not unduly inhibit foreign competition. Plaintiffs would still find it difficult to win a predatory pricing case. In addition to a showing that the difference between the alleged predator's home market and export prices persisted over a considerable period, say one year, the plaintiff also would have to show that the defendant possessed monopoly power in the home market. Finally, the plaintiff would have to show that the defendant had gained a significant share of the U.S. market, say at least 10 percent.

One objection to the proposal is that a monopolist may discriminate in price without predatory intent. Since the effect on the domestic industry is the same, however, innocent intent should not excuse the behavior. In purely domestic cases the problem of intent may be unavoidable, because vigorous competitive pricing may destroy rivals, and there is no equivalent of a home market price standard. The courts may have to undertake a large investigation. But the problem of intent should not interfere with protecting domestic industries against foreign monopolists. Yet, as the law stands now, the courts may be unable to avoid assessing intent. As chapter 9 reports, although *Matsushita* involved Section 1 of the Sherman Act, the Supreme Court required plaintiffs to show that the defendants acted with predatory intent. Legislation may be needed to implement the home market price standard.

Moreover, excess capacity should not excuse persistently low export prices. If the overcapacity is due to overestimates of demand, then the exporter should bear the consequences without inflicting losses on competitors in the export market. In addition, overcapacity due to forecasting errors cannot be distinguished from predatory capacity.

To capture the economies of scale a monopolist in a small home market may set low export prices. Only a defendant that is a single-firm monopoly, however, could offer this defense. Several defendants joined together in a cartel, each operating its own plant or plants, could not justify price discrimination on this ground. Nor would this defense justify discrimination when the defendant's home market consumption exceeded the output of an optimally utilized plant of minimum efficient size.

An adequate learning curve defense also would be difficult to make. The defendant would have to show that the learning curve for the manufacturing processes in question was steep and that it was not already well along on the learning curve. Moreover, the argument would be valid neither for a group of independent companies nor for a company with a large, protected home market. The company could achieve the learning economies by expanding its home market sales or simply by selling in the home market over a longer period. Finally, the learning curve economies have not been shown to be large enough for many products to warrant losses over a long period.

Since the courts may not want to apply the home market price standard, I offer a fallback position, which is the AC standard. The home market price standard would challenge monopoly power abroad and provoke foreign governments' protests against applying U.S. laws to their countries, and they may argue that the low export price is nonpredatory. But even in a monopoly model AC is an appropriate standard. A nonpredatory monopolist will not persistently export at prices that are below AC. More important, we do not want a large firm that is willing to accept losses to gain a monopoly to drive efficient firms out of business.

Although it is the less strict standard, it may be harder to show that export prices are less than AC than to show that they are less than home market prices. Chapter 7 estimates the AC of Japanese TV manufacturers on the basis of data on defendants' overall profits in *Matsushita*. Without such data the task of estimating the AC-export price difference may be impossible. Yet even the adoption of the AC standard would improve the law.

Conclusion

My economic analysis of foreign-based predatory pricing suggests that the standard should be the home market price. I propose AC as an alternative standard.

CHAPTER 5

The Cartel in the Domestic Market

Strategic trade theorists have suggested that oligopolists selling differentiated products will set export prices below their home market prices, but they do not specify the conditions necessary for firms to maintain price discrimination. They simply assume that an oligopolist faces a lower demand elasticity in the home market than in the export market, from which they infer the profit-maximizing prices. The theoretical analysis in chapter 3 suggests that independent, profit-maximizing oligopolists will not maintain persistent, substantial domestic-export price differences. The description of TV manufacturers' activities in the home market in the present chapter shows that the manufacturers needed a cartel to maintain high domestic prices. The manufacturers' representatives had to meet frequently to fix prices and outputs. In addition, as the next chapter shows, the domestic-export price differences were very large. It is doubtful that independently competing oligopolists would have exported at as low prices relative to those they received in the home market.

Indeed, it is remarkable that the cartel was able over a long period to maintain a large domestic-export price difference in the face of disappointing expectations concerning the growth of demand. Because the home market demand for monochrome receivers did not grow continuously, as early as 1956 retailers cut their prices below the levels suggested by the manufacturers, putting pressure on the manufacturers to reduce their prices, and in 1965 sales of monochrome receivers dropped sharply (see table 6.6, p. 113). The manufacturers did not always agree on the appropriate prices, they competed for retailers' support by using rebates to shade their nominal prices, and, although they were eager to fix monopoly prices, they were reluctant to reduce their output to the necessary level. Nevertheless, the cartel remained effective. How was this accomplished? Regular, frequent meetings, at which manufacturers' representatives negotiated outputs and prices at the retail, wholesale, and manufacturer's levels, were an important element of the success. In addition, to help maintain discipline the manufacturers exchanged detailed information on their respective outputs, sales, and inventories. What is more, they established groups of high-level executives to resolve disagreements. Another source of discipline was the manufacturers' participation in other cartels dealing with other products. Breaking ranks risked retaliation in other lines of business. Moreover, the companies probably had developed habits and expectations of cooperation. As chapter 4 reports, Japan has a long tradition of cartels, cartels are numerous, and the Antimonopoly Law has been ineffective. Such long-established, large, multiproduct companies as MEI, Hitachi, MELCO, Toshiba, Sanyo, and Sharp probably had participated in other cartels.

The story of the cartel shows that it would have been an impossible venture had the FTCJ possessed more power. The members were continuously renegotiating complex, detailed agreements at numerous meetings, which did not escape notice by the FTCJ, and the commission did take action. Vigorous enforcement would have encouraged more caution, but some meetings could not be avoided. The members tended to produce more than their allotted quotas, so retail and wholesale price competition kept erupting. Prices and outputs could not be kept fixed. The agreements did not put an end to changes in demand and in costs, and the members did not stop introducing new models.

Moreover, the story indicates that a U.S. cartel would not have succeeded. According to critics of the U.S. antitrust laws, collusive price setting is difficult to distinguish from independent oligopolistic behavior. Independently, and without consultation, firms may decide to follow a price leader and thus escape penalties. Consultation reduces the uncertainty of rivals' behavior at the risk of an antitrust suit, but, if other firms' reactions are highly predictable, they need not take the risk. The Japanese cartel's behavior, suggests, however, that the U.S. laws can be relied on to deter collusion in markets for complex, differentiated goods, such as TV receivers. Even the members of a disciplined, collusive group, with a tradition of cooperation, would have had to communicate with one another. It is evident that the agreements were too complex to be negotiated by signals, which go undetected by the antitrust authorities. The Justice Department would have had to be pretty somnolent not to have discovered similar activities by an even more discreet group.

For convenience this chapter confines its attention to the Japanese market, leaving the U.S. market to the next chapter; the division does not signify separate, independent decisions by cartel members for each market. The basic source for the description of the activities of the Market Stabilization Council, with which I begin, is the 1957 decision of the FTCJ in the "Case against the Home Electric Appliance Market Stabilization Council." I then go on to other cartel groups, including the Tenth-Day, Palace, and Okura groups, the information for which comes from defendants' answers to plaintiffs' interrogatories in *Matsushita* and from documents in the FTCJ's proceedings in "Case No. 6, 1966 against Sanyo Electric Co. Ltd. and Five Other Companies," which has been called the Six-Company Case.

These cases reveal that the manufacturers organized so many groups that met so frequently that the demands on the participants' time must have been enormous. Dealers, as well as manufacturers, sent representatives to the groups formed first, and, while these joint groups continued, the manufacturers established their own private ones. Thus, several groups, some with dealers' representatives and some without, negotiated distributors' margins, retail and wholesale prices, and other matters pertaining to distribution. The manufacturers' exclusive groups also agreed on outputs, which posed even more difficult issues, and doubly to forestall competition the members set sales and inventory quotas. Making matters even more complicated, to ensure coordination the groups setting domestic prices also discussed export prices. There were also higher-level groups. The different companies' TV business managers, who ran the cartel, were sometimes at loggerheads, so the cartel needed a mechanism for settling conflicts. Moreover, the TV manufacturers participated in other cartels. We will see that the Market Stabilization Council restricted competition in radios, washing machines, and fans as well as in TV receivers. Chapter 2 reports that the JMEA operated export cartels in other product markets, and it is likely that the TV manufacturers, with their broad product lines, participated in them. To resolve conflicts among the middle-level executives running the different cartels the manufacturers' higher executives met regularly.

The Market Stabilization Council

Problems arose chiefly from three sources: new manufacturers entering the consumer electronic and electric appliance industries, the wholesalers' and retailers' lack of cash, and the manufacturers' unwillingness to restrict their output. The manufacturers of heavy electrical equipment, which had completed their huge postwar power projects, saw a great opportunity in consumer appliances. At the same time the tight credit policy was especially hard on wholesalers, who had been accepting retailers' promissory notes while paying their own bills promptly. Short-term credit from the manufacturers provided inadequate relief. Because the wholesalers were cutting prices and pressing them for faster payments, in 1954 the retailers began to cut prices of the older products, washing machines and fans. In addition, losing sales to the new entrants, the manufacturers competed more fiercely for retailers' support with higher margins, rebates that increased more than proportionally with sales, more generous credit, and prizes to good performers, and, despite distributors' protests, they began to sell directly to consumer unions and to companies offering electric appliances as prizes in lotteries.

To head off what they considered unbridled competition in 1956 the manufacturers and distributors organized a cartel through the Electronic Industries Association of Japan (EIAJ). The founding members of the Home Electric Appliances Market Stabilization Council included the All-Japan Federation of the Associations of Radio and Electric Appliance Dealers, and, among other manufacturers, MELCO, MEI, Toshiba, Sharp, Hitachi, Sanyo, and Fuji Electric. Sony joined later.

I digress to comment on Sony. A maverick in the industry and among large Japanese corporations generally, Sony was not heavily leveraged. Founded after the war, Sony lacked the access to bank credit that the older, large companies had, and in the early period earnings financed its growth. The company, which was less dependent on foreign technology than the other manufacturers, developed the Trinitron tube set, the tape recorder, and other products. Between 1967 and 1972 its share of the Japanese color TV market grew from 1.0 percent to 11.7 percent and in the next two years to 22.7 percent.[1] Unlike the other TV manufacturers, who sold their products to U.S. mass merchandisers for resale under private label, Sony developed its own distribution outlets in the U.S. and marketed products under its own brand name.

The Market Stabilization Council notwithstanding, retail price cutting continued. In 1956, calling for free competition, three department stores in Nagoya reduced their prices below the suggested level for washing machines, fans, and TV receivers, which by now too were being discounted. After some negotiations the manufacturers allowed the Nagoya discounters to cut prices by 8 percent for TV receivers and washing machines and by 5 percent for fans. The troubles spread to Tokyo, where nine department stores, which were discounting, answered the manufacturers' protests by accusing them of selling directly to an association of government employees. No agreement was reached.

Attempting to keep the thousands of retailers and wholesalers in line, the manufacturers and dealers agreed to the "Nine Essential Points of Implementation." To reveal discounters retailers were to display their prices on tags and posters. Wholesalers were not to make retail sales, and to identify themselves retailers were to wear badges. A price maintenance committee was to enforce the observance of list prices. Finally, recognizing the disruptive effect of their own competition, the manufacturers agreed to convene presidents' meetings to control both prices and outputs.[2]

The cartel members added the "Eight Essential Points of Implementation" to set distributors' margins. Retailers' margins were fixed at 22 percent of the retail price set by the manufacturers, except for "compelling circumstances" when the margin could be raised to 23 percent. The agreement allowed manufacturers to grant an additional 2 percent to retailers providing

---

1. Nehmer Report, vol. 1: table VII-9.
2. Zenith Radio Corp. v. Matsushita Electric Industries Co., 513 F. Supp. 1100 (1981), at 1223–24.

after-sales service, and it gave retailers a monopoly of such service. The struggle for distributors' support had led to a slew of bonuses to retailers, including allowances for coupons, coprosperity tickets, and incentive moneys, so the agreement limited the total of such allowances to 1 percent of sales. In addition, a limit was set on the provision by manufacturers of cheap credit to dealers. To provide additional assurance, the agreement called for a joint price maintenance campaign by manufacturers and dealers.[3]

The agreement set the wholesalers' margin at 1 percent of the manufacturer's selling price, but an "exceptional circumstances" provision allowed a supplemental 1 percent. In addition, the wholesalers were to receive a discount not exceeding 5 percent of the manufacturer's price.[4] The Eight Points also prohibited manufacturers from selling home appliances for use as premiums and to consumer and mutual aid societies.

To enforce the resale prices the Eight Points established a fund to buy up articles offered for less than the list prices. In addition, the manufacturers of discounted goods were to trace the wholesale sources and threaten them with suspension unless they stopped shipments to the discounters.

The companies set up an executive committee and various subcommittees to manage the cartel. The TV Subcommittee, made up of the manufacturers' business managers, was to enforce the retail price agreement. The Market Supervisory Committee was to ensure that manufacturers carried out the enforcement procedure against discounters.

The prohibition of the sale of appliances as lottery prizes was immediately invoked against Hitachi, which had agreed to sell one thousand washing machines to the toothpaste manufacturer, Shiseido, for this purpose. Under pressure Hitachi agreed to sell the products at normal prices through its wholesale and retail dealers.[5] Another problem came up in February 1957, when wholesalers in Tokyo made retail sales of MEI and Sanyo products at discount prices. The manufacturers suspended shipments to these dealers.[6] In Hiroshima Daiichi Sangyo and other retailers began to reduce prices. According to the FTCJ Decision No. 5, these retailers substantially undercut the list prices of washing machines because they purchased supplies at low prices. Being large, they could obtain sizable rebates by buying in big quantities.

In response to other retailers' protests, the Market Stabilization Council had the manufacturers force their wholesalers to suspend shipments to Daiichi

3. 513 F. Supp. 1100 (1981), at 1223–24.

4. DePodwin Report, vol. 1: IV-5–6; *The Decisions of the Fair Trade Commission,* 1958, 9:26–30, app. 2.

5. DePodwin Report, 15–16, vol. 1, Appendix Exhibit 1; Fair Trade Commission of Japan, "Cases involving Home Electric Appliances Market Stabilization Council and One Other Person," Decision (Recommendation) No. 5, 1957.

6. DePodwin Report, 22–23, vol. 1, Appendix Exhibit 1; FTCJ, "Cases."

Sangyo, which then, under a false name, obtained merchandise from distant wholesalers. But, after tracing the sources, the manufacturers suspended shipments to them. Daiichi Sangyo then promised to observe the list prices, and the suspension was lifted. Daiichi Sangyo, however, then discounted the prices of space heaters, and another suspension was followed by another reinstatement. According to the FTCJ, the Association of Radio and Electric Appliance Dealers of Hiroshima attributed the problem to the high rebate rates available to large retailers.[7] As noted earlier, the wholesale margin in the Eight Points did not vary with the size of shipments to retailers but, rather, was uniform for all shipments.

Problems arose, partly because of excessive output. In September 1956 the council began to control output, but, since demand kept changing, the manufacturers had difficulty agreeing on the total output and on their shares. The companies promised to maintain the shares that they had during the period from May to July 1956 and also to reduce aggregate production of fans, washing machines, and TV receivers.[8] The council decided that production would be curtailed by 30 percent. According to the FTCJ, "some manufacturers carried out a production cutback at that time."[9] Evidently, the cutback was not fully met, and, as chapter 6 reports, the manufacturers proceeded to dump radios abroad.

The attempt to maintain monopolistic prices without limiting output had created stocks of obsolete products, but the sellers were not eager to sacrifice sales. The introduction of TV receivers with a ninety-degree deflection Braun tube rendered those having seventy-degree deflection obsolete. The TV Subcommittee decided that the list prices of the stock of the obsolete models should be maintained. It also decided to prohibit general discount sales of obsolete models of all home electric appliances. Another problem arose when MEI introduced a new washing machine model. The Washing Machine Panel of the Market Stabilization Council decided that the prices of new models were to be high enough not to force a fall in the prices of older models.[10]

Intervening in September 1957, the FTCJ decided that the Market Stabilization Council had violated the Antimonopoly Law, and the council members did not contest the ruling. The commission ordered them to abrogate the Eight Points and, in particular, to refrain from suspending shipments to discounters. On the other hand, the FTCJ refrained from ordering the members to dissolve the council or to desist from fixing prices.

---

7. FTCJ, "Cases," 20–29. Cited by Nehmer Report, vol. 1: III-11.
8. DePodwin Report, vol. 1: VI-7, 37.
9. FTCJ, "Cases," 20–29. Cited by Nehmer Report, vol. 1: III-12.
10. FTCJ, "Cases," 20–29. Cited by Nehmer Report, vol. 1: III-13.

The Tenth-Day and the Television Study Groups

Both because the Market Stabilization Council was busy disciplining distributors and the dealers' participation complicated matters, the manufacturers decided to set up new groups, arranged in a hierarchy. The midlevel executives, who managed the TV businesses and were familiar with the details of prices, production, inventories, and retail and wholesale margins, negotiated the agreements. When their disagreements reached an impasse the problems were passed on to higher-level groups. At the lowest hierarchical level stood the Tenth-Day, the Television Study (TS), and the MD groups, along with the TV Subcommittee of the Market Stabilization Council. The Palace Preparatory, the Palace, and the Okura groups ranked successively higher. The company presidents met in the Okura Group, the peak group, and the senior managing directors, the executives ranking immediately below the presidents, met in the Palace Group. The Palace Preparatory Group decided which issues merited the managing directors' attention.[11] The Palace Group resolved issues in cartels dealing with products other than TV receivers as well as with this product line. The available information features the Tenth-Day Group, which attended to the domestic TV business. The jurisdictional lines not being exact, the MD and the Tenth-Day groups' activities overlapped, but the Tenth-Day Group made most decisions. The MD Group served mainly as the center for the exchange of information.

The manufacturers' representatives at the Tenth-Day Group also attended the meetings of the TV Subcommittee and the TS Group, and the three groups' discussions overlapped.[12] The TV Subcommittee's discussions focused on distribution, as we have seen. The other two groups discussed prices, retail margins, and outputs. The decisions that came out of the smaller group of large companies meeting in the Tenth-Day Group were brought to the TS Group for the other companies' approval. The Tenth-Day Group included MEI, Toshiba, Hitachi, MELCO, Sanyo, and Sharp, while the TS Group also included Nippon Columbia, Shin Nippon Electric, Yao, Japan Victor, Osaka Onkyo, and Sony.[13] Japan Victor was a subsidiary of MEI. Sony may not have been a member of the Tenth-Day Group, because, as

---

11. 513 F. Supp. 100 (1981), at 1197.

12. Kozo Yamamura, "The Pervasive Use of Collusive and Company Group (Keiretsu) Activities in Achieving the Rapid Increase in Japanese Exports of Television Receivers to the United States" (Prepared for plaintiffs' counsel in the Japanese Electronics Product Antitrust Litigation M.D.L. 189, 81 [hereafter referred to as Yamamura, "Pervasive Use"]). The discussion of the testimony at the FTCJ proceedings in Case No. 6 will be based on Yamamura, "Pervasive Use," 80–87, 89, 91–96, 100–108, 111–12, 115–16, 140–41, except as noted.

13. DePodwin Report, vol. 1: IV-12.

mentioned, in 1967 it had only 1.0 percent of the sales in the domestic market.

The Tenth-Day Group companies sent the same representatives to both groups, and the two groups talked about the same issues. The Tenth-Day Group members, which in 1963 controlled 79.7 percent of the total output, would more readily see their common interests than the other companies, which among them controlled 20.1 percent of the total output. The market shares of the individual members of the Tenth-Day Group were as follows: MEI (including Victor) 24.4 percent, Toshiba 15.0 percent, Hitachi 11.0 percent, MELCO 10.9 percent, Sanyo 9.6 percent, and Sharp 8.8 percent.[14] Disagreements were more easily resolved in the small than in the large group, and the large companies were in a strong position to dominate the other companies. A small company could gain market share and profits by undercutting the cartel's prices, but it might not survive the cartel's retaliation. Through their *keiretsu* groups the cartel members might have retaliated by making it more difficult for a troublemaker to get bank loans and to sell its products to retailers. Moreover, as a group, it was as much in the interest of the small companies to cooperate as it was for any of the large companies.

Tadashi Kamakura, the director of Toshiba's TV division, appealed for the FTCJ examiners' sympathy at the hearings in Case No. 6 by testifying that the Tenth-Day Group was organized in 1964 after the depression set off severe price competition, which nearly bankrupted the companies. Kamakura suggested that the manufacturers were innocent because they wanted only to avoid ruinous competition, not to squeeze monopoly profits from consumers. Judge Becker's interpretation of this and similar testimony was that it contradicted the plaintiffs' assertion that the manufacturers accumulated monopoly profits in the home market. Chapter 8 evaluates Judge Becker's arguments.

The members of the Tenth-Day Group did more than merely exchange ideas. Thus, Judge Becker said that the Tenth-Day Group conducted serious discussions about a variety of business matters, their primary concern being "prediction of demand, so as to avoid overproduction, oversaturation, and further price decline." The meetings also discussed "bottom prices" and wholesale, retail, and rebate margins. Confirming that the decisions affected the companies' plans, Seiichi Yajima, manager of the Second Section of Toshiba's TV Business Department, said that he reported the discussions to his superior, Mr. Kamakura, and that he could "more or less guess each company's moves."[15] Demand and cost changes forced frequent meetings to

---

14. DePodwin Report, vol. 1: III-46.
15. 513 F. Supp. 100 (1981), at 1202–3.

reconsider and renegotiate prices. Hitachi's TV manager, Kaoru Adachi, said that price agreements were limited to six-month periods.

I will comment first on the discussions pertaining to monochrome, or black-and-white sets. Mamoru Yamamoto of Hitachi testified that in February 1965 the group agreed to the minimum cash normal retail prices, to a retail profit margin of 22 percent, and to a wholesale profit margin of 8 percent. This agreement was extended at subsequent meetings.[16]

It is significant that the margins were the same for all retailers, despite the economies of scale in retailing, and the wholesale margins were the same, regardless of shipment size. Moreover, the rebates to retailers only in part reflected the economies of large shipments. Since the rebate rates depended on the size of total shipments over a period rather than on the size of individual shipments and were cumulated over different products supplied by the same manufacturer, they were not designed only with a view to reflecting economies of either wholesaling or of manufacturing. Chapter 2 suggests that a major purpose of the rebates was to promote the loyalty of retailers. Since they differed among the manufacturers, they were a continuing source of aggravation. The companies set common retail profit margins, but their rebates differed. The issue may have been difficult to resolve because the rebate rates were based on a retailer's sales of all the manufacturer's products, not only those of TV receivers. Nevertheless, as Adachi testified, the manufacturers reached an agreement to set an upper limit to the rebate rates, 8 percent of the wholesale price to the retailer. The average rebate rate for each manufacturer in 1970 appears to have been in the range of 4 to 5 percent. As we will see in chapter 8, Judge Becker interpreted the problems with rebates to signify that the collusion did not succeed in maintaining prices.

The cartel members also had to contend with problems raised by product differences, new models, and price differences. The Tenth-Day Group had to evaluate the price equivalents of product differences. On March 24, 1966, Sanyo, Hitachi, Toshiba, Sharp, Fuji Electric, and MEI agreed that the price of a monochrome console set with a seventeen-inch screen and one speaker was to be ¥ 54,000, the premium for one additional speaker was to be ¥ 5,000, and that for a second additional speaker was to be ¥ 3,000.[17] But the issue became so complicated that in the summer of 1966 the members decided to disregard the number of speakers. In addition, new models repeatedly caused friction. Six months prior to their introduction companies submitted proposed retail prices. If the group rejected the proposed price as too low, the company would either raise it or withdraw the model.[18] Even small price

---

16. DePodwin Report, vol. 1: V-28.
17. DePodwin Report, vol. 1: V-28.
18. DePodwin Report, vol. 1: V-31 and Appendix Exhibit 2.

differences caused trouble. According to Adachi, when the bottom price of a particular monochrome screen size was ¥ 59,000, one company said that it was not underselling the others by setting a price of ¥ 58,000.

None of the witnesses testified that an explicit agreement fixed the manufacturers' prices at the factory. None was necessary, since the agreements on retail prices, retail and wholesale margins, and rebates effectively fixed the factory prices. The retail price of a nineteen-inch table monochrome receiver was set at ¥ 58,000 on July 21, 1966. The rebates and profit margins agreed to resulted in a manufacturer's selling price of ¥ 38,292. In reaching this figure, a maximum rebate of 8 percent is assumed.[19]

To turn to the prices of color sets, Adachi testified that the companies first discussed such prices in the spring of 1965, when the prices of sixteen-inch and seventeen-inch sets were respectively about ¥ 190,000 and ¥ 230,000. The members decided that to popularize color television they had to reduce prices sharply, which they did by adopting the formula of ¥ 10,000 per inch of screen size. This agreement was extended at subsequent meetings.

The notebook of Seiichi Yajima, manager of the Second Section of Toshiba's TV Business Department, reported some details of the discussion at the meeting on November 22, 1965:

> Discussion of sales profit and profit margin for color TVs produced by Hitachi, Matsushita, Mitsubishi, Toshiba, Sanyo, and Hayakawa.
>
> Toshiba: We should refrain from competing in lowering bottom prices. . . . Concerning margin, rebate, installation fees and service charges, if leading manufacturers pay them, the rest of the manufacturers will follow, and will be influenced by the sales industry. Manufacturers need to reach agreement on this.
>
> Sanyo: After January 26 until June 1966, the current bottom (prices), margins and rebate will be maintained. It is feared that installation fees and service charges will be included in margin, so a countermeasure must be established for it.
>
> Hayakawa: Margin, rebate and the rate of interest ("cash" rebate) should be clearly determined.
>
> Sanyo: The prices do not matter for the current consumers constant price changing is a bigger problem. Will maintain the present condition.
>
> . . . Would be better if each company were to discuss margins. Each company should not decide them on its own, but it would be better to keep pace with the others.

The decision was reached that each member was to bring a proposal to the next meeting.

---

19. Nehmer Report, vol. 2: VII-9.

The discussion covered the following topics: (1) the bottom prices of TVs, (2) margins (including rebates), (3) installation fees, service charges, and ways of applying them, (4) monthly installment prices and number of installments for color TVs, (5) service for black-and-white TVs, (6) sales of TVs with built-in UHF, (7) production and shipment of TVs in October (for six companies), and (8) the blast-proof Braun tube. Following the reference to the Braun tube, Yajima noted: "will ask the Ad Committee to propose suggestions which will be submitted to the TS Group."

The notes on the meeting of December 14, 1965, included references to a survey on the production, shipments, and stocks of black-and-white and color TVs for November, a demand estimate for 1966, the prices of black-and-white and color TVs after January 20, and the service coupon system for black-and-white TVs. Those in attendance included Hitachi, MELCO, Sanyo, Toshiba, and MEI.

Toshiba raised the issue of pricing color table models. Before Toshiba introduced its product the color models had all been consoles, and, as we have just seen, the price was set at ¥ 10,000 per inch of screen size. According to Seigo Narita, senior managing director of Toshiba Shoji Company, his company, which planned to sell a color table model in July or August of 1966, proposed to set a lower price for the table model than the bottom price for the console model of the same screen size. At the meeting on April 5, 1966, Kamakura proposed a bottom price for the nineteen-inch color table model of ¥ 180,000, which was only 5.3 percent less than the price of the corresponding console model. Although, as Narita said, the table model cost less to produce than the console, the other members did not agree to the request. When the problem came before the Palace Group on April 8, however, the group did make the price concession.[20]

The Tenth-Day Group also agreed to retail profit margins for color receivers. According to Adachi, in August 1966 the margin was raised from 18 to 20 percent. To prevent companies from gaining an early advantage no announcement was to be made before October 1. Adachi reported that, while Hitachi raised its retail margin as of September 21, the announcement was delayed until after October 21.

As in the case of monochrome receivers, rebates to retailers were a problem. Adachi reported that at the outset no rebates were paid on color TV sales. But competition kept erupting, and companies preferred to pay rebates rather than cut prices to retailers. MEI started to pay an average rebate of 2 percent on total sales with a maximum rate of 4 percent, and other companies followed. The meeting in August 1966 adopted MEI's average and maximum rates as the standards for the industry.

As chapter 6 reports, export prices were the domain of the Television

20. DePodwin Report, vol. 1: V-27; Yamamura, "Pervasive Use," 100–101.

Export Council. Nevertheless, Yajima's notebook reported a Tenth-Day Group discussion of export prices on September 6, 1965, at MEI's Tokyo branch office. The MEI representative said: "Regarding export prices, not necessary to have connection with domestic prices." This quotation suggests that MEI judged that the domestic market was insulated against foreign competition. The group again discussed export prices on December 14, 1965. Yajima's notes include the following: "agreed prices":

Under	10 inches	FOB $42.00
	12–11 inches	$43.00
	16 inches	$54.00
	19 inches	$60.00[21]

Despite the frequent meetings of the various groups and the apparent ease with which the members reached agreements they were wary of one another. To assure themselves that their competitors were observing the agreements they exchanged price information.[22] These exchanges were in addition to those made through the MD Group, which will be discussed later.

The group tried to protect the prices that it set by regulating the total output, which entailed setting output quotas. To prepare the output agreements the conspirators exchanged information on outputs and shipments. Historical market shares were the basis for the output agreements. Using Igo stones, which are "poker-like chips," the members voted on production quotas.[23]

The group also paid attention to inventories, which tended to accumulate and threaten the agreed prices. On March 31, 1966, the MELCO representative proposed adjusting output quotas for inventories as well as for past shipments. In addition, the members adopted common policies on advertising, installment sales, installment fees, service, warranties, and the disposition of inventories of current and obsolete models.[24]

One other item should be mentioned. Despite the weak enforcement of the antimonopoly law, the members tried to conceal the group's proceedings from the FTCJ. On learning of the commission's investigation, they took steps to destroy incriminating evidence. Yajima's notebook referred to a meeting on January 16, 1966, at Toshiba's offices, during which the members discussed measures to be taken to avoid exposure of the group's activities. The following is a quotation from the notes: "To burn all documents. Do not take minutes; burn all documents. Change the name of the Palace Group. Also change the place of meeting."[25]

---

21. Yamamura, "Pervasive Use," 140–41.
22. DePodwin Report, vol. 1: IV-11.
23. Yamamura, "Pervasive Use," 108.
24. DePodwin Report, vol. 1: IV-10–11.
25. Yamamura, "Pervasive Use," 116–17.

The MD Group

Through the MD Group the cartel members exchanged detailed records of production and shipments. To prevent excessive inventories the conspirators tracked one another's shipments as well as output. The data were broken down as follows: by domestic and export, by monochrome and color receivers, and by screen size categories. The reports also covered inventories. The exchanges, which were more complete and detailed than those transmitted through the Tenth-Day Group, guarded against a member increasing its market share beyond the agreed percentage, and they served as a basis for the agreements. MD members included Hitachi, MELCO, MEI, Sony, Pioneer Electric, Sansui Electric, Sanyo, Toshiba, Sharp, Japan Victor, Trio Kenwood, and Nippon Columbia.[26] Information also was transmitted on other consumer electronic products, including radios and tape recorders, indicating that the cartel restricted competition in these other products.

The MD Group also shared decision making with the Tenth-Day Group. The manager of planning and research at the Victor Company, Mr. Koguri, reported that on December 23, 1970, the members of the MD Group, which accounted for 90 percent of the market, voted to permit Victor a market share of 6.4 percent.[27]

The Palace Preparatory and the Palace Groups

The intermediate group, the Palace Preparatory Group, screened and funneled issues to the Palace Group.[28] The Palace Group, consisting of the senior managing directors of Hitachi, MEI, MELCO, Sanyo, Sharp, Toshiba, and Fuji Electric, held monthly meetings from 1964 to 1977.[29]

According to Yasuo Ito, managing director at MELCO, the Palace Preparatory Group performed the essential agenda service of screening many issues transmitted by different groups. Confirming Ito's testimony, Yajima reported that the Palace Group dealt with the whole home appliance field, but, since the FTCJ investigation confined itself to TV receivers, we have no testimony on other markets. Narita did testify, however, that the meeting on April 8, 1966, discussed the retail margin for refrigerators.

According to Yajima, because the TV business managers were intimately familiar with the market, the Tenth-Day Group did not always refer unresolved issues to the higher group. Sometimes its members brought the matters back to their own group after only consulting with their superiors, rather than

---

26. DePodwin Report, vol. 1: IV-14.
27. DePodwin Report, vol. 1, Appendix Exhibit 5.
28. 513 F. Supp. 100 (1981), at 1202–3.
29. DePodwin Report, vol. 1: IV-14.

leaving the final decision to them. Indeed, some division directors had complete authority over manufacturing and sales and might not report the issues to their companies' Palace Group representatives.

Prices were the main topic of discussions at the Palace Group. Narita said that after discussions at the Tenth-Day Group the Palace Group usually set what was to be the lowest price for a period of six months. Also, Kamakura reported that the Palace Group always reviewed the Tenth-Day Group's price decisions.

According to Narita, the Palace Group also discussed production quotas. In confirmation Ito said that a meeting in 1965 discussed setting quotas from the spring of 1965 to the spring of 1966 on the basis of certain estimates prepared by the Electronic Industry Group.

In addition, the Palace Group took up retail margins. The reason it did so was that each retailer carried a range of a manufacturer's products, not only TV receivers. The manufacturer set retail margins for all of its products; it did not allow the individual product divisions to set their own retail margins independently. According to Ito: "I think the reason the profit margin rate was decided at the Palace Group meeting was that the general retail stores dealt with many products from each company." He went on to say: "For example, if our company's rate is 15 percent and another company's is 17 percent, naturally the retail store would be attracted by 17 percent. That is why we needed to arrange it." Moreover, Yukio Koishi, managing director of Fuji Electrical Home Appliance Company, Ltd., reported that after the retailers had demanded a higher margin for color receivers at the Four-Group Council and in the Diet the Palace Group took up the issue. The demand was made on the ground that color receivers required five or six service calls for adjustments. Narita testified that at the meeting of April 8, 1966, MEI proposed an increase from 18 percent to 20 percent, and it was agreed that the increase would take effect on September 21.

Surprisingly, for a high-level group dealing with a broad range of products the Palace Group also discussed problems relating to warranty tags, old models, and maintenance service for color receivers. The group got into the details of specific competitive problems.

The Okura Group

The Okura Group consisted of the presidents of Toshiba, MEI, Sharp, Hitachi, MELCO, Sanyo, and Fuji, and it too dealt with a wide range of products. It met regularly from August 1964 through at least September 1974.

Konosuke Matsushita, the president of MEI and the group's initiator, chief spokesman and defender, argued in a lecture on January 1, 1966, that the companies had to cooperate to pull the electric appliance industry out of its unsatisfactory condition, which was due to overproduction and the resulting excessive competition and chaos. He referred to the whole electric appliance industry, not to the TV receiver industry alone. According to Matsushita, there were similar groups in other industries, and it was strange that presidents' meetings had not taken place earlier in the electric appliance industries. Matsushita reported that the Okura Group had been meeting monthly and that the main questions concerned production. The group took some care in discussing the production plans, since it studied inventories and demand forecasts and reached agreements on the basis of these examinations.[30]

Conclusion

The cartel operated through an elaborate set of groups that restricted competition by regulating inventories, outputs, retail and wholesale margins, as well as retail prices. The groups found it necessary also to curb competition in advertising, warranties, and installment financing.

None of the company officials testifying at the FTCJ hearings suggested that the cartel had failed to maintain prices or to restrict output. The companies had to reduce prices to popularize color receivers, not because of an outbreak of competition. They had recognized that a cut in prices by the industry as a whole would raise profits for all the companies. The FTCJ testimony indicates that the cartel succeeded in restricting competition.

---

30. DePodwin Report, vol. 1: IV-18–20.

CHAPTER 6

The Cartel in the U.S. Market

As chapter 3 shows, the Japanese TV manufacturers were unlikely to export persistently at prices substantially less than the home market prices without a home market monopoly and restrictions on competition in the U.S. Having described how the cartel maintained monopoly control of the home market in chapter 5, we turn to its activities in the U.S. To avoid the enormous costs of unrestrained competition the manufacturers colluded to take a large share of the U.S. market and perhaps even to capture monopoly power. Not only did the cartel members dump their receivers over a long period, but their exports over at least part of the period were at loss prices. Inasmuch as they added capacity, which increased their fixed costs, the losses cannot be attributed to innocent efforts to utilize excess capacity or to spread the heavy fixed-cost burden over a larger output. Moreover, it is unlikely that the manufacturers would have invested as heavily as they did in capacity to supply the U.S. market without reducing the risk of losses by restricting competition among themselves in the U.S.

The TV manufacturers were not the only group to restrict competition in exports. As chapter 2 reports, the Japan Machinery Export Association (JMEA), formed in 1952, organized collusive schemes in other export markets as well as in that for TV receivers, and other trade associations did the same for their members. Moreover, the defendants in *Matsushita* and Japanese publications referred to restrictions in other markets. My information is limited, however, to TV receivers and radios. The defendants in *Matsushita* participated in agreements covering both U.S. markets, and the TV agreements resembled those for radios.

The Radio Export Agreements

When the rapid growth of domestic shipments of radios came to a halt in 1956 (table 6.1), exports jumped more than sixfold, and a high rate of growth continued in 1957 and 1959. In the latter year exports accounted for as much as 71 percent of the total shipments, with two-thirds of the exports going to the U.S.[1] The closeness in time of the leap in exports to the cartelization of the

---

1. Nehmer Report, vol. 1: VI-15.

home market in 1956 was no accident, for, as chapter 5 reports, the Market Stabilization Council called for a reduction in output. The level of prices that the radio manufacturers were trying to maintain was inconsistent with full-capacity utilization, and exports were an obvious solution.

To sell in the U.S. the manufacturers had to cut their export prices below their home market monopoly prices, and they had to accept losses. Losses on exports were, however, not unusual, for, as an article in *Association News*, the JMEA's publication, by Giichi Tanaka indicated, the radio manufacturers were following an established pattern. Quoting some members of the audience at a speech by the chairman of the association, the article said:

> In the case of export about 10 years ago when an association as a promotion-body to expand our country's plant export in the direction indicated by the ideology of trade structure was created along with a strong request by the government, I remember that the Chairman of the Association had spoken in his inaugural address that the "secret of expansion of our export has to be that of transactions which raise proper (just) profits to be shared by every business, which is useful to the balance of international payments, and is contributive to the social development of a client nation." The majority of persons who attended this meeting were either executives or directors from various firms who were aware of the actual situation of exporting machinery. They, hearing this address, felt that "the address was truly foolish, and exporting of machinery cannot be easily done according to his statement. The first priority is to develop the market in some way, even with the expectation of loss. For this purpose, a reasonable sacrifice is a necessary loss."

TABLE 6.1.   Japan: Radios—Total Shipments, Domestic Shipments, Exports, 1953–59 (in thousand units)

	Total	Domestic	Exports	Exports as Percentage of Total
1953	1,383	1,378	5	0.4
1954	1,418	1,411	7	0.5
1955	1,776	1,684	92	5.2
1956	2,971	2,394	577	19.4
1957	3,568	2,436	1,131	31.7
1958	4,940	1,152	3,788	76.7
1959	9,903	2,874	7,030	71.0

Source: Economic Consulting Services Inc., *Economic Analysis of Evidence relating to Japanese Electronic Products Antitrust Litigation,* Civil Action Nos. 74-2451 and 74-3247, U.S. District Court for the Eastern District of Pennsylvania, September 11, 1979, table VI-2.

The author, who was writing in 1966, was referring to a meeting ten years earlier. He went on to say:

> stubbornly maintaining that improvement of profit and loss was only a step beyond, we were over-awed by a gradual wave of depression, and coining such new phrases as "prosperity flourish without profit," and we rolled from side to side in struggle. A policy cut off from business profit that took a disregard for profit and loss as something acceptable for the purpose of developing the export market ended up in completely losing its own substantiation.

Further:

> I think that the markets developed by a mixture of excessive and just competition in the past have brought some compensation to sacrifices that were paid. But, in the future we ought to utilize this great loss.[2]

There is also evidence that in 1954 the manufacturers of sewing machines took losses to raise their exports by 50 percent over the level of the preceding year. According to an article in the *Japan Economic Year Book, 1955*, these were "sacrifice" exports.[3] Export losses were not uncommon.

To promote collusion in the export radio market, the JMEA established the Transistor Radio Export Examination Committee, which drafted the export agreement, effective in 1958. The justification was as follows: "It seems that export growth can be fully realized through pricing cooperation among the businessmen concerned."[4] The agreement, which covered the six-month period from July 1958 to December 1958, set the following minimum export prices f.o.b. Japan for radios having the number of transistors indicated: four transistors $11.50; five transistors $13.30; six transistors $14.00; seven or more transistors $16.10.[5] It was renewed for successive periods up to April 1961. The part of the agreement covering price was not renewed for the period from 1961 to 1964. Minimum prices were again agreed to in 1964 for periods lasting through most of 1965.

The agreements, however, were not observed. The check prices established in 1958 were reduced in 1960, because, according to the JMEA, they had been circumvented by the manufacturers by paying rebates.[6]

---

2. Case record of 513 F. Supp. 1100. Doc. Sony 0689-1,2,3,4, pp. 15–16. Quoted by Nehmer Report, vol. 1: VI-18–19.

3. *Japan Economic Year Book, 1955,* The Oriental Economist, 1955, 105. Cited by Nehmer Report, vol. 1: VI-18.

4. Nehmer Report, vol. 1: VI-20.

5. Nehmer Report, vol. 1: VI-21, 27.

6. *Television Digest* 16, no. 12: 21. Cited by Nehmer Report, vol. 1: VI-29.

The manufacturers divided the market. New rules setting market shares came in 1962 at the start of an export drive. According to an article quoted by the Nehmer Report, the manufacturers wanted to set their market shares, because "the industries should become one body, avoiding meaningless excessive competition, and taking the national viewpoint into consideration; we should take an attitude which seeks cooperation with each other."[7] The joint interest of the group was associated with the national interest. The participants agreed to their total export volume and to their shares, which were based on exports in an earlier period. To allow changes in prices as market conditions changed the agreements expired at six-month intervals. Clauses allowing transfers of allocations between export areas and between manufacturers provided additional flexibility.

The agreement established a verification procedure. For each shipment a manufacturer had to submit an application for the validation of the export volume.[8] In 1963 tighter rules mandated that the applications show brand names and model numbers and that the companies register their export customers.[9] The cartel could monitor shipments from each exporter to each U.S. customer.

The radio cartel set up several committees, including the Transistor Radio Export Stabilization Committee, which was to administer the quotas. Still, the workhorse, the Transistor Radio Export Examination Committee, implemented the rules and settled conflicts over the registration of export customers and trademarks and other issues. This active committee met as frequently as every two weeks at least through 1970.

In 1965 a new market-sharing agreement, known as the Five-company Rule, prohibited each cartel member from selling to more than the indicated number of direct customers. They were the mass merchandisers, such as J. C. Penney, Sears Roebuck, Macy's, and S. S. Kresge; smaller customers did not buy directly from the home offices. Replacing the earlier quota system, the Rule, which was in force through 1969, was a simple, direct method of market allocation. It eliminated the need for advance estimates of total exports, members were no longer forced to refuse orders on reaching their quota, and the enforcement agency no longer had to keep a cumulative total of each manufacturer's exports.

The Television Export Agreements

Although the defendants in *Matsushita* claimed that the agreements were designed to protect U.S. manufacturers against a sharp decline in prices, the

---

7. Nehmer Report, vol. 1: VI-54.
8. Nehmer Report, vol. 1: VI-38.
9. Nehmer Report, vol. 1: VI-41–42.

first agreements came before the TV manufacturers had begun to take a significant fraction of the U.S. market and well before complaints by the U.S. industry about dumping or pressure by the U.S. government. In addition, the agreements resembled those for radios, which came earlier. The first Manufacturers' Agreement setting minimum export prices for monochrome receivers was signed in 1963. Imports from Japan only accounted for 2 percent of U.S. consumption of monochrome receivers in 1962 and in 1963 for 5 percent (table 6.7, p. 114), which was not large enough to prompt serious complaints. But they were exporting a significant fraction, 14 percent, of their output. If they were to expand their exports and avoid the costs of competition, it was time to negotiate agreements. It will be recalled that the cartel had controlled the home market since 1956.

The Agreements covered minimum prices of color receivers beginning in 1964, a year after those for monochrome receivers were first set. Exports to the U.S. still were too small to be reflected by the U.S. import statistics. Nevertheless, the manufacturers, with MITI's encouragement, agreed to minimum prices for color receivers.

The market-sharing agreement came in 1967. By this time imports from Japan accounted for as much as 21 percent of the U.S. consumption of monochrome receivers (table 6.7, p. 114). The U.S. TV manufacturers were being hurt, and the dumping had become a serious problem. Imports of color receivers from Japan still were not a significant threat to U.S. manufacturers, accounting for only 6 percent of U.S. consumption (table 6.5, p. 111). Exports to the U.S., however, made up a large proportion of Japanese output, 26 percent (table 6.4, p. 110). The restriction was important for the Japanese manufacturers, particularly since their sales were concentrated in the segment of the U.S. market served by the mass merchandisers. In addition, they presumably expected to take a larger share of the U.S. market.

More important, the market-sharing agreements reduced the cost of enlarging the Japanese manufacturers' share of the U.S. market. They had begun to take a large enough share of the U.S. market for competition among themselves to reduce significantly their selling prices. The Rationale of the initial Rules governing exports to the U.S. sets out the purpose clearly:

> Thus, the businessmen involved have decided that, acting as one body, they will strive to maintain export order and, furthermore, to aim for steady expansion of exportation. With respect to regions other than the U.S., separate measures shall be devised as needs arise.[10]

The statement expressed the fear of unchecked price competition and the hope that the agreement would facilitate the growth of exports.

---

10. 513 F. Supp. 1100 (1981), at 1231.

Beginning in 1963, seventeen Agreements, covering consecutive periods varying from one month to two years, set minimum or, as they were called, "check" prices—and specified quality standards. The Television Export Council, to which all manufacturers sent representatives, was to administer the Agreements.[11] In addition, the JMEA adopted Rules, which were to be administered by the Television Export Examination Committee. Beginning in 1967, again following the example of the radio agreements, the Rules limited each exporter to five U.S. customers, and they barred the manufacturers from acquiring customers already buying from another manufacturer. Article 6 of the Rules read as follows:

> The members of the Association, when they are going to export applicable goods to an applicable area, shall register in advance the export customer with the Association in conformity to attached Form (1), and shall also notify the Association of the trademark (expressed by means of letters, symbols or a combination of both, and hereinafter referred to as "trademark") to be used for the applicable goods in conformity to attached Form (1).
>
> 2. Application for registration pursuant to the provisions of the above paragraph must be such that the export transaction referred to in the application satisfies each of the following conditions:
>
> (1) An export contract has been concluded or a long-term, continuous trading relationship has been maintained; and, as a principle, the number of such customers shall not be more than 5 companies for the First Zone. . . .[12]

The Rules also provided that: "The export customers registered with the Association shall not be changed within the applicable period; provided, however, that this shall not apply if a legitimate reason applies."[13] Thus, a cartel member was prohibited from obtaining new customers, unless it did not take sales away from other members. Judge Becker argued that there was no evidence in the record that this limitation applied before 1973 or that it was enforced.[14] I will consider this point later.

Going even further, the 1973 Rules explicitly forbade more than a single manufacturer from selling to a customer, unless the Television Export Examination Committee deemed that there was no "likelihood of disturbance to order in export transactions."[15] When a customer had been buying from two

---

11. 513 F. Supp. 1100 (1981), at 1187–90.
12. 513 F. Supp. 1100 (1981), at 1189.
13. 513 F. Supp. 1100 (1981), Doc. No. MJ000377. Cited by Nehmer Report, vol. 2: VII-15.
14. 513 F. Supp. 1100 (1981), at 1189 n. 118.
15. Nehmer Report, vol. 2: VII-18–19.

cartel members, however, the arrangements were allowed to continue, as in the case of Sears, which had been supplied by both Toshiba and Sanyo.[16]

The Rules placed severe limits on both manufacturers and customers. Apart from Sony, which developed its own U.S. distribution system, the manufacturers were blocked from competing aggressively for direct customers. Because the five included a manufacturer's own sales company, the Five-company Rule really limited the manufacturers to four direct customers. The sales company resold to small distributors, which did not send buyers to Japan. The mass merchandisers, which were the direct customers, were prohibited from buying directly more than one manufacturer's receivers of a given color category and screen size. They could not promote their TV department by displaying a wide range of products, unless they bought from other manufacturers' sales subsidiaries at higher prices. Also, however popular a product was, no more than four customers could buy it directly from the home office.

Including the sales subsidiaries among the five did not cancel the Rule's effectiveness. The price elasticity of demand of Sears Roebuck's customers was higher than that of the small distributors' customers. The small electronics and other specialty stores' appeal depended much more on convenience and service at point of sale.

The Antiraiding Rule, which was especially important, reduced the manufacturers' costs of acquiring a large share of the U.S. market by enhancing their bargaining power against the mass merchandisers. For the purpose of dealing with these buyers the Rule's effect was to merge the manufacturers. It prevented a large buyer from beating prices down to marginal costs by playing the manufacturers off against one another. Moreover, a manufacturer was assured of all of a customer's purchases over an extended period. Without this assurance a manufacturer was less likely to make the initial price cuts necessary to win a customer. Under fully competitive conditions a manufacturer's deep price cuts need not have won a customer's loyalty.

This restriction was at the heart of the conspiracy. Without it the prospect of unrestrained competition might have deterred the manufacturers from attempting to acquire a large share of the U.S. market. They were prepared to take some losses, but the losses entailed by full competition would have been much higher. As we see later, the manufacturers built a large capacity to supply the U.S. market. If they had not entered the market-sharing agreement and had made the same investment in additional capacity, the competition among them would have driven prices down to lower levels than necessary to take a large share of the U.S. market, and it would have resulted in large losses. It is doubtful that the manufacturers would have made the investment without the agreement.

---

16. 513 F. Supp. 1100 (1981), Doc. No. 50488, 1973; JMEA Agreement, "Guidelines for Registration, Attachment," No. 2. Cited by Nehmer Report, vol. 2: VII-16.

Further, the prospect of a monopoly, even if it had to be shared, may have been attractive. For an independent competitor the probability of monopoly power was nil. No one of the manufacturers could have won such power without at least the tolerance of the others, and no one of them had the necessary production and financial capacity. Since, as a group, they did, the restrictions on competition enhanced the probability. The prospect of monopoly profits may have encouraged the cartel members to accept losses. The restrictions may have led the manufacturers to expect to gain a monopoly. The Rationale of the Rules did say that, acting as one body, they would aim for steady expansion of exports.

To enforce the Rule, as in the case of radios, the members agreed to provide detailed information on each export shipment. The Application for Confirmation of Shipment reported the names and addresses of the importer, the exporter, and the manufacturer; the names, numbers, and trademarks of the models being shipped; and for each model the quantity and the home market and export prices. In addition, the cartel members obtained in advance the written certification by the council or by the Television Export Examination Committee that a shipment or transaction did not violate the Agreements or Rules. [17]

Why did the buyers not protest against being at the mercy of a single supplier, who would be free to raise prices? I can only guess. The manufacturers may have been stubborn, and they may have blamed MITI's orders, as they did in *Matsushita*. There was also the excuse that competition and the resulting even lower prices would provoke the U.S. to take protectionist measures, which it eventually did. In addition, joining the manufacturers in an illegal rebate scheme to evade antidumping duties weakened the buyers' bargaining position. To conceal the true export prices from the U.S. Customs Service the manufacturers paid rebates by check to the customers. Also, of course, the after-rebate prices were less than the U.S. manufacturers' prices.

Another question is: Why was the Five-company Rule agreed to as well as the more restrictive Antiraiding Rule? Members may have feared being pushed out. Without this limitation MEI, the largest member, might have blocked other manufacturers from gaining a foothold by quickly winning a long list of customers. Also, with the cooperation of a customer a member might evade the Antiraiding Rule by having that customer switch from another supplier after a delay of a few months.

Not disputing the existence of the Agreements and Rules, the defendants in *Matsushita* only denied that these "Arrangements," as they called them, harmed the plaintiffs. The defendants also claimed that MITI's participation in designing the Agreements and Rules gave them immunity from U.S. antitrust

---

17. DePodwin Report, vol. 1: V-17.

laws under the doctrines of acts of state and sovereign compulsion and the principles of international comity. The plaintiffs did not dispute MITI's participation, but they denied that the TV manufacturers acted under compulsion.[18] Chapter 8 takes up these issues.

The defendants' sovereign-compulsion arguments indicated that the restrictions on export competition were not confined to the TV industry. According to the defendants:

> These restrictions are imposed by the Ministry of International Trade and Industry of the Japanese government ("MITI"), the agency responsible for formulating and implementing Japan's foreign trade policy, and include price, quantity and/or quality restrictions upon a wide variety of products. Over the years hundreds of products such as bicycles, binoculars, glassware, batteries, ceramic wall tile and cameras, as well as radios and television receivers have been the subject of such restraints.[19]

Observance of Check Prices

The check prices were not observed. Since the check prices, which were also those shown on the invoices, failed to meet the competition of U.S. suppliers, rebates were paid. In their correspondence the manufacturers attempted to conceal the rebates by using such euphemisms as "difference money," "loyalty discount," and "warehousing." The manufacturers knew of one another's rebates, and the purchasers knew that other purchasers also were receiving rebates, as the defendants in *Matsushita* conceded.[20]

The rebates varied in magnitude. In 1969 Sears received rebates from Sanyo on monochrome and color receivers amounting to 5.0 and 4.6 percent, respectively. Unusually high in 1972, Sanyo's rebates to Sears amounted to 13.1 and 11.1 percent, respectively. In the same year MEI paid J. C. Penney rebates amounting to 3.2 and 3.1 percent, respectively, and its rebates that year to W. T. Grant came to 3.2 and 2.6 percent, respectively.[21] On the whole the rebates were not large, but even before the rebates the check prices were below prices in the home market and were less than average cost. Also, the market-sharing agreements kept them from being higher.

The check prices evidently were intended to evade antidumping duties. The Japanese manufacturers appear to have been under the impression that the

---

18. 513 F. Supp. 1100 (1981), at 1191–95.

19. Brief of Appellees, U.S. court of Appeals 3d. Cir., Japanese Electronic Products Antitrust Litigation Nos. 81-2331, 81-2332, 81-2333, D.C. Civil No. 189 M.D.L., 10.

20. 513 F. Supp. 1100 (1981), at 1241–45.

21. DePodwin Report, vol. 1: V-49.

U.S. Treasury would have found that the check prices met the less-than-fair-value (LTFV) test.

In any case, the price agreements may have been unnecessary. Apart from the early period, when they were striving for their first orders, the cartel members avoided deep price cuts by refraining from raiding one another's customers. To gain sales they only had to cut slightly below U.S. prices. Further, the precautions were in vain, for the U.S. manufacturers uncovered the dumping and complained to the Customs Service.

Observance of the Market-Sharing Rules

Denying the effectiveness of the Five-company and Antiraiding Rules, Judge Becker argued that they were turned into hollow restrictions by the inclusion among the five of manufacturers' sales subsidiaries.[22] Judge Becker did not consider, however, that these buyers were mass distributors, whose appeal was based on price and whose customers were especially price sensitive.

Judge Becker also argued that the Five-company and Antiraiding Rules were not observed. The evidence indicates, however, that the TV manufacturers did comply with the Five-company Rule, which came into effect in 1967. In no year did MELCO, MEI, Sharp, Hitachi, and Sony supply more than three U.S. customers, not including their sales subsidiaries.[23] The manufacturers also conformed to the Antiraiding Rule. Except for four minor instances of violations of the Rules, no importer received supplies from more than a single Japanese manufacturer. During the period from 1967 to 1973 both MEI and MELCO supplied W. T. Grant. Yet MEI, the major supplier over this whole period, did not have reason for much concern. It sold a full line of TV's to W. T. Grant, except for a fifteen-inch color portable, which MELCO supplied. This was the only model that W. T. Grant bought from MELCO. Both MEI and Toshiba sold twelve-inch black-and-white transistorized sets to J. C. Penney; otherwise, the two companies avoided each other. Both Toshiba and Sanyo sold to Sears Roebuck, but each supplied different screen sizes, while covering almost every available screen size between them. Moreover, as we saw earlier, the Rule did not apply to the sales by these companies to Sears, because they had supplied Sears before the Rule was instituted. Both Sharp and MELCO sold to Midland, but, except for the twelve-inch black-and-white tube model, they supplied different products.[24]

---

22. 513 F. Supp. 100 (1981), at 1189–90.
23. DePodwin Report, vol. 1: V-53–54.
24. DePodwin Report, vol. 1: V-54–55.

Domestic Prices Greatly Exceeded Export Prices

We have the evidence of the U.S. Treasury Department that the Japanese TV manufacturers' export prices were less than their home market prices. As chapter 7 reports, after a lengthy investigation, on December 4, 1970, the Treasury concluded that the Japanese manufacturers had been dumping goods in the U.S. market.[25]

The *Matsushita* plaintiffs submitted three sets of price comparisons, which also showed that dumping had occurred. Judge Becker agreed with the defendants' objection that the comparisons did not allow for quality differences other than in screen size and color category, and he decided not to admit the comparisons into evidence. But, as we will see, the average cost of the export and home market models within the same screen size and color category were nearly the same. If the home market models on the whole had been more costly to manufacture, this would have resulted in substantial differences in average costs.

The third study, the one carried out by a staff of engineers under the direction of Vito Brugliera, Zenith's manager, Value Engineering, allowed for physical differences in great detail.[26] The study was carefully designed to withstand objections at trial. The prices studied were the factory home market and export prices of Sanyo, Toshiba, and MEI over a period from 1966 to 1977. The paired transactions were for technically comparable sets of the same screen size, which were sold within eighteen months of one another.

Two sets of comparisons were made: one was based on domestic prices as reported in commodity tax returns, and the other on those reported in answers to Interrogatory No. 46(c) in *Matsushita*. Export prices were from documents obtained from U.S. purchasers and from defendants' answers to Interrogatory No. 46(c) and Supplemental Interrogatory No. 11. Table 6.2 reports the comparisons of the arithmetic mean prices. The estimates based on the commodity tax returns are reported in panel 1 of the table. The average percentage differences for monochrome sets were between 46 and 50 percent of the export price. Those for color sets were higher—between 55 and 71 percent.

The range was wider for the averages based on answers to interrogatories, which are reported in panel 2. For monochrome sets the range was 39 to 75 percent, and for color sets it was between 33 and 75 percent. These estimates establish that the export prices were much lower than the home market prices.

25. *Federal Register* 35 (1970): 18594.
26. 513 F. Supp. 100 (1981), at 1236.

TABLE 6.2. Percentage by which Average Home Market Price Exceeded Average Export Price, by Color Category and Company, January 1966 to February 1977

	Monochrome	Color
(1) Based on Commodity Tax Returns		
Sanyo	47	65
Toshiba	50	55
MEI	46	71
(2) Based on Answers to Interrogatory no. 46(c) and Supplemental Interrogatory no. 11		
Sanyo	75	75
Toshiba	39	33
MEI	57	73

Source: Based on Horace J. DePodwin, David Schwartzman and Marcia Texeira, *Economic Study of the Japanese Television Industry,* Civil Action Nos. 74-2451 and 74-3247, U.S. District Court for the Eastern District of Pennsylvania, September 1979, vol. 1: 6.42, 43.

The large domestic-export price differences persisted over too long a period to be dismissed as promotional. The differences, especially for monochrome receivers, persisted after the products were well established in the U.S. market. By 1971 the Japanese TV manufacturers were supplying as much as 36 percent of the total number of monochrome receivers sold in the U.S. (table 6.7).

Attacking the home market price estimates based on their interrogatory answers, the defendants said that these answers reported suggested retail prices. The appropriate prices were at the factory, and the actual prices after rebates were less than the suggested prices.[27] From his own reading of the answers Judge Becker concluded that they reported prices at several levels of distribution and that these were list prices, not "actual" prices. Moreover, he could not tell which prices the plaintiffs had compared.[28]

Refusing to agree to the estimates of home market prices based on their commodity tax returns, the defendants said that the prices to which the tax

27. This discussion is based on Zenith Radio Corp. v. Matsushita Electric Industrial Co., 505 F. Supp. 1313 (1980), at 1355–56.
28. 505 F. Supp. 1313 (1980), at 1355.

was applied usually were calculated by multiplying the retail price by a fixed percentage, based on an estimate of the cost of distribution from the manufacturers to the retailers. The judge, who did not attempt to evaluate the argument, ruled that the resulting estimates were inadmissible, because they were hypothetical. According to the judge: "The commodity tax formula does not purport to be a reliable guide to the actual prices charged in the Japanese market, but is instead intended as an industry-wide construct which avoids the computation of actual prices for countless transactions."[29]

Concerning the estimates based on the interrogatory answers, the plaintiffs replied that they referred to factory prices.[30] They also said that the defendants had described the prices in the interrogatory answers as the most accurate and relevant prices. According to the plaintiffs, the defendants had admitted in court that "there is no such thing as an actual price." They had conceded that the concept of an actual price was a fiction, which they had invented. They had admitted that any price other than that provided in the answers to the interrogatories was "irrelevant" and "unnecessary" and would be "artificial."[31] The plaintiffs inferred that the comparisons were valid.

Moreover, we note that, although the defendants claimed that the export prices reported in the answers to interrogatories were true prices—that no rebates had been paid—in fact, the importers had received rebates. Yet, even though it would have raised the estimates of the domestic-export price differences, the plaintiffs did not subtract the rebates paid to importers from the prices reported in the interrogatory answers.

Concerning the commodity tax returns, which showed factory prices, the plaintiffs' brief said that they had used the prices reported by defendants on these returns. In support, the plaintiffs said that, since a low price resulted in a low tax, the reported prices were low estimates. In addition, the prices reported on the tax returns for the period between February 1, 1971, and September 30, 1973, were actual transaction prices, and since the estimates for this period differed very little from those for other periods, the latter estimates contained negligible errors. In any case, the comparisons based on the interrogatory answers also showed large domestic-export price differences.[32]

The plaintiffs' defense of their price comparisons based on the commodity tax returns appears to be adequate. There appear to be errors in the estimates of home market prices based on the interrogatory answers owing to the failure to allow for rebates to retailers. The defendants' answers did not

---

29. 505 F. Supp. 1313 (1980), at 1356.
30. Brief of Appellants, 116ff.
31. Brief of Appellants, 117.
32. Brief of Appellants, 121–22.

adjust the reported home market prices for rebates. As chapter 5 mentions, the average rebate to retailers appears to have been in the range of 4 to 5 percent. Since the estimates of the domestic-export price differences far exceeded this amount, the error does not invalidate the conclusion that the differences were large. The small inaccuracy did not warrant the ruling of inadmissibility.

Because of the differences between the estimates based on the two sources, both of which are defensible, we cannot conclude on the basis of panel 1 of table 6.2 that Toshiba's average domestic-export price difference between January 1966 and February 1977 for monochrome receivers was 50 percent of the export price. Panel 2 shows it to have been 39 percent. Since both estimates are large, however, it is safe to conclude that Toshiba's home market prices greatly exceeded its export prices. The same is true for the other companies' prices of monochrome receivers and for the prices of color receivers.

Export Prices Were Less than Average Cost

The plaintiffs' experts estimated the difference between average costs and export prices, but we also have the evidence of statements by executives of the Japanese manufacturers. A memorandum dated March 3, 1973, by Mr. Kamura, a senior managing director of the Sanyo Trading Company, addressed to President Iue reads in part as follows:

> we expounded our idea that the Japanese side, in the worst event, would shoulder approximately 50 million yen of loss for units, thereby maintaining the present price level and subsequently have the American side receive the goods.[33]

Also, A. Saeki and Y. Fukao of Sharp told R. A. Noreen of Montgomery Ward at a meeting on February 14, 1975, "Sharp is trying to supply products for Wards at best possible costs which could be as low as break-even without profit."[34]

The plaintiffs' experts' estimates of the excess of average costs over export prices referred to the period 1967 through 1970 and the five companies—MEI, MELCO, Hitachi, Sanyo, and Toshiba—for which data were available.[35] The following data were used: operating profits and sales for each TV plant of each of the companies, unit values of home market, export, and total

---

33. 513 F. Supp. 100 (1981), Doc. No. ZSX-0234. Cited by Nehmer Report, vol. 2: VII-21.

34. 513 F. Supp. 100 (1981), Doc. No. 006266. Cited by Nehmer Report, vol. 2: VII-21.

35. This discussion based on DePodwin Report, vol. 1: VI-71–87.

sales by screen size and color category for each plant. Defendants in the antitrust case supplied data on plants' profits and sales. Calculations of average unit values were based on defendants' answers to plaintiffs' Interrogatories Nos. 45 and 46(c). The cost data referred to operating costs, that is to say, those at the plant. Central office costs were excluded. The operating costs included all costs at the plant, fixed as well as variable. The District Court distinguished between operating costs and production costs. As we will see, operating costs may have included costs other than production costs, which covered direct material costs, direct labor costs, and manufacturing overhead. Since the average production costs of domestically sold and exported sets were nearly identical, differences in these costs do not present a problem. The exclusion of central office overhead results in an overstatement of the actual profits on home market sales and an understatement of the actual losses on exports. The operating profits were before taxes. Thus, the profits on sales, which ranged from 5 to 10 percent before taxes, were lower after taxes.

The following assumptions were made. The average unit values of exports by color category and screen size were the same for all plants of each company, and similarly for domestic sales. The average operating cost to produce each TV receiver sold domestically was the same as that of the corresponding export receiver. The average operating profit rate, covering domestic and export sales, of the different product classes of a plant was the same. The last assumption may be incorrect, but differences in average profit rates were unlikely to distort seriously the overall comparisons of the export prices and costs.

The data for the Iberagi TV Business Division of MEI will illustrate the procedure for estimating losses on exports. In 1969 the average operating profit on total sales for twelve-inch black-and-white TV receivers was 5.0 percent, and the average unit value for total sales was $59.95, yielding an average operating profit of $3.00 (table 6.3). Average unit value minus average profit per unit was average operating cost, $56.95. Assuming that the average cost of exports equaled the average cost of domestic sales, this was the average cost for exports (table 6.3, panel 1). The average profit for exports per unit was the average unit value of exports, $43.65, minus the average cost, $56.95, yielding a loss of $13.30 per unit. As a percentage of the average unit value, the loss was 30.4 percent.

The profit for domestic sales was calculated as follows. The average unit value of domestic sales, $76.78, minus the average cost, $56.95, equaled the average profit, $19.83. As a percentage of the average unit value of domestic sales, $76.78, this profit was 25.8 percent.

The Iberagi plant's export sales of twelve-inch black-and-white sets were not exceptional. Estimates of profits and losses were made for exports for each year, for each screen size group, and for each operating unit. The total number of estimates was 110. Almost 40 percent of the estimates indicate losses of 50 percent or more on export sales. In over 55 percent of the cases the losses came to 25 percent or more. As we have just seen, these estimates err on the low side, since the basic data do not include corporate overhead charges. Moreover, the export prices are not net of rebates to importers. The estimates of export prices and average costs indicate that the manufacturers lost money on their export sales generally.

Judge Becker ruled that the evidence relating to costs and export prices was inadmissible on two grounds. The first was that the assumptions underlying the cost estimates were implausible. Again, the assumptions were as follows. For each company the average unit values by color category and screen size of exports were the same across plants, as it was for domestic sales. The average operating cost of a domestically sold receiver was the same as that of the export receiver in the same color and screen size category. The average operating profit rates of the product classes, including domestic and export sales, of a plant were the same. Judge Becker said that the assumption that the cost of domestic models equaled the cost of corresponding export models was critical. He cited an affidavit by Kenji Yamagishi, an MEI executive, that this assumption was incorrect. According to Yamagishi, during the 1967–70 period MEI's average operating costs were never the same for sales of television models in domestic and export markets. The sets sold in the U.S.

TABLE 6.3. Profits and Losses of the Iberagi Plant
of MEI on Total, Domestic, and Export Sales
of the 12-inch Black-and-White TV Receiver in 1969

	Total	Domestic	Export
(1) Assume equal domestic and export average operating cost			
% profit on sales	5.00	25.80	−30.40
Unit value ($)	59.95	76.78	43.65
Profit per unit ($)	3.00	19.83	−13.30
Average cost ($)	56.95	56.95	56.95
(2) Assume that average operating cost of domestic product exceeds that of export product by 20%			
% profit on sales	5.00	18.60	−19.30
Unit value ($)	59.95	76.78	43.65
Profit per unit ($)	3.00	14.31	−8.41
Average cost ($)	56.95	62.47	52.06

Source: Author's calculations. (See text.)

included a higher proportion of economy models than those sold in Japan.[36] Judge Becker also cited the figures in the DePodwin Report showing that there were differences in costs between domestic and export models. As he said: "It is plain that in some cases the domestic production costs are greater than export production costs, while in many other cases the opposite relationship exists. These results hardly support his thesis that export and domestic production costs are identical."[37]

If Yamagishi's affidavit concerning the proportion of export and domestic sales consisting of economy models were correct, then the average cost of domestic models as a whole would have exceeded the average cost of exported models as a whole. The difference, however, 0.02 percent, between the two average production cost estimates was too small to be significant. The basic source for the production cost estimates referred to MEI and consisted of that company's submissions on its production costs to the U.S. Treasury Department in antidumping proceedings.[38] True, the estimate of the difference between average cost and average export prices assumed that the average cost of export and domestic models was the same, and this was not literally correct. But the estimates were of the overall losses for screen size and color categories, not of the losses on individual models. A more accurate statement of the assumption underlying the estimates is that the average cost of the domestic models within a category was equal to the average cost of the export models within the same category. Moreover, and this point needs emphasis, the export losses were large, so a small error would not invalidate the conclusion that the TV manufacturers were exporting at a loss.

The more serious objection based on the Yamagishi affidavit was that the average operating cost was estimated on the basis of profit-and-loss statements of the defendants' plants and on unit values for each company as a whole for receivers by screen size and color category. The average *operating* cost so calculated, according to Yamagishi, differed from the average *production* cost, because it included in addition to the production cost direct selling expenses in Japan and other expenses associated with domestic sales but not with exports. The average operating cost for domestic sales exceeded the average operating cost for exports. Accordingly, the average operating cost for exports was overstated. The implication was that the export price may not have resulted in losses. This error in the estimation of the average cost of exports may be offset, however, by the other error pointed to earlier resulting from the exclusion of central office overhead from the operating expenses of

---

36. 505 F. Supp. 1313 (1980), at 1359.
37. 505 F. Supp. 1313 (1980), at 1360.
38. 505 F. Supp. 1313 (1980), at 1360.

exports. In addition, the export prices were overstated, since the data in the defendants' interrogatory answers did not subtract the rebates paid to U.S. customers.

Moreover, we may have other doubts about the treatment of selling expenses. It is strange that certain central office expenses and overhead were not included in the operating costs of plants, but that others, such as selling expenses for domestic sales, were. Such doubts might have been resolved by a cross-examination of Yamagishi at trial. But Judge Becker's summary judgment denied the opportunity. Yamagishi's assertion was part of an affidavit submitted to the Court after discovery was completed, so plaintiffs did not have the opportunity to investigate the statement.

Moreover, the errors that may have arisen due to selling expenses incurred in the domestic market probably were too small to invalidate the conclusion that the export prices were below costs. The U.S. Federal Trade Commission (FTC) Line of Business reports covering the years 1974–77 showed that the U.S. TV manufacturers' selling costs were on the average over the four years 7.8 percent of sales.[39] The Japanese TV manufacturers may have had higher selling costs. To show the effect of a generous allowance for the selling costs in their home market panel 2 in table 6.3 demonstrates the effect on the estimates of profits and losses of a 20 percent difference between the domestic and export models in average operating costs. We can see that the loss on sales of the export model is reduced from 30.4 percent to 19.3 percent and the profit on the sales of the domestic model from 25.8 percent to 18.6 percent. Thus, even a high estimate of the domestic-export difference in costs does not change the conclusion that exports were made at losses.

Judge Becker also ruled the estimates of price-cost differences inadmissible because they relied on estimates of average prices by screen size categories.[40] He held that the original ruling, which applied to the comparison between export and domestic prices, also applied in the present context. But, as we have seen, there is no basis for believing that the price comparisons were biased by the physical differences.

Judge Becker also objected to what he called the "mathematical construction" offered to show that the manufacturers exported at a loss.[41] This objection was not one of his grounds for the ruling, but the judge expressed it strongly enough to give the impression that it had influenced his decision. According to the judge, "the plaintiffs and their expert eschewed the particularized actual cost data which was available to them in favor of a mathemati-

39. Federal Trade Commission (FTC), *FTC Statistical Report: Annual Line of Business Report,* 1974, 1975, 1976, 1977, table 2.7.

40. 505 F. Supp. 1313 (1980), at 1357–58.

41. 505 F. Supp. 1313 (1980), at 1357–58.

cal construction of what is obviously at best a rough estimate of defendants' costs."[42] It is unlikely that detailed data on costs of particular models would have improved the estimates of average cost-price differences of screen size and color categories significantly. The mass of data tendered by the defendants may not have included the pertinent data.[43] In addition, allocations would have had to be made of overhead expenses between models. The cost data that were used were the defendants' own estimates of their average operating costs.

The losses on exports cannot be excused as the result of promotional selling or the extra costs of entry into the U.S. market. According to the estimates, in 1970 the Japanese manufacturers were still selling monochrome receivers at a loss when they already had 34 percent of the U.S. market (table 6.7, p. 114). With 16 percent of total sales they also were well established in the U.S. color TV market (table 6.4). Moreover, the evidence of predatory pricing would be even stronger were it based on total costs rather than on operating costs.

Capacity Expansion

We must consider the possibility that excess capacity and the associated high fixed costs forced the TV manufacturers to sell abroad at low and possibly loss prices. Lower home market sales over short periods than those planned and the resulting excess capacity may have induced the manufacturers to export at a loss. At low rates of capacity utilization a monopolist may export at low prices. Control over the home market combined with excess capacity might encourage a cartel to export at prices that did not yield a profit. However, low demand was not the explanation. The number of color TV units sold in the home market increased over much of the period. It declined only toward the end. Moreover, and more important, production capacity expanded.

I begin with color TV receivers, for which capacity expansion data are available. Japan began producing color receivers in significant quantities in 1962 (table 6.4). Output grew enormously, and in 1969 Japan produced 5.0 million sets, in 1972 output amounted to 8.4 million and in 1977 to 9.7 million (tables 6.4 and 6.5.) From the beginning the manufacturers exported a

---

42. 505 F. Supp. 1313 (1980), at 1358.

43. Commenting on the U.S. Customs Service's problem of assessing costs in the dumping case, Prestowitz says:

The Customs Service had only a small staff, which the Japanese consciously overwhelmed with literally miles of documentation, much of it conflicting. No one in the United States understood Japanese accounting, and acrimonious debate erupted over the different accounting procedures. At one point, Japanese producers justified lower prices in the United States by saying they used only young workers on U.S.-bound sets, which were therefore of poorer quality than those made by older workers for Japanese use. (*Trading Places,* 356)

TABLE 6.4. Japan: Color Television Receivers—Total Shipments, Domestic Shipments, Total Exports, Exports to United States, 1962–77

Year	Shipments		Exports	
	Total	Domestic	Total	United States
	Thousands of Units			
1962	12	12	0	0
1963	16	16	0	0
1964	60	43	17	17
1965	107	63	43	43
1966	510	258	252	240
1967	1268	927	341	324
1968	2785	2017	769	736
1969	5021	4017	1003	939
1970	6452	5444	1008	887
1971	7681	6104	1577	1259
1972	8401	6553	1849	1147
1973	9322	7230	2092	1122
1974	7833	5545	2289	1012
1975	8321	5565	2756	1223
1976	10941	5691	5251	2975
1977	9699	5277	4423	2149
	Percentages			
1962	100	100	0	0
1963	100	100	0	0
1964	100	72	28	28
1965	100	59	40	40
1966	100	51	49	47
1967	100	73	27	26
1968	100	72	28	26
1969	100	80	20	19
1970	100	84	16	14
1971	100	79	21	16
1972	100	78	22	14
1973	100	78	22	12
1974	100	71	29	13
1975	100	67	33	15
1976	100	52	48	27
1977	100	54	46	22

Source: Based on DePodwin Report, vol. 2: tables 3 and 12.

TABLE 6.5. **United States Color Television Receivers: Apparent Consumption, Domestic Shipments, Total Imports, Imports from Japan, 1962–77**

Year	Apparent Consumption	Domestic Shipments	Imports Total	Imports From Japan
		Thousands of Units		
1962	438	438	0	0
1963	747	747	0	0
1964	1340	1340	0	0
1965	2689	2689	0	0
1966	4988	4748	240	200
1967	5323	4995	328	315
1968	6232	5566	666	662
1969	5993	5081	912	879
1970	5430	4513	914	851
1971	6889	5606	1281	1191
1972	8103	6785	1318	1094
1973	8828	7429	1399	1059
1974	8010	6728	1282	916
1975	6742	5527	1215	1044
1976	8579	5744	2835	2530
1977	9283	6745	2538	2029
		Percentages		
1962	100	100	0	0
1963	100	100	0	0
1964	100	100	0	0
1965	100	100	0	0
1966	100	95	5	4
1967	100	94	6	6
1968	100	89	11	11
1969	100	85	15	15
1970	100	83	17	16
1971	100	81	19	17
1972	100	84	16	14
1973	100	84	16	12
1974	100	84	16	11
1975	100	82	18	15
1976	100	67	33	29
1977	100	73	27	22

Source: Based on Nehmer Report, table VII-2.

substantial proportion of the total output to the U.S., and the exports grew rapidly until 1971. In 1976 exports to the U.S. reached a one-year, very high peak. The Orderly Marketing Agreement (OMA) came into force in 1978, putting a stop to further growth. The drop was partly offset by an increase in exports from Taiwan and South Korea, much of which came from Japanese manufacturers' offshore plants. Nearly all of Taiwan and South Korea's output was exported, none of it going to Japan. In 1977, including their exports from offshore plants, the Japanese manufacturers' share of the U.S. color receiver market probably was about 25 percent. This is not the picture of an industry that is exporting at low prices because it is afflicted with excess capacity.

Data are available on the capacity expansion of the leading firms between 1967 and 1970. Over this period MEI, Toshiba, Hitachi, Sony, Sharp, MELCO, and Victor together expanded their annual capacity to manufacture color TV receivers from 1.2 million units to 8.2 million units, or sevenfold.[44] This increase in capacity clearly was intended for the export market. In 1970 domestic shipments of color TV receivers amounted to only 4.5 million units, and total shipments, including exports, amounted to 5.4 million units. Domestic shipments did increase to 7.2 million units in 1973, but this was a one-year peak. In the subsequent years domestic shipments did not go above 5.7 million units.

We have no data on Japan's monochrome TV capacity. We have only the data on domestic and export shipments. Exports grew to too large a fraction of total output, however, merely to be the result of surplus capacity. Domestic shipments reached a peak of 4.5 million receivers as early as 1961 (table 6.6), but exports continued to grow. In 1971 exports made up 70 percent of total shipments. In the same year 47 percent of total shipments went to the U.S. It is reasonable to infer that capacity was built to supply the U.S. market.

Imports from Japan reached a peak of 36 percent of the U.S. apparent consumption of monochrome receivers in 1971 (table 6.7). The share of the U.S. market taken by Japanese manufacturers was much larger. Most of the imports from other countries came from offshore plants owned and operated by the Japanese manufacturers in Taiwan and South Korea. In 1974, 71 percent of imports of monochrome receivers came from Taiwan and 9 percent from South Korea.[45] Of the total 1972 output in Taiwan of such receivers Japanese manufacturers accounted for 24 percent. In South Korea the corresponding figure was 77 percent.[46] We can estimate that, in 1974, 17 percent of the total imports of monochrome receivers manufactured by Japanese companies came from Taiwan and South Korea. Accordingly, the Japanese manufac-

44. DePodwin Report, vol. 1: III-34, table III-16.
45. DePodwin Report, vol. 2: 96, table 64.
46. DePodwin Report, vol. 1: III-38, table III-18.

TABLE 6.6. Japan: Monochrome Television Receivers—Total Shipments, Domestic Shipments, Total Exports, Exports to United States, 1960–77

Year	Shipments		Exports	
	Total	Domestic	Total	United States
		Thousands of Units		
1960	3586	3540	45	10
1961	4573	4486	87	23
1962	4751	4489	262	NA
1963	4881	4198	686	NA
1964	5095	4112	984	770
1965	4226	2769	1457	1089
1966	5014	3171	1843	1321
1967	5516	3593	1923	1248
1968	6420	3659	2761	1771
1969	7033	3747	3287	2305
1970	6228	2513	3715	2467
1971	5610	1674	3936	2609
1972	4291	1106	3188	3188
1973	3745	1473	2273	2273
1974	3592	1203	2389	775
1975	3286	999	2287	647
1976	4543	938	3606	1385
1977	4658	975	3683	1662
		Percentages		
1960	100	99	1	0
1961	100	98	2	1
1962	100	94	6	NA
1963	100	86	14	NA
1964	100	81	19	15
1965	100	66	34	26
1966	100	63	37	26
1967	100	65	35	23
1968	100	57	43	28
1969	100	53	47	33
1970	100	40	60	40
1971	100	30	70	47
1972	100	26	74	74
1973	100	39	61	61
1974	100	33	67	22
1975	100	30	70	20
1976	100	21	79	30
1977	100	21	79	36

Source: Nehmer Report, table VII-6.

TABLE 6.7. United States: Monochrome Television Receivers—Apparent Consumption, Domestic Shipments, Total Imports, Imports from Japan, 1962–77

Year	Apparent Consumption	Domestic Shipments	Imports Total	Imports From Japan
		Thousands of Units		
1962	6365	6206	159	127
1963	7378	6987	391	389
1964	8088	7373	715	711
1965	8248	7200	1048	1047
1966	8276	6913	1519	1434
1967	5913	4738	1290	1216
1968	6999	5061	2043	1637
1969	7269	4247	3121	2209
1970	7221	3700	3596	2441
1971	7138	3046	4166	2549
1972	8102	3188	4989	1777
1973	8030	3080	5049	983
1974	6768	2226	4659	884
1975	4641	1757	2975	639
1976	5952	1625	4483	1417
1977	6759	1186	5726	1717
		Percentages		
1962	100	98	2	2
1963	100	95	5	5
1964	100	91	9	9
1965	100	87	13	13
1966	100	84	18	17
1967	100	80	22	21
1968	100	72	29	23
1969	100	58	43	30
1970	100	51	50	34
1971	100	43	58	36
1972	100	39	62	22
1973	100	38	63	12
1974	100	33	69	13
1975	100	38	64	14
1976	100	27	75	24
1977	100	18	85	25

Source: Based on Nehmer Report, table VII-1.

turers supplied a total of 30 percent of the U.S. market. Thus, in 1974 the share of the U.S. monochrome market taken by Japanese manufacturers was nearly as high as in 1971. Evidently, they now were supplying the U.S. from offshore plants. A similar estimate for 1977 puts the Japanese share of the U.S. market for monochrome receivers at 45 percent. In the 1970s the cartel was supplying a large and growing share of the U.S. market for monochrome receivers.

The difference between home market and export prices for both color and monochrome receivers thus was not the result of surplus capacity. The Japanese TV manufacturers built the capacity deliberately to supply the U.S. market. We can only conclude that the price difference expressed a deliberate policy. When the manufacturers built this capacity they were aware of the prices of TV receivers in the U.S. and in Japan. They knew that their export prices would have to be much lower than their home market prices and that the exports would incur losses. Moreover, it is unlikely that unbridled rivalry led to the capacity expansion. As chapter 4 reported, MITI was aware of the dangers of excessive capacity. During the 1960s, when much of the capacity was built, MITI exercised control over construction.

Since 1977 Japanese companies have increased their share of the U.S. color TV market. By 1986 the share of U.S. companies had fallen to 43 percent, while that of Japanese companies had risen to 34 percent. Much of this share came from plants based in Taiwan and South Korea. Some continued to come from Japan itself. As table 2.1 (pp. 32–35) shows, even in the late 1980s Japanese manufacturers were still dumping receivers manufactured in Japan. The share of companies based in the Netherlands, South Korea, Taiwan, and other countries was 23 percent. These figures refer to the companies' shares, not to the place of manufacture. Some sets and components sold in the U.S. by RCA and Zenith were manufactured by offshore plants that they operated. In 1987 General Electric, which had acquired RCA in 1985, sold its consumer electronics business to the French company Thomson. As a result, Zenith, with a market share of 15 percent in 1987, was the sole surviving TV manufacturer based in the U.S.[47]

Conclusion

The TV manufacturers restricted competition among themselves in the export market. They limited the number of direct U.S. customers to which each could sell, and they did not allow any member of the cartel to take a customer

---

47. David H. Staelin et al., "The Decline of U.S. Consumer Electronics Manufacturing: History, Hypotheses, and Remedies," in *The Working Papers of the MIT Commission on Industrial Productivity* (Cambridge, Mass.: MIT Press, 1989).

away from another member. By so controlling competition, they gained a large share of the market at a much lower cost than if they had competed freely.

To gain a large share of the U.S. market for both color and monochrome receivers the cartel set export prices that were much less than the home market prices. This was possible because the cartel exercised monopoly power in the home market. In addition, the export prices of the receivers were less than the average costs. That the low prices and the losses were not the product of temporary surplus capacity also seems clear. The members of the cartel deliberately built the capacity for exports. The losses were not the result of excess capacity due to overestimating the home market demand.

CHAPTER 7

The Antidumping Proceedings

On March 22, 1968, the Electronic Industries Association filed with the commissioner of Customs a petition under the Antidumping Act of 1921, alleging that Japan was exporting monochrome and color TV receivers to the U.S. at less-than-fair value (LTFV). Although the Treasury approved the petition and the Customs Service assessed large dumping duties, the final settlement was trivial.

The administration under Nixon, Ford, and Carter was unwilling to enforce what was in its view a protectionist measure, inconsistent with the policy of trade liberalization being implemented through the various GATT rounds of tariff reduction and negotiations for opening markets. The large volume of goods dumped, and the involvement of the Japanese government made the TV case particularly nettlesome. In the administration's view—the main problem being to open Japan's markets to exports—TV dumping was not worth a nasty confrontation, which risked wrecking the negotiations. In addition, being hostile toward antidumping petitions generally, the administration was unwilling to devote adequate resources to the effective enforcement of the law. The Customs Service could not speedily handle the problems of product comparability and determining the fair value of the goods in hundreds of import entries of TV receivers, especially with the Japanese manufacturers concealing the true prices with false invoices and obstructing the collection of information. Moreover, the fear of disturbing relations with the Japanese government inhibited penalizing the exporters for their fraudulent practices. To deal with the exporters' obstructionist tactics the Customs Service finally adopted a novel method of estimating fair value, prompting threats of litigation. After a decade of haggling the administration negotiated a settlement imposing small penalties.

A History of the Proceedings

Delays set in immediately after the TV petition was filed. It was not before December 5, 1970, twenty months after the filing, that the Treasury made the LTFV determination. Since this preliminary determination was based on the petitioners' submissions, problems of valuation did not cause the delay. On March 9, 1971, the Tariff Commission (the ITC's predecessor) determined that the dumping had injured the domestic industry, and the Treasury then published a finding of dumping.[1]

More than five years after the finding, in October 1976, the agency made an assessment and then only for the period between September 1970 and March 1972. The assessment was only about $1 million.[2] The General Counsel of the Department of Commerce in 1980, Homer E. Moyer, Jr., said that Customs had been slow in calculating the dumping duties owed.

One reason the assessment was so small was that before 1977 the Customs Service accepted the invoice prices and did not subtract the rebates to the importers, even though it knew of them. The agency only recognized the rebates officially early in 1977, when, in making a voluntary tender of duties, Gamble Skogmo, an importer, disclosed that Mitsubishi (MELCO) had entered false prices on the invoices. Customs then began a large investigation.

The investigation found that, except for Sony, the major Japanese TV manufacturers had made rebates, some of which were large. Alexander's, Inc., which was the first importer to be sentenced by a court, admitted that it had received a rebate of $25.18 on sets for which the import price was $71.95.[3] According to Customs officials, the civil penalties against the importers found guilty of customs fraud could equal the value of the imported goods, which would come to at least $1 billion.[4]

Although it was their invoices that had shown the false prices, the Japanese manufacturers claimed innocence. According to an official of EIAJ, because the rebates were not illegal, the only issue was whether they had been disclosed, and disclosure was the responsibility of the importers and Customs, not of the Japanese manufacturers.[5]

The reluctance of the Japanese manufacturers to supply correct information and their delaying tactics led Customs to calculate the fair values using the "best information available," which was based on the commodity tax formula.[6] Under this method the foreign market value would be estimated as

---

1. "Statement of Facts pertaining to the Finding of Dumping of Television Receivers from Japan," Office of Chief Counsel, Regulations and Rulings, Operations, and Investigations, U.S. Customs Service, n.d. (hereafter referred to as "Statement of Facts").

2. Department of Commerce, Briefing by Homer Moyer, general counsel, Department of Commerce, and Sal Caramagno, director of Classification and Value, U.S. Customs Service, April 28, 1980, 2 (hereafter referred to as Moyer Memorandum).

3. *Wall Street Journal,* March 30, 1979. Cited by John W. Rosenblum and Bruce R. Scott, *Zenith Radio Corporation v. the United States: 1978–1980* (Cambridge, Mass.: Harvard Business School Cases, 1980), 3.

4. Seymour M. Hersh, "Testimony on Fraud in Importing TV Sets," *New York Times,* January 24, 1979. Quoted by Rosenblum and Scott, *Zenith Radio Corporation,* 5.

5. Hersh, "Testimony on Fraud in Importing Sets." Quoted by Rosenblum and Scott, *Zenith Radio Corporation,* 5.

6. Memorandum dated April 1978 (App-2-04-6:D:T LB ln) from acting assistant commissioner (Operations) to the commissioner of Customs. Quoted by L. J. Holroyd, representing

the factory prices for domestic shipments by subtracting from Japanese retail prices a percentage based on the formula used by the Japanese Ministry of Finance. The factory prices so estimated would be compared with the export prices. Applying the commodity tax method, in 1978 Customs estimated the antidumping duties due on imports through March 1977 at $382 million.[7] Yet, although the Treasury Department agreed to the use of the commodity tax method, it was reluctant to carry through the assessment of the duties. On March 28, 1978, at the request of the Japanese embassy, Treasury and Customs officials heard the TV manufacturers' protests against the use of the formula. As a result, there were further delays. Seven years had passed since the antidumping order, but no assessment had been made.

Following the meeting, the Treasury Department decided that Customs should not assess dumping duties for entries beyond June 30, 1973. According to Moyer, "For various reasons, Treasury and Customs determined that it would be inappropriate to assess this amount all at once."[8] The two main considerations were the novelty of the commodity tax method and that the assessment would cause great hardship for some importers. Despite Moyer's statement, Customs opposed the delay. Customs commissioner Robert E. Chasen objected that to delay assessing duties through 1977 would cause administrative difficulties,[9] and senior Customs attorneys attributed the postponement to the Treasury Department's acquiescence to the Japanese embassy's pressure and its insufficient sensitivity to the interests of unemployed U.S. workers. Protesting the decision, Congressmen Charles A. Vanik and Dan Rostenkowski said:

It is unfortunate that the Treasury Department thought it appropriate to consult both with counsel for the importers and representatives of the Japanese government as to its proposed action in this case but did not see fit to consult with Congress or representatives of the domestic industry.[10]

These protests did not alter the Treasury Department's decision, and on March 31, 1978, Customs made an assessment for entries only through June 30,

---

Midland International Corp., House, Subcommittee on Trade, Committee on Ways and Means, Hearings, September 21, 1978, *Administration of the Antidumping Act of 1921,* 157–58. Midland was an importer. (These hearings will hereafter be referred to as House Subcommittee on Trade Hearings 1978.)

7. Moyer Memorandum, 2.

8. Moyer Memorandum, 2.

9. House Subcommittee on Trade Hearings 1978, Paul D. Cullen, "Statement of the Electronic Industries Association, Imports Committee of the Tube Division," 84–85 (hereafter referred to as Cullen Memorandum).

10. Statement of congressmen Charles A. Vanik and Dan Rostenkowski on the TV antidumping case, April 10, 1978. Quoted by Seymour M. Hersh, "Testimony on Fraud in Importing TV Sets." Quoted by Rosenblum and Scott, *Zenith Radio Corporation,* 7.

1973, which was approximately $46 million.[11] Two more assessments were made, totaling $32 million.[12]

Anticipating legal challenges to the use of the commodity tax formula, Treasury instructed Customs to explain and justify its use at a disclosure meeting which took place on May 3. Irving W. Smith, Jr., chief of the Value Branch of Customs, said that the similarity of the manufacturers' submissions regarding market values and the unreliable information provided by a substantial number led Customs to doubt the veracity of all the submissions. The widespread rebates and other invoicing irregularities added to the doubts. Some manufacturers failed to respond at all to repeated requests for information, many submissions were incomplete, and some TV models exported to the U.S. were not covered at all. A significant number of the submissions on foreign market value were so dubious that accepting them at face value would have required Customs to believe that receivers were being sold at a loss in the home market. Another source of doubt was that in many cases the home market sets that the manufacturers identified as most comparable to the exported sets were not as the manufacturers claimed but were, in fact, quite different. Finally, Customs decided that, since the usual process could not fulfill the purpose of the Antidumping Act, it required a more expeditious method. The decision was made after considering the mass of data submitted, the extended period of time already spent on the case, and the additional time that would be required to verify new data.

Smith also explained the procedure for estimating factory prices for home market sales based on the commodity tax formula. The Japanese tax authority estimated the factory price by multiplying the retail price by 0.62, and, to remove the commodity tax included in the gross wholesale price, it then multiplied the result by 0.87. Customs applied the same formula to the suggested retail list prices, which it obtained from the Green Book, newspaper advertisements by nondiscount retail stores, and manufacturers' brochures as well as information received directly from the manufacturers. To establish the comparability of export and home market receivers only the home market prices of those sets sold in the same quarter in which the set in question was exported were used. To determine the physical comparability of the export and home market sets electronics engineers compared the schematics for receivers sold in the U.S. published by Sams Photofax with those for models sold in Japan published by Dempa.

The export prices were estimated from the invoices. Customs subtracted from the prices shown allowances for freight, insurance, inland freight in

---

11. Memorandum from Robert E. Chasen, commissioner of Customs, to Don Furtado, acting undersecretary, Department of the Treasury, "Japanese Televisions—Antidumping," February 19, 1980, 3 (hereafter referred to as Chasen Memorandum, 2/19/80).

12. Moyer Memorandum, 2.

Japan, and brokerage fees to arrive at the factory price. Where they were submitted Customs used the data on rebates to arrive at exporters' sales prices. Where data was not supplied Customs estimated the ratio of exporters' sales prices to invoice prices from known prices and applied the ratio to the invoice prices.[13]

Affirming Smith's message, Commissioner Chasen blamed the TV manufacturers for the long delay. He also blamed the administrative procedures requiring the collection and analysis of vast amounts of information. According to Chasen, the delays negated Congress's purpose.[14]

Despite the Customs Service's statement, the long delay in arriving at the March 31 assessment for only the period prior to June 31, 1973, and the deceit by the Japanese manufacturers, the Treasury Department led the Japanese government to believe that even that assessment was provisional and would probably be reduced after Customs received more data. In a memorandum dated April 18 several Customs attorneys protested against Treasury statements suggesting that the assessment of $46 million was not final. They said that the exporters and importers anticipated that the assessment would be reduced through informal government-to-government negotiations or contacts between manufacturers and the Treasury.[15]

The Japanese manufacturers and the importers filed hundreds of detailed objections to the March 31 assessment. These involved the comparability of models and the differences in circumstances of sales between the domestic and the export sales.

The Customs Service staff attorneys assigned to estimate the reduction in the March 31 assessment defended the original assessment. The adjustments proposed by the manufacturers were based on information for a small number of model matches, generally three per manufacturer, which were not selected on the basis of their statistical representativeness. They were selected because Customs and the manufacturers agreed on the technical equivalence of the home market and export models. The attorneys said:

> Therefore, these "estimates" are highly unreliable when applied to the total dumping duty assessed (on entries made prior to June 30, 1973) against each importer (by manufacturer) on March 31, 1978. For a variety of reasons, the unreliability of these "estimates" is further compounded when applied to post-June, 1973 entries.[16]

13. Based on quotations in Hersh, "Testimony on Fraud in Importing TV Sets." Quoted by Rosenblum and Scott, *Zenith Radio Corporation,* 8–13.

14. Memorandum by Chasen, dated October 18, 1977, to the undersecretary and general counsel of the Treasury. Quoted by Cullen Memorandum, 85.

15. Cullen Memorandum, 88.

16. Memorandum to file from staff attorneys on "'Estimated' Reduction of Dumping Duties Assessed against Televisions Imported from Japan (T.D. 71–76); Adjustments to Foreign

In addition, the staff attorneys said that the adjustments were recalculated to allow for "all claimed circumstance of sale adjustments which appeared to meet the legal test of being directly related to the ultimate sale of the televisions in question."[17] Customs did not check the veracity of the claims. The on-site verification did not determine whether the alleged services to customers were, in fact, offered. Nor were the claims concerning costs verified. The assumption underlying the estimation procedure was that all claims had to be established by the manufacturer to the satisfaction of Customs. As they said in their memorandum, however, the claims were not substantiated to the satisfaction of the staff attorneys assigned to make the estimates.[18]

Apart from the problems of product comparability, there were two main general issues. According to H. William Tanaka, representing Sony, by changing the rules five or six years after the dates of the imports, the Customs Service retroactively created liabilities, contrary to the purpose of the act. He argued that the act was intended to operate prospectively to prevent injury to a domestic industry, not to penalize past dumping activities.[19] Tanaka also protested against the use of the commodity tax formula, which was based on the suggested retail price. According to Tanaka, retailers did not sell TV receivers at list prices. Further, the Antidumping Act required allowances to be made for differences in circumstances of sale, including differences in advertising costs, warranty costs, rebates, discounts, and credit terms. Using the commodity tax formula did not allow for these differences.[20]

Whether the retail list price was the actual retail price was, however, immaterial. The fair value was defined as the factory price in the exporting country. The commodity tax was assessed on the same price. The Japanese government estimated the factory price as the retail list price less 38 percent and an allowance for the commodity tax. It did not estimate the factory price on the basis of the actual retail price.

Market Value Due to Differences in Circumstances of Sale," dated March 2, 1979, signed by Irwin Altschuler, David Amerine, Berniece Browne, Dinah Flynn, Steven Kersner, Robert Seely, Craig Walker, Barbara Graham, Bill Brooks, 1–2 (hereafter referred to as Staff Attorneys' Memorandum).

17. Staff Attorneys' Memorandum, 2.

18. The conflict between Treasury and Customs resulted in some organizational changes. Treasury general counsel Mundheim transferred the antidumping functions from the Customs Office of Regulations and Rulings to his own office. The senior Customs staff attorney involved in the TV case, Thomas L. Delaney, was shifted to looking after Freedom of Information applications "Hot Duel over Dumping," *Time*, March 26, 1979, 64; Seymour M. Hersh, "Dumping Vigilance Debated. . . ," *New York Times*, January 26, 1979. Quoted by Rosenblum and Scott, *Zenith Radio Corporation*, 8–9.

19. Statement of H. William Tanaka, House, Subcommittee on Trade Hearings, 1978, 172 (hereafter referred to as Tanaka).

20. Tanaka, 175.

In December 1979 Treasury representatives suggested a settlement of $50 million for the dumping duties and the civil fraud claims. The Treasury tried to gain Congressional support by expressing concern for the U.S. retailers who would have to pay penalties of $1 billion for the charges of fraud in addition to hundreds of millions of dollars for the dumping charges. A memorandum from Customs, listing estimates of the dumping duties, was used to support the appeal. In addition, Treasury officials said that imposing the original assessment might set off a trade war while the multilateral trade agreement was being negotiated. The members of the U.S. House Ways and Means Committee, approached by the Treasury, rejected the proposal, which would have allowed importers to pay less than 10 percent of the dumping duties and would have waived civil penalties.[21]

Contrary to the recommendation of the Customs attorneys charged with evaluating the manufacturers' protests, the Department of Commerce, which replaced the Treasury, reduced the original assessment of $46 million to under $8 million.[22] Taking this reduction into account, in April 1980 Commerce estimated that the maximum claim for dumping duties that could be made for the period from 1971 to 1979 was $138.7 million.[23] If the original assessment of $46 million had been allowed to stand and antidumping duties had been assessed on imports after 1973 on the same basis as this assessment, the claim for duties would have been approximately $800 million. This estimate is arrived at by multiplying $138.7 million by 46/8.

On the basis of the adjusted assessment plus other considerations Commerce negotiated a settlement with MITI, acting for the importers and the Japanese manufacturers, for antidumping duties over the period from 1971 through 1979. Moyer announced a settlement of $66 million. The settlement of the civil fraud cases by Customs and Treasury would add $9 to $11 million, making a total of between $75 and $77 million.[24] Since $66 million was 48 percent of the adjusted assessment, the other considerations appear to have been important.

These other considerations included the possibility that further protests would reduce the estimate of $138.7 million, the risk of litigation reducing the amount collected, and the demand on the resources of the Customs Service. The legal defensibility of the commodity tax formula was questionable, ac-

21. Department of Treasury, U.S. Customs Service, Memorandum to Robert H. Mundheim, general counsel, from chief counsel, on "Television Sets from Japan—Collection of Dumping Duties," March 6, 1978, 1–2. Seymour M. Hersh, "Testimony on Fraud in Importing TV Sets," *New York Times,* January 24, 1979. Quoted by Rosenblum and Scott, *Zenith Radio Corporation,* 7–8.

22. Moyer Memorandum, 3.

23. Moyer Memorandum, 5.

24. Moyer Memorandum, 1.

cording to Moyer. He said that the Justice Department took the view that the formula was sustainable in the courts only if it was demonstrated that the prices so estimated were *identical* to the actual sales prices in Japan.[25] If a court ruled that the formula could not be used, then the claims would have to be dropped, or they would have to be reestimated using the traditional method, which would require substantial additional resources and take up to three years. The new estimates would themselves be open to both administrative and judicial challenges.[26]

Barbara Babcock, Assistant Attorney General, advised a settlement, because, if the importers were to litigate the dumping cases, they were likely to prevail, and contesting the suits would demand significant government resources. According to Babcock, the plaintiffs could demonstrate that the commodity tax formula did not produce accurate estimates. They could easily get sellers and purchasers to testify that the estimated prices differed from the actual prices, while the Department of Justice would be unable to persuade Japanese retailers to testify at all. It was not sufficient to demonstrate the reasonableness of using the commodity tax formula to deal with the falsification of the data by the manufacturers. The Department of Justice had to demonstrate that the actual prices in Japan were identical to those that were estimated by the formula.[27] Other legal issues included the following: the comparability of models sold in Japan with those sold in the United States, the adequacy of the adjustments for differences in the circumstances of sale, and the differences in prices caused by the rise in the value of the yen.[28]

The basic issue was the validity of the Customs Service's March 31, 1978, assessment of dumping duties, based on the commodity tax formula, of $138.7 million, and the Commissioner of Customs and the General Counsel of the Department of Commerce believed that it would not withstand challenges in the courts.

Protesting the settlement, Congressman Vanik, chairman of the House Subcommittee on Trade, questioned whether the adjustment claimed for a color TV model within a screen size group would match that for a monochrome receiver of a different size. Evidently, an adjustment that Customs agreed to for a particular model was applied to a wide range of models. Moreover, it was his understanding that Customs intended to verify the data submitted only as needed, giving the Japanese manufacturers the benefit of the doubt. Vanik assumed that concern for the size of the penalties that importers

25. Moyer Memorandum, 6.

26. Moyer Memorandum, 6.

27. Letter by Barbara A. Babcock, assistant attorney general, Civil Division, Department of Justice, to Robert E. Chasen, commissioner of Customs, December 19, 1978.

28. Moyer Memorandum, 6–7.

would have to bear was partly responsible for the lenient treatment. Vanik disagreed with the assessment by the Commerce Department of the chance of success in the courts. He argued that, because the Antidumping Act provided that adjustments were to be made only if they were "established to the satisfaction of the Secretary," Commerce had a strong case.[29]

It should be noted that the Japanese manufacturers undertook to pay the penalties under the settlement for the importers.[30]

Discussion

The length of time taken by Customs to do its work contributed to its ineffectiveness. To accomplish the objective of deterring dumping the enforcement agency had to act swiftly to raise the importer's cost back to what it would have been without dumping. The long delays encouraged the exporters to doubt that the duties would ever be collected. Failure promptly to collect antidumping duties undermined the act's remedial purpose.

It took Customs five years to issue its first assessment of duties. It was 1976 before Customs assessed the duties for 1970–72. The later proceedings also were delayed. Not only did Customs have to deal with the problems created by the double invoicing by Japanese manufacturers, but the manufacturers also delayed the proceedings by overwhelming the Customs staff with large stacks of documents containing inconsistent information. The administration's opposition to the goal of the Antidumping Act also played a part. The administration viewed antidumping proceedings generally as protectionist efforts. Because the dominant view within the administration was that the major U.S.-Japan trade problem was to open up Japanese markets, it preferred to deal with the dumping problems by negotiation with the Japanese government and reaching a settlement.

A stronger commitment to enforce the act would have sped up the proceedings, if for no other reason than that it would have devoted more resources to the task. Assessing antidumping duties created a large and growing workload for the Customs staff, which did not grow proportionally. The increase in the volume of imports of complex manufactured goods added to the burden. TV receivers have many minor differences, for which Customs must make allowances when appraising dumping margins. In 1977 the Gen-

---

29. Charles A. Vanik, chairman, House, Subcommittee on Trade, Committee on Ways and Means, letter to Robert Chasen, commissioner, U.S. Customs Service, March 19, 1979.

30. Memorandum to Homer Moyer, from Ted Hume, Office of the U.S. Trade Representative, March 25, 1980; attached background paper No. 2, Jordan Luke's notes of discussions in November 1978 with MITI, 4, 15.

eral Accounting Office (GAO) estimated that the average delay in assessing dumping duties was 3–3.5 years.[31] To do the job Customs collected information from the exporters, analyzed the information, and issued instructions to the field offices. The questionnaires to the exporters related to home market sales, U.S. export sales, and circumstances of sales, such as discounts, advertising, warranties, and distribution costs. A backlog of assessments accumulated.[32] More resources were required to achieve quick results, without which the act did little to deter dumping.

In addition, a more committed administration would have been willing to confront the exporters and the Japanese government. The administration allowed the manufacturers to protest the application of the commodity tax formula on the ground that it represented a change in the rules, even though its use was provoked by their own false invoicing. A more outraged administration would have pursued the matter in the courts.

There were also other instruments available, which the administration was reluctant to use. Section 337 of the Trade Act of 1930, amended by the Trade Act of 1974, provides sanctions against unfair methods of competition when these tend to destroy or substantially injure an industry or to restrain or monopolize trade in the U.S. The sanctions include prohibition of imports that are in violation and cease-and-desist orders. Before 1974 the International Trade Commission (ITC) could only recommend sanctions to the president, who made the final decision. The 1974 Trade Act authorized the ITC to issue the orders directly. The president may revoke an order for policy reasons, but otherwise it goes into effect. Congress strengthened the ITC's authority because of pressure from industries suffering losses due to dumping, and the administration was opposed to reliance on Section 337.[33] The president still could block the use of Section 337, but at a greater political risk.

While trade liberalization was the administration's dominant policy, compromises were necessary to protect badly injured domestic industries. The administration preferred to rely on bilateral agreements to restrict imports rather than on the Antidumping Act. These included Orderly Marketing Agreements (OMAs) and Voluntary Export Restraints (VERs). In May 1977 an OMA limiting exports of color TV receivers to the U.S. for three years was

---

31. "Results of the U.S. General Accounting Office Review of Selected Aspects of the Administration of the Antidumping Act of 1921," Hearings, House, Subcommittee on Trade, Committee on Ways and Means, "Unfair Trade Practices," September 5, 1978, 24 (hereafter referred to as House Subcommittee on Trade Hearings, 9/5/78).

32. House Subcommittee on Trade, 9/5/78, 22–23.

33. Matthew J. Marks, "Dealing with Unfair Competition" (Speech before Conference Board, New York, May 11, 1978); printed in House Subcommittee on Trade Hearings 9/5/78, 125–26 (hereafter cited as Marks Statement).

entered into with Japan. The limit was placed at 1.75 million receivers. President Carter secretly promised in exchange for the agreement to end the ITC investigation of customs fraud and dumping and the related antitrust investigations by the Department of Justice.[34] On their side the Japanese government agreed to encourage the TV manufacturers to invest in assembly plants in the U.S.[35] In December 1978 the administration negotiated OMAs limiting imports from Taiwan and South Korea.

Despite the OMA, in September 1977 Zenith said that it would shift much of its production of color TV receivers to Taiwan and Mexico. The other leading American producer, RCA, had shifted its production offshore several years earlier.[36] The movement offshore would have occurred eventually, even if the antidumping proceedings had been effective. The failure to stop dumping sooner spurred the movement.

During the 1970s Congress became impatient with the way in which the Antidumping Law was being administered, particularly in the TV case. Reflecting this impatience, the 1974 Trade Act required the Treasury to reach a final determination in antidumping cases within nine to twelve months. It also specified in detail the deductions and additions permitted in calculating the purchase price or exporter's sales price. In addition, if an exporter was found to sell at prices below average total costs over an extended period, then it would be found to be dumping.[37] The Trade Act of 1979 further shortened the time for the final determination of dumping. The new limit was 235 days. In addition, the act required annual reviews of the antidumping duties.

A more important change was shifting the administration of the law from the Treasury to the Commerce Department. The Treasury had been favorable to trade liberalization. Commerce, on the other hand, was more likely to sympathize with American manufacturers claiming to have been injured by unfair foreign trade practices.

The Trade and Tariff Act of 1984 permitted Commerce to use averages in calculating the export prices. The International Trade Administration (ITA)

34. David H. Staelin et al. "The Decline of U.S. Consumer Electronics Manufacturing: History, Hypotheses, and Remedies," Consumer Electronics Sector Working Group, MIT Commission on Industrial Productivity, December 1988, 27.

35. James E. Millstein, "Decline in an Expanding Industry: Japanese Competition in Color Television," in *American Industry in International Competition: Government Policies and Corporate Strategies,* ed. John Zysman and Laura Tyson (Ithaca, N.Y.: Cornell University Press, 1983), 135.

36. Millstein, "Decline in an Expanding Industry," 136.

37. This discussion relies heavily on Robert E. Baldwin and Michael O. Moore, "Political Aspects of the Trade Remedy Laws," in *Down in the Dumps; Administration of the Unfair Trade Laws,* ed. Richard Boltuck and Robert E. Litan (Washington, D.C.: Brookings Institution, 1991), 256–63.

now could compare the average export price with the average home market price to determine the dumping margin. In most dumping cases, however, the ITA continues to compare the average home market price with individual export transaction prices.[38]

The Omnibus Trade and Competitiveness Act of 1988 sought to close some loopholes that exporters were exploiting. Exporters began to assemble in the U.S. the parts of a final product subject to an antidumping order. Alternatively, they shipped the parts to a third country for assembly there and exported the assembled product from that country to the U.S. Another device for circumventing the restrictions was to make minor alterations in the product for sale in the home market or in the U.S. The act permitted an antidumping order to include imports of the parts of a product as well as the assembled product, parts assembled in third countries, and slightly altered products.

Since Commerce took over its administration, the Antidumping Act has become more effective. The proceedings have been speeded up, and where necessary estimates of fair value have been based on "best information available." As chapter 2 reports, the number of antidumping orders issued against Japanese products has grown, and the dumping margins in many cases have been found to be large. The stricter enforcement does not appear to have curtailed dumping by Japanese manufacturers. The number of antidumping cases and the large size of the dumping margins noted in chapter 2 indicate a continuing serious problem. Another problem may be that the exporters can circumvent the antidumping law by exporting products that are not identical to those sold in the home market. The 1988 act attempts to deal with this problem. It is difficult to know how successful it has been.

---

38. Baldwin and Moore, "Political Aspects of the Administration of the Trade Remedy Laws," 260.

CHAPTER 8

The Lower Courts

This chapter reviews the case in the district and appeals courts involving the 1916 Antidumping Act as well as that under the Sherman and Wilson Tariff acts. It will be recalled from Chapter 4 that a breach of the Wilson Tariff Act is also a breach of the Sherman Act.

The plaintiffs relied chiefly on their allegedly direct evidence of a conspiracy. They apparently hoped to avoid the difficult task of demonstrating motivation and of showing that the conspiracy theory was more plausible than alternative theories, which a circumstantial evidence case would have entailed. The plaintiffs apparently also planned to persuade the potential jurors with the story of numerous clandestine, conspiratorial meetings and the shady, secret rebates to U.S. customers, and so avoid confusing the jurors with a recondite economic analysis. Economic issues could not be avoided entirely, but the facts of the agreements were to be the main pillar.

Hindsight suggests, however, that the strategy erred. To get to a jury the plaintiffs first had to persuade the district and higher courts of a plausible motive and that the conspiracy had caused them injury, which was impossible without an economic analysis.

As chapter 9 reports, the Supreme Court could see no plausible motive other than to monopolize the U.S. market. To deliberately take losses the conspirators would have had to expect to recoup them later, which would have required monopoly profits. A plausible case demanded a plausible motive, which could be only the goal of monopoly. Thus, the Section 1 case became a Section 2 case. The Court demanded that the plaintiffs show an attempt to monopolize. Since, in its view, the plaintiffs failed to meet this requirement, the Court deemed the alternative explanation of the defendants' conduct— vigorous competition—to be more plausible. The Court reversed the appeals court and affirmed the district court.

The Plaintiffs' Case

The direct evidence of the cartel's operations in the domestic market referred to documents and records of discussions at the Market Stabilization Council and the Okura, Palace, Tenth-Day, TS, and MD groups and the testimony at

the FTCJ hearings of participants in these groups (fig. 8.1.)[1] The direct
evidence of the export agreements included the minimum-price agreements,
the Five-company Rule, the Antiraiding Rule, and the Application for the
Validation of Shipment.[2] Following *American Tobacco* (1946), the plaintiffs
argued that the Agreements and Rules showed "a unity of purpose or a
common design and understanding, or a meeting of minds in an unlawful
arrangement."[3] The agreements setting domestic prices and market shares
were part of the same conspiracy. The domestic monopoly profits enabled the
manufacturers to set low enough export prices to "reduce or eliminate U.S.
competition while maintaining an acceptable rate of return overall."[4] Pursuant
to *Poller,* this evidence, which showed a genuine issue, precluded summary
judgment.[5]

Although the direct evidence was their main support, the plaintiffs also
offered the economic argument that the defendants' monopoly profits were
protected by barriers to entry, providing a cushion for losses in the export
market. In addition, they produced the Brugliera study (see chap. 6), revealing
persistent domestic-export price differences. The study showed that Sony, as
well as the other defendants, had discriminated in price between the two
national markets.[6]

According to the plaintiffs, the predatory scheme made sense of the defendants' behavior. The goal being to eliminate U.S. competitors by depressing U.S. prices, the conspiracy produced excess profits in the home market,
the domestic prices exceeded the export prices, and the conspiracy restricted
competition in the export market. The defendants had acknowledged the goal
in the Rationale of the first set of Rules, setting out the aims of maintaining
export order and expanding exports.[7] Chapter 6 quotes the Rationale.

The plaintiffs stressed the secret rebates to importers. The actual
prices—the check prices minus the rebates—which were below the dumping
level, had to be hidden. The importers paid the false prices entered on the
invoices and the customs entry documents, and the manufacturers made secret
money transfers.[8]

The injury argument invoked studies by the U.S. Tariff Commission,

---

1. Brief of Appellants, Zenith Radio Corp. and National Union Electric Corp., U.S. Court
of Appeals 3d Cir., Japanese Electronic Products Antitrust Litigation, Nos. 81-2331, 81-2332,
81-2333, D.C. Civil No. 189 M.D.L., 36–38 (hereafter referred to as Brief of Appellants).
2. Brief of Appellants, 15–17.
3. Brief of Appellants, 63–64.
4. Brief of Appellants, 95.
5. Brief of Appellants, 53.
6. Brief of Appellants, 38–40.
7. Brief of Appellants, 19–20.
8. Brief of Appellants, 21.

Charges:
1. The Japanese TV manufacturers conspired to expand their U.S. market share by depressing prices and driving U.S. manufacturers out of business.
2. The Japanese TV manufacturers conspired and attempted to monopolize the U.S. market.

A. *Arguments Relying on Direct Evidence and Supporting Arguments*
   1. Basic Argument: Competition among Japanese manufacturers was restricted by Agreements and Rules and by activities of groups controlling the domestic market. This evidence presented genuine issue of conspiracy meriting trial under *Poller*.
   2. Supporting Arguments
      a. Economic Arguments
         i. Monopoly of domestic market assured by closed entry. Excess profits funded predatory attack on U.S. market.
         ii. Conspiracy's effectiveness in maintaining high domestic prices and low export prices shown by Brugliera study.
         iii. Conspiracy concentrated the force of Japanese manufacturers' efforts against U.S. competitors.
         iv. Japanese share of U.S. market grew rapidly.
      b. Statement in Rules expressed aim of maintaining export order and expanding exports.
      c. Japanese manufacturers concealed their rebates to U.S. importers from customs service.
B. *Argument Relying on Circumstantial Evidence*
   1. Interdependence of defendants
      a. Shown by nonenforcement of check prices.
      b. Shown by concerted efforts to conceal prices from U.S. customs.
   2. Supporting arguments: same as under A.
   3. Conspiracy motivated by the cartel's power to depress U.S. prices.
C. *Injury Argument*
   1. Conspiracy depressed prices in United States, as shown by Brugliera study.
   2. Conspiracy deprived plaintiffs of sales. Data on Japanese share of U.S. market.

Fig. 8.1. The plaintiffs' Sherman Act case

which showed a decline in prices, the loss of sales by the U.S. TV industry to imports from Japan, and low profits earned by U.S. manufacturers. The Brugliera study also supported the claim that the Japanese exports had injured the plaintiffs by reducing U.S. prices.

The circumstantial case highlighted the evidence of collusion. Independently competing firms would have reported their competitors' rebates to importers to the Television Export Council and the U.S. Customs Service, but, acting in concert, the defendants had concealed this behavior. Moreover, that there was an issue did not depend only on the Agreements and Rules.

Although these expired in 1973, the defendants continued reporting higher prices on Customs Service documents.[9]

Attending to the issue of motivation, the plaintiffs pointed to the good economic sense of the conspiracy in light of the greater strength of the combination than of any one company. A single firm could not achieve sufficient sales volume to reduce U.S. prices severely, but the combination could.[10]

Although the plaintiffs did file the Section 2 charge of a conspiracy and an attempt to monopolize the U.S. market, they made little effort to support it.

The plaintiffs neglected four issues raised by the defendants. First, there was the question whether unbridled competition would have produced lower export prices. The reply would have required an economic analysis, such as the one in chapter 3, to show that the conspiracy lowered export prices more than unrestrained competition would have done. Second, the plaintiffs did not contest the argument that international price discrimination did not imply collusion. The argument in chapter 3 was needed to show that independent competitors would not persistently have sold at substantially different prices in the two markets. Third, were the secret rebates relevant to the antitrust charges? The defendants correctly contended that they were not. The rebates supported the charges under the 1916 Antidumping Act but not those under the Sherman Act. Fourth, the plaintiffs ignored the defendants' argument that they were unlikely to have conspired to monopolize the U.S. market.

Moreover, relying on the facts relating to the agreements, the plaintiffs did not emphasize the evidence of below-cost pricing in the DePodwin Report. Judge Becker ruled this evidence inadmissible, but a careful argument defending the estimates would have strengthened the case.

The Defendants' Case

To avoid the consequences of a ruling that the Agreements and the Rules were direct evidence the defendants placed a great deal of emphasis on their claim to immunity under the doctrine of sovereign compulsion (fig. 8.2). They said that MITI had ordered restrictions on competition for "hundreds of products such as bicycles, binoculars, glassware, batteries, ceramic wall tile and cameras, as well as radios and television receivers."[11] Accordingly, between 1963 and 1973 MITI imposed the check prices and, beginning in 1967, the Five-

---

9. Brief of Appellants, 66.

10. Brief of Appellants, 67–70.

11. Brief of Appellees, U.S. Court of Appeals, 3d. Cir., *in re* Japanese Electronic Products Antitrust Litigation Nos. 81-2331, 81-2332, 81-2333, D.C. Civil No. 189 M.D.L., 10 (hereafter referred to as Brief of Appellees).

1. Defendants immune from prosecution for conspiracy in export market, because MITI directed them to adopt Agreements and Rules.
2. Discussions at Television Export Council and Television Export Examination Committee meetings implemented MITI export controls. They were not part of a conspiracy.
3. Conspiracy relating to domestic market out of bounds for U.S. courts.
4. Evidence relating to domestic collusion inadmissible.
5. Economic Arguments
   A. Rebates revealed competition.
   B. Proof of interdependence required showing that defendants' acts were contrary to their own interest and that they had motivation. Plaintiffs did not provide such proof.
   C. Independently defendants decided to sell at lower prices in the United States than in Japan.
   D. If Agreements and Rules had any effect, it was to raise prices.
6. Summary judgment warranted under *Cities Service*. Record lacked specific facts to support a prima facie case for plaintiffs.

Fig. 8.2. The defendants' case

company Rule, as a letter from the Japanese embassy attested. Further, since some exporters granted rebates to U.S. purchasers, the agreements were ineffective.[12]

Not only were the agreements ineffective, but, as subservient minions, the defendants had not conspired: they were not independent agents. The Television Export Council and the Television Export Examination Committee meetings, to which MITI sent representatives, merely implemented the ministry's controls.

Moreover, the home market was not subject to U.S. laws, and no evidence showed a unified, single conspiracy embracing both the home and export markets. The FTCJ testimony revealed no discussions of exports at the Tenth-Day and other home market groups, and the documents relating to the home market did not refer to exports. Moreover, the FTCJ Market Stabilization Case of 1957 came well before the export of TV receivers to the U.S.[13] Also, because the plaintiffs had refused to conform to the usual practice of taking depositions to establish the authenticity of the diaries, memoranda, and other documentary evidence, the documents relating to the home market were inadmissible.[14] Further, the Market Stabilization Council had not set monopoly prices but, rather, had only tried to curtail intense retail price-cutting. Similarly, the record of the Six-Company Case showed only that in a period of

---

12. Brief of Appellees, 10–11.
13. Brief of Appellees, 68–71.
14. Brief of Appellees, 91–92.

severe price-cutting the manufacturers discussed lowering their prices to increase sales.[15]

A major economic argument concerned interdependence. *Cities Service* had ruled that a conspiracy theory, which is confronted by an alternative, equally attractive inference, is unreasonable.[16] The manufacturers' different rebates signified independent decisions.[17] Given that competitive conditions differed in the two markets, independently, the defendants asked lower prices in the United States than in the home market.[18]

Concerning injury, an effective conspiracy would have raised prices, so it could not have injured the plaintiffs.[19]

I comment on the sovereign-compulsion defense. According to the plaintiffs' expert on Japanese law, John O. Haley, MITI could legally make only nonbinding recommendations, so it could not compel the defendants to enter the agreements. Moreover, the defendants were subject to the Sherman Act if they did not act under compulsion, and the permissive language of the Manufacturers' Agreements allowed the defendants to withdraw from them upon notice to the Television Export Council. MITI's role was informally to encourage and approve of activities initiated by the defendants.[20]

The sovereign-compulsion defense was inconsistent with the argument that the defendants did not abide by the agreements. If they were not conspirators because they were following MITI's orders, then they would not have broken the agreements. The evidence indicated that the defendants sold at prices below the agreed check prices. Thus, they broke the agreements and were not simply MITI's agents. They did not break the market-sharing rules, but the defendants could not both claim to be MITI's agents with respect to the rules and disclaim this role with respect to the price agreements.

The District Court

According to Judge Becker, the chief issue was the existence of a conspiracy to take over the U.S. markets for consumer electronic products, including the market for TV receivers. Following the organization of the opinion, I discuss his views on the export and home markets separately (fig. 8.3).

Much of the evidence was ruled inadmissible. Judge Becker decided that much of the DePodwin Report and other plaintiffs' experts' reports was not helpful to the fact finder. According to the judge, an economist, who was not

---

15. Brief of Appellees, 68–71.
16. Brief of Appellees, 29.
17. Brief of Appellees, 22–23.
18. Brief of Appellees, 44–62.
19. Brief of Appellees, 63–66.
20. 513 F. Supp. 1100 (1981), at 1194–95.

Motion for summary judgment against plaintiffs granted.
1. Evidentiary Rulings
   A. Large parts of experts' reports excluded, including evidence of domestic-export price differences and of cost-export price differences.
   B. Evidence of domestic-export price differences from U.S. Tariff Commission excluded.
   C. Testimony before FTCJ excluded.
2. The Export Market
   A. Evidence of domestic-export price differences and of cost-export price differences excluded.
   B. Defendants independently set lower export than home market prices.
   C. Defendants did not observe market-sharing rules.
   D. Minimum-price agreements and market-sharing rules, which raised prices, did not harm plaintiffs.
   E. Since the prospect of a U.S. monopoly was poor, defendants did not conspire to gain monopoly.
3. The Home Market
   A. Home market relevant to case only as source of monopoly profits to pay for predatory losses.
   B. There was no monopoly, since prices fell, not rose.
   C. Profits in home market low.
   D. Agreements did not set actual prices but only list prices. Rebates to retailers expressed competitive efforts.
   E. Since the defendants did not exchange information on latest plans, profit margins, and costs, they did not conspire.

Fig. 8.3. The district court opinion

a "conspiracyologist," should not assume the jury's task of evaluating what went on at the meetings of the various groups.[21] The court also found that the plaintiffs had not properly authenticated the FTCJ and the Tariff Commission documents.

The Export Market

The Court's Analysis
Categorizing the evidence as circumstantial, Judge Becker appraised the inferences of home market monopoly power and of a conspiracy affecting the U.S. market. He adopted the defendants' arguments that they had set low export prices independently, that they had not observed the Five-company and Antiraiding Rules, and that observance of the rules, which tended to raise prices, would not have harmed plaintiffs.

Despite his ruling that the evidence of domestic-export price differences was inadmissible, Judge Becker considered whether such differences implied

---

21. 505 F. Supp. 1313 (1980), at 1342.

collusion. He decided that they did not, because, since the competitive conditions differed, independent competitors would have discriminated in price. He said: "Price differences between two markets where competitive conditions, income and spending patterns, and products differ are to be expected and therefore do not support an inference that the lower price is the result of an agreement."[22]

Having excluded the evidence of below-cost pricing, Judge Becker did not appraise its significance. As chapter 6 reports, he decided that the estimates erroneously assumed the equality of the operating costs of the home market and of the corresponding export models. Judge Becker accepted the defendants' contention that the TV manufacturers' selling costs in the home market were higher than in the export market.

Moreover, because the Manufacturers' Agreements set minimum export prices, they did not harm the plaintiffs.[23] Nor did the Five-company Rule cause them harm. First, it did not restrict competition. Inasmuch as the U.S. sales subsidiaries resold to other customers, the rule did not limit the number of each manufacturer's U.S. customers. Second, some defendants sold to more than five direct customers at a time.[24] Third, and more important, even if it was observed, the Rule would not have harmed the plaintiffs and may have benefited them, for it raised prices.

The judge also decided that, with so poor a prospect of a monopoly, there was no motivation to conspire, so the defendants had not conspired. Together, Zenith and RCA's market share was 50 percent, and there were a large number of manufacturers. As Judge Becker said:

> To put it charitably, the analytical possibilities of a nexus between plaintiffs' evidence and the concerted predatory pricing conspiracy theorized by plaintiffs range from nonexistent to gossamer, especially given the onus of a rule of reason test.[25]

As chapter 9 shows, this analysis was critical for the Supreme Court's decision.

Further, Judge Becker said that, if the defendants were predatory conspirators, then they would not have restricted their output. They would have

---

22. 513 F. Supp. 1100 (1981), at 1239. In n. 205 on the same page the Court noted that establishing a precedent of inferring a conspiracy from a domestic-export price difference would have serious international trade consequences as well as consequences for antitrust policy. Such an inference and the threat of treble damages might inhibit competition, a result contrary to the intention of the antitrust laws.

23. 513 F. Supp. 1100 (1981), at 1157–62.
24. 513 F. Supp. 1100 (1981), at 1189–90.
25. 513 F. Supp. 1100 (1981), at 1213.

done the opposite. To depress prices they would have flooded the market. Output-limiting agreements impede predatory pricing.[26]

Comments

A conclusion that the defendants had conspired based only on the fact that meetings took place would not have helped the hypothetical jury, and Judge Becker would be right. But the economist looks at the subjects discussed at the meetings to determine their significance, and he or she puts the evidence into a context. Thus, there was the evidence of substantial domestic-export price differences. This evidence did not prove the existence of a conspiracy, for a monopolist might ask similar prices in the two markets. The additional information that there were several manufacturers and that they met and discussed prices, outputs, and other subjects was necessary to show that there was a conspiracy. Concerning the effectiveness of the conspiracy, the details of the discussions concerning the allocations of outputs, the resale prices, the rebates, and the exchanges of information supported the conclusion based on the domestic-export price differences. An economist is likely to be more aware of the importance of these details than a judge or a juror.

Having discussed in chapter 6 the exclusion of the evidence on domestic-export price differences, I will deal with it only briefly here. Small errors in the estimates of home market prices due to rebates to retailers did not invalidate the conclusion that the domestic-export price differences were large, especially since the commodity tax method allowed for the rebates. The court weighed small errors too heavily.

The persistence of large domestic-export price differences testified to monopoly power in the home market, which Judge Becker implicitly recognized by attributing the price discrimination to differences between the two markets in competitive conditions. As he also said, however, the price differences alone did not imply collusion, which was what the charge alleged. But, since monopoly power required collusion, the price discrimination attested to a conspiracy in the home market as well as to monopoly power. Noncolluding oligopolists might have discriminated in price between Japan and the U.S., but it is highly unlikely that they would have maintained as large price differences as the defendants had. In any case, the discussions at the meetings of the Tenth-Day and other groups supported the inference of a conspiracy. While the plaintiffs contended that the conspiracy also embraced the export market, this did not follow from the analysis of the domestic-export price discrimination. That conclusion would have to rest on other grounds.

Judge Becker ruled that the Manufacturers' Agreements and the Five-company and Antiraiding Rules did not restrict competition and also that in

---

26. 513 F. Supp. 1100 (1981), at 1213.

any case they did not harm the plaintiffs. True, the defendants did not observe the prices specified in the Manufacturers' Agreements. But, as chapter 6 shows, the Rules were effective. Despite the use of sales subsidiaries, the Rules limited competition for sales to the mass distributors, preventing them from driving prices down to marginal costs.

By limiting competition, the restrictions reduced the costs of a predatory campaign. Indeed, the restrictions harmed the plaintiffs by reducing the costs to an acceptable level. Had the manufacturers anticipated unrestricted competition and the resulting large losses, they probably would not have invested as heavily as they did in capacity to supply the U.S. market. The Rule prohibiting customer raiding encouraged a manufacturer to make the price cuts necessary to win a customer, since that customer was permanently off-limits to the other Japanese manufacturers. Further, the combination improved the manufacturers' prospects of achieving a monopoly, which added to the inducement to accept losses. As we have seen, the manufacturers said that, acting as a group, they could expand their sales more rapidly.

According to Judge Becker, the plaintiffs' theory was inconsistent, because predators do not restrict output. If the statement is interpreted literally, any price above zero implies innocent intentions. Any price, predatory or not, entails some limit to output. Moreover, a price lower than necessary to eliminate competitors would have meant unnecessary costs. Finally, Judge Becker ignored the monopoly in the home market, which required reducing output to below the competitive level.

His assessment of the prospect of a Japanese monopoly in the U.S. persuaded the judge that the defendants had not preyed. But the Section 1 charge was only that the cartel had depressed prices to eliminate some U.S. competitors. The charge did not imply an attempt to monopolize.

Moreover, since the defendants need not have expected large predatory losses, it did not require unreasonable optimism for them to seek a monopoly. Zenith's and RCA's large market shares were not an effective shield against a tight group's predation. In addition, their large shares, which entailed large immediate losses, made them vulnerable to the defendants' predatory activities. Their immediate losses would be larger than those the defendants suffered. Further, as chapter 4 shows, a predator need not wait to raise its prices until all of the competitive capacity disappears. An overly sanguine view of the prospects was not essential for the cartel to risk a predatory campaign. Also, the defendants may have been willing to take losses, because their goal may have been a reasonable overall rate of return, which the domestic monopoly permitted. Although the discussion of motivation necessarily is speculative and thus less than overwhelming, the intent to gain monopoly power is not inconceivable.

In any case, clearly the Japanese manufacturers acted jointly to take a large share of the U.S. market. As the Ninth Circuit pointed out in *Inglis*, such action may establish the specific intent to monopolize.[27] In *Matsushita* there was enough evidence of conduct attesting to such an attempt to merit a trial. Not only did the manufacturers form a cartel, but also their export prices were below their costs. The absence of direct testimony by the defendants' officers that they sought a monopoly did not justify summary judgment.

Further, concerning the Section 2 charge, Judge Becker did not deny that the defendants lost money on their exports over a long period. Had he admitted the evidence, he might have allowed a trial even on this charge. The evidence of losses is persuasive, if not certain. Chapter 6 shows that allowing a difference in operating costs of producing TV receivers of as much as 20 percent between the home and the export markets would not alter the conclusion that costs exceeded export prices. Other problems might have awaited a review at trial. Because it was produced after discovery, the plaintiffs could not challenge the affidavit that the cost estimates were based on inappropriate production cost data or show that the appropriate data would not have affected the conclusions. The summary judgment precluded further investigation.

In any case, the alleged error did not warrant a summary judgment on the Section 1 charge, which rested on the evidence of the agreements, of the observance of the market-sharing agreements, of the domestic-export price differences, of the conspiracy in the home market, of the defendants' monopoly power in the home market, and of the construction of capacity to supply the export market as well as in the cost-export price comparisons.

The Home Market

The Court's Analysis
Although for the court the alleged home market monopoly mattered only as a possible source of funds for a predatory campaign,[28] much of the opinion was taken up with this issue. Granting that the Tenth-Day, Palace, Okura, and other groups were more than innocuous, the judge nevertheless decided that they did not wield monopoly power, set monopoly prices, or earn high profits.[29] The basis was the testimony at the FTCJ hearings and the public statements by K. Matsushita, the head of MEI.

According to Judge Becker, testimony in the Six-Company Case had shown that the industry's profits had been low and that the aim of the collaboration was to prevent large losses.[30] Further, the conclusion that the manu-

---

27. See chapter 2.
28. 513 F. Supp. 1100 (1981), at 1197.
29. 513 F. Supp. 1100 (1981), at 1202–3.
30. 513 F. Supp. 1100 (1981), at 1205.

facturers feared losses was supported by the fact that it was retailers' competition that had provoked the meetings. The previously innocent social groups became more serious near the end of 1964 or in early 1965, when market saturation caused "tremendous retail price-cutting competition."[31]

Further:

> The period from 1960 to 1965 had seen a steady decline in the price of monochrome TVs, so that there was already a relatively low price threshold, and the manufacturers were concerned about the possibility that the retail market might collapse. Accordingly, they entered into serious discussions at the Tenth Day Group about a variety of business matters. It is apparent that their primary concern was prediction of demand so as to avoid overproduction, saturation, and further price decline. However, there was also discussion at the Tenth Day Group meetings of so-called "bottom prices" and of wholesale, retail, and rebate margins.[32]

Profits could not have been high, because TV prices were falling. According to Judge Becker:

> It is plain that the thrust of whatever price discussions there were was not to keep prices high, but rather to keep them from going all the way down. Thus, the minimum price which was being set was not a high price, but was rather as low a price as the manufacturers could bear without letting their retail market collapse, i.e., a price consistent with protecting retail margins. As one witness stated, they were talking about targets for the maximum price *cut*.[33]

In support, Judge Becker cited Yajima's testimony that Toshiba's proposed bottom price of ￥175,000 for a table-top color model meant going into the "red." The manufacturers were trying only to maintain prices, and they failed.[34] Thus: "Indeed, according to the record, throughout the relevant period, bottom prices went down, not up!"[35] So ineffective was the Tenth-Day Group that the members did not agree on a bottom price. According to the judge:

> The evidence is strong that there was no agreement on bottom price and that ultimately everyone was free to proceed with whatever bottom price

31. 513 F. Supp. 1100 (1981), at 1202.
32. 513 F. Supp. 1100 (1981), at 1202–3.
33. 513 F. Supp. 1100 (1981), at 1204.
34. 513 F. Supp. 1100 (1981), at 1204.
35. 513 F. Supp. 1100 (1981), at 1204.

he wished; however, for purposes of the motion for summary judgment, we assumed that there was such an agreement.[36]

Thus, in Judge Becker's view there was no collusion and, hence, no monopoly power.

Matsushita had said that the meetings were intended to protect the companies against themselves by ensuring that competition did not become too intense.[37] He also had said that the general business recession and the manufacturers' stupid, fierce competition had reduced profits to half the former levels.

Indeed, by raising the retail margins to protect retailers and thus reducing their own profits, the companies acted contrary to their own interest. Thus:

> However, insofar as margins are concerned, the only evidence is that there was considerable pressure to *increase* the margins, and that the companies during the relevant period agreed to increase the margins, particularly the retail margins, so as to protect the retailers from collapse. This, of course, would have the effect of *decreasing* the manufacturer's profit, the opposite of what plaintiffs posit in support of their theory of high profit in Japan to war-chest a predatory export raid on the U.S. market.[38]

There was also Yajima's testimony that the Tenth-Day Group did not discuss their companies' latest plans, profit margins, cost of production, and product line details.[39]

In addition, the agreements set only "bottom" list prices, which, because the companies paid rebates to retailers, exceeded the actual selling prices. Yajima had identified a variety of rebates paid by Toshiba, so fixing only the bottom prices and the profit margin rates did not automatically determine the price of TV sets marketed.[40]

Comments

Judge Becker advanced the remarkable theory that collusion to prevent a fall in prices is not setting monopoly prices, implying that monopoly prices never fall. Obviously, however, monopolists are not immune from a decline in demand. No less than competitive firms, they prosper or decline with changes in demand. Moreover, even when demand drops their prices and profits will

---

36. 513 F. Supp. 1100 (1981), at 1203.
37. 513 F. Supp. 1100 (1981), at 1205.
38. 513 F. Supp. 1100 (1981), at 1204.
39. 513 F. Supp. 1100 (1981), at 1203.
40. 513 F. Supp. 1100 (1981), at 1203.

exceed those of competitive firms under similar conditions. Firms maximize profits, not prices, and they will adjust prices accordingly. They may even lose money, but their losses will be less than those a competitive firm would experience.

Judge Becker's ready acceptance of allegedly ruinous competition as an excuse for collusion broke with long-standing antitrust law. Since *Trans-Missouri Freight Association* (1897) the courts have rejected loss prevention as a defense, recognizing that Congress intended that competitive markets rule prices.

The judge erred even on what was for him the critical issue of whether the home market could support a predatory campaign. Carried away by the vision of the defendants teetering on the brink of losses, Becker confused total with home market profits. It was total profits that were low, not home market profits, and it was export losses that kept total profits low. The judge unintentionally stood the plaintiffs' argument on its head by implying that export losses forced defendants to maintain high home market profits.

The difficulties over retailers' rebates also impressed Judge Becker, for whom anything less than perfection apparently was failure. Initially, competition did focus on rebates, but, as chapter 5 reports, the manufacturers reached an agreement, which specified a maximum of 8 percent. Also, for Judge Becker the Market Stabilization Council's efforts were worthless, despite the fixing of service and installation fees and of coupon rates, the decisions about the disposition of obsolete models, the imposition of fines of ¥ 5,000 on retailers who violated the agreements, the cutting off of supplies to discounters, and the manufacturers' monitoring one another's production and shipments. In the judge's view all this added up to competition.

The judge misunderstood the significance of the manufacturers' agreement to raise retail margins. The increase did not imply that the companies did not conspire to maintain their own prices or that they lacked the power to do so. On the contrary, the evidence confirms that they had the power. Of course, given the retail price, a rise in the retail margin meant a decline in the manufacturer's price. But, being forced to concede higher retail margins did not exclude the possibility that the lower manufacturers' prices were at a monopoly level. Also, the manufacturers may have maintained or raised their own prices by raising retail prices. Neither the original retail prices nor the original retail margins may have been optimal from the manufacturers' standpoint. I do not know whether they raised their retail prices, but the possibility should not be excluded. In addition, a rise in the retail margins benefited the manufacturers by relieving the pressure by the retailers on individual manufacturers to reduce their own prices. Persistent clamoring for lower manufacturers' prices might have broken the discipline among the manufacturers to maintain their prices. They managed to agree on a limit to rebates, but the agreement might not have succeeded in maintaining discipline without a general rise in retail margins.

Pointing to Yajima's testimony that the companies did not exchange information on their latest plans suggested the novel requirement of a showing of complete disclosure for proof of a violation of Section 1. Moreover, according even to Yajima's testimony, as paraphrased by Judge Becker, the exchanges were sufficient for the conspiracy to be effective:

> Yajima testified before the FTCJ that he would report to his superior, Mr. Kamakura, the bottom price and demand forecast figures disclosed at the Tenth Day Group meeting. Having discussed these matters at the meeting, Yajima said that he could "more or less guess each company's moves."[41]

It is also clear that the court ignored evidence of the cartel's effectiveness. Contrary to Judge Becker, a manufacturer could not choose any bottom price. As chapter 5 shows, the Palace Group had to decide the price of the color table model. Also, surely the companies did not over a long period waste their representatives' time at numerous meetings that failed. It is even harder to believe that the conspiracy failed when the participants agreed on prices, on retail and wholesale margins, rebates, market shares, outputs, advertising, prices of obsolete equipment, and on machinery to enforce the agreements and exchanged information on outputs, shipments, and inventories. The great detail of the agreements, the frequency of the meetings, the effort to keep the prices up to date by renewing the agreements at six-month intervals, and the enforcement of retail margins strongly suggest that the enforcement was effective. Finally, the evidence of the large domestic-export price differences shows that the defendants exercised monopoly power in the home market and that they colluded to achieve this power. As chapter 3 shows, independently competing oligopolists were unlikely to have asked as low export prices in relation to their home market prices as the TV manufacturers did.

The Court of Appeals

The Court of Appeals for the Third Circuit reversed the district court's summary judgment with respect to the Japanese defendants, excluding Sony. The appeals court decided that the district court had broken with the traditional standard by substituting its own interpretation of the record for a reasonable jury's. According to the Third Circuit, it was not beyond reason that the

---

41. 513 F. Supp. 1100 (1981), at 1203.

Reversed the district court. Found that there was sufficient evidence to warrant trial.
1. Evidentiary Rulings
   A. Reversed district court's exclusion of large parts of the experts' reports, FTCJ documents, and findings of U.S. Tariff Commission.
2. Direct Evidence
   A. Direct evidence of conspiracy consisted of evidence of home market conspiracy, especially the evidence of exchanges of production and inventory data.
3. Circumstantial Evidence
   A. Export Market
      i. Motivation for conspiracy
         a. TV standards compatible in Japanese and U.S. markets.
         b. U.S. market large.
         c. Defendants had excess capacity.
         d. Home market conspiracy and Five-company Rule evidence of intent to price predatorily while eliminating competition among defendants. Neither resales by sales subsidiaries nor tendency of agreements to raise prices excluded possibility of intent to price predatorily.
      ii. Home market conspiracy and export conspiracy enabled defendants to price predatorily.
      iii. Export losses implied predatory pricing.
      iv. Combination of home market conspiracy and customer allocation in the United States would permit defendants to inflict losses on plaintiffs, which would permit plaintiffs to recover damages.
      v. Sovereign compulsion uncertain. Japanese government may not have ordered Five-company Rule or determined export prices.
   B. Home Market
      i. High market concentration and barriers to entry made home market conspiracy feasible.
      ii. Conspiracy shown by evidence of frequent meetings.
      iii. High home market prices enabled manufacturers to subsidize exports.

Fig. 8.4. The court of appeals opinion

Japanese manufacturers had conspired to destroy U.S. manufacturers. The appeals court affirmed with respect to the American defendants, Sears Roebuck and Motorola (fig. 8.4).

The court reversed the district court's evidentiary rulings, excluding large parts of the experts' reports, documents relating to the FTCJ cases, and the findings of the U.S. Tariff Commission.[42]

---

42. Japanese Electronic Products Antitrust Litigation, D.C. M.D.L. No. 189, U.S. Court of Appeals, 3d Cir., October 21–22, 1982, 723 F.2d 238 (1983), at 255–303 (hereafter referred to as 723 F.2d 238 [1983]).

The Direct Evidence

The court said that the circumstantial evidence, to be discussed shortly, was not by itself sufficient for a finding of conspiracy. It only suggested circumstances motivating a price conspiracy, the feasibility of a conspiracy, and export prices consistent with the existence of an agreement. Referring to the findings of the FTCJ, which it held admissible, the court said that these provided direct evidence of a conspiracy. Contrary to the district court, the appeals court described the plaintiffs' case as an accumulation of both direct and circumstantial evidence. In the Market Stabilization case the FTCJ found that the manufacturers agreed to set high prices and to enforce the agreement. In the 1967 case the FTCJ found that MEI enforced high resale prices by its wholesalers. In addition, there was evidence that the defendants reached price agreements at meetings and of the exchange of production and inventory statistics, which, the court said, would be necessary for the agreement to be implemented.[43] In response to Judge Becker's argument that the home market price-fixing would only increase the wholesalers' and retailers' margins, the Third Circuit said that the exchanges of production and inventory data suggested much more than that. Judge Becker had selected only one of several permissible inferences. A reasonable fact finder could conclude that no manufacturer would participate in such an agreement unless it also protected its own profits.[44]

The Circumstantial Evidence

The Export Market
The court decided that, after hearing testimony that the defendants had built more capacity than the home market needed, a reasonable juror might conclude that the defendants had an incentive to conspire to gain large sales in the U.S. Also, the evidence of a home market price conspiracy suggested a motive to cut prices to eliminate American firms.[45] In addition, the home market agreement combined with the Five-company Rule supported the allegation that the defendants intended to concentrate their competitive efforts against American companies. Concerning this effect of the Five-company Rule, the Third Circuit held that neither the resales by sales subsidiaries nor the tendency of the rule to raise prices was sufficient to exclude the possi-

---

43. 723 F.2d 238 (1983), at 308.
44. 723 F.2d 238 (1983), at 308.
45. 723 F.2d 238 (1983), at 310.

bility.[46] Therefore, the court reversed the dismissal of the evidence relating to the Five-company Rule.

Turning to the ability to sustain predatory losses, the court had no trouble with the inference that the manufacturers could price predatorily from the evidence of concerted action and of high home market prices.[47]

Emphasizing the evidence of below-cost pricing, the Third Circuit reversed the district court on its admissibility, because the combination of export losses and the Five-company Rule might have probative value. A reasonable juror might infer intentional predatory pricing from the evidence that over a long period export prices produced losses often as much as 25 percent of sales.[48]

Concerning injury, the court said that, although an agreement to allocate customers violates Section 1, ordinarily competitors, who remain free to compete for all customers, cannot expect to win standing to sue. But a home market conspiracy changed the effect of the agreement. Customer allocation combined with a home market monopoly would permit the Japanese manufacturers to prey on individual U.S. competitors. Insulated from Japanese competition at home and in the U.S., the manufacturers could place the full brunt of their competition on American TV manufacturers. Accordingly, a finding of a conspiracy in both markets would permit plaintiffs to recover damages.[49]

The court rejected the sovereign-compulsion defense. The district court did not reach this issue, because it granted summary judgment on other grounds. Citing *Alcoa,* the court said that U.S. laws reached conduct in foreign markets that had an impact on U.S. commerce.[50] While it assumed that the Sherman Act did not apply to a government-mandated export cartel arrangement, it held that, because the agreements were used as evidence of a low-price conspiracy, such an exemption did not warrant summary judgment. Moreover, it was not certain that the Japanese government determined the minimum prices. The defendants themselves may have fixed their export prices, and the government may merely have provided a basis for an exemption from Japanese antitrust laws. In any case, that the cartel arrangements were not mandated was evident from the fact that some defendants secretly broke the price agreements. In addition, no evidence showed that the government ordered the Five-company Rule. Finally, a conspiracy in the home market violated the laws of Japan.[51]

---

46. 723 F.2d 238 (1983), at 311.
47. 723 F.2d 238 (1983), at 310.
48. 723 F.2d 238 (1983), at 311.
49. 723 F.2d 238 (1983), at 306.
50. 723 F.2d 238 (1983), at 306.
51. 723 F.2d 238 (1983), at 315.

The Home Market

The appeals court held that barriers to entry and high market concentration may have made the home market conspiracy feasible. The record included evidence of government-imposed barriers to the entry of U.S. and other foreign firms, including high tariff rates, import deposits, limitations of foreign investment, and cumbersome inspection and testing procedures. The *keiretsu*, which controlled distribution channels, also may have created barriers.[52]

The evidence also suggested that the leading manufacturers' representatives met regularly to exchange information about capacity, inventories, and pricing. So there may have been opportunities for concerted action on home market prices, permitting exports at low enough prices to absorb excess capacity.[53]

Finally, there was the evidence that the home market prices exceeded the export prices. This evidence might persuade a fact finder that each manufacturer was confident that it could subsidize export sales out of high-price home sales.[54]

The court affirmed the summary judgment pertaining to Sony, Sears, and Motorola. According to the court, the record contained no direct evidence that these defendants had acted with the intent to injure or destroy a U.S. industry. In addition, the circumstantial evidence against these companies was weak. It showed only that they sold TV receivers at substantially lower prices in the U.S. than in Japan, that they knew that the other defendants were engaged in similar activities, and that they knew that concerted dumping could injure or destroy the U.S. industry. The evidence supported a finding of general intent, but it was not sufficient to create a genuine issue of fact.

Comments

I comment on the court's affirmation of the summary judgment with respect to Sony. Since the company participated in the meetings of the TS Group, it was a member of the cartel, and it discriminated in price between the Japanese and U.S. markets. On the other hand, the cartel agreements were less important for Sony than for the other participants. As chapter 5 reports, its share of the Japanese market grew rapidly in the 1960s and early 1970s. In addition, unlike the other defendants, it did not sell directly to U.S. mass merchandisers. Its only direct customers were its own sales company and General Distributors Company.[55] These companies resold the TV receivers to the mass merchandisers and other retailers.

---

52. 723 F.2d 238 (1983), at 307.
53. 723 F.2d 238 (1983), at 307–8.
54. 723 F.2d 238 (1983), at 308.
55. DePodwin Report, vol. 1: V-52.

The available evidence on the differences between Sony's home market and export prices for color sets is limited to those for twelve-inch receivers in 1970, when the average difference was 11.1 percent. More information is available for monochrome sets. In 1968 the average price differences by screen size groups varied from 3.9 percent of the export price for the seven-inch group to 14.3 percent for the twelve-inch group.[56] In evaluating these differences, we should note that Sony claimed that its Trinitron product was superior to its competitors', and its promotional efforts were greater than those of its competitors. It did not sell directly to mass distributors for resale under their brand names, as the other TV manufacturers did. Chapter 3 suggests that a strong brand may enable a manufacturer to discriminate in price between the home market and the export market. Moreover, Sony's domestic-export price differences were smaller than the average price differences for MEI, Sanyo, and Toshiba (reported in table 6.2).

Thus, the evidence that Sony participated in a conspiracy to eliminate some U.S. manufacturers to capture a large share of the U.S. market was not as strong as it was for the other defendants.

Claims under the 1916 Antidumping Act

The Antidumping Act of 1916 declares that it is unlawful commonly and systematically to import, sell, or cause to be imported or sold goods at a "price substantially less than the actual market value or wholesale price of such articles" in the home market "with the intent of destroying or injuring an industry in the United States." Injured parties may recover treble damages.[57]

Despite its age, there had been no extensive judicial discussion of the 1916 act prior to Judge Becker's opinion. The court had to decide the appropriate standards for the comparability of the imported and home market products for the imported products to come under the act. Judge Becker's reading of the act's legislative history led him to regard it as an antitrust law, not as a protectionist measure. Congress's intention was to place exporters under the same restrictions with respect to price discrimination as the Clayton Act (1914), amended by the Robinson-Patman Act (1936), placed domestic firms.[58] It should be noted that the court asserted this about the 1916 Antidumping Act, despite the Robinson-Patman Act's much later date.

According to the plaintiffs' expert's reports on the technical comparability of the imported and home market TV receivers, the differences were of two kinds. In Japan VHF broadcasts were on frequencies ranging from 90 to 108 MHz and from 170 to 222 MHz. In the U.S. the frequency ranges were

---

56. DePodwin Report, vol. 1: VI-11–13.

57. 15 U.S.C. §72. Quoted in Zenith Radio Corp. v. Matsushita Electric Industrial Co., et al., 494 F. Supp. 1190 (1980), at 1194–95, n. 4.

58. 494 F. Supp. 1190 (1980), at 1197.

54 to 88 MHz and 174 to 216 MHz. In addition, the particular TV channels had different specific frequencies. Thus, channel 2 in the U.S. was assigned a frequency of 55.25 MHz for the picture and 59.75 for the sound, while in Japan the same channel was assigned frequencies of 97.25 and 101.75 MHz. Consequently, TV receivers exported to the U.S. could not receive most broadcasts in Japan, and the home market receivers were useless in the U.S. Also, in Japan power was supplied at 100 volts, while in the U.S. the voltage was 120. The difference would prevent imported and home market receivers from being operated interchangeably. According to Zenith's expert, Brugliera, these differences were not technologically significant and did not result in a significant cost difference.[59]

Relying on interpretations of the word *such* in similar contexts in cases in the customs courts, the defendants contended that the act required the comparison of the prices of identical products.[60] The plaintiffs replied that Congress had proscribed unfair competition and, therefore, that the act required the comparison of products in broad categories.[61] The defendants also argued that the act called for plaintiffs to show predatory intent, which, following Areeda and Turner, required the plaintiffs to show "that each defendant sold its products below its marginal cost, . . . or that the defendant had a sizable share of the market."[62]

Granting the motion for summary judgment on the dumping claims, the court said that the home market products were not of "like grade and quality" as the imported products, since the physical differences affected "consumer use and preferences or marketability."[63] The 1916 act imposed the same standards of comparability as the Robinson-Patman Act, which applied to price discrimination within the U.S. Moreover, the home market value of the imported merchandise referred to merchandise that had to be "commercially interchangeable" with the imported articles. By using the phrase "actual market value or wholesale prices," Congress adopted the valuation provision of the Tariff Act of 1913, which required commercial interchangeability. Since a product sold in Japan was of no practical use to a consumer in the U.S., the products sold in one country were not marketable in the other.[64] Judge Becker ruled that the product differences were legally significant.

The appeals court reversed the district court's summary judgment, because the technical differences between the TV receivers sold in Japan and those exported could not explain the price differential.[65]

---

59. 494 F. Supp. 1190 (1980), at 1204–9.
60. 494 F. Supp. 1190 (1980), at 1200.
61. 494 F. Supp. 1190 (1980), at 1201.
62. 494 F. Supp. 1190 (1980), at 1200.
63. 494 F. Supp. 1190 (1980), at 1197.
64. 494 F. Supp. 1190 (1980), at 1197.
65. 723 F.2d 319 (1983), at 326.

Concerning the issue of specific intent, the court said that the plaintiffs had to show that the defendants set export prices with the intent of destroying or injuring an industry. It decided that whether the defendants had acted with this intent was a genuine issue of fact.[66]

The Third Circuit decided that the plaintiffs' case was too strong to warrant summary judgment. On virtually all of the major issues of the case the appeals court agreed that the plaintiffs' case was at least arguable.

Conclusion

Judge Becker's economics led him into a complex, twisted rationale for the Japanese manufacturers' conduct. The observation that the main purpose of the home market collusion was to prevent prices from falling does not deny that the prices were set at monopoly levels. Hence, it does not challenge the further inference that these efforts enabled the defendants to bankroll their predatory activity in the U.S. Moreover, as chapter 3 shows, were the Japanese TV manufacturers independent competitors, the differences between the home market and export prices would not have been as large as those observed.

Judge Becker's argument that the export conspiracy benefited the plaintiffs by raising prices also is invalid. The market-sharing agreements enabled the defendants to limit the price reductions necessary to increase their share of the market. They did not have to suffer price reductions resulting from competition among themselves. This restriction on competition injured the plaintiffs by increasing the incentive of the Japanese manufacturers to undertake predatory pricing.

Because Judge Becker regarded his theory that the defendants were competing energetically as more plausible than the predation theory, he granted a summary judgment. It is difficult to see how competition is consistent with the pattern of behavior of market allocation, higher home market than export prices, below-cost pricing, and capacity expansion. Collusion to expand the Japanese manufacturers' joint share of the U.S. market appears to be a more plausible explanation of the behavior. In any case, the evidence should have been sufficient to allow a trial. Even those who find Judge Becker's theory persuasive may have difficulty defending the summary judgment.

---

66. 723 F.2d 319 (1983), at 329.

CHAPTER 9

The Supreme Court

The Petition for a Writ of Certiorari

The defendants' petition to the Supreme Court posed three issues: (1) whether their conduct was more consistent with their independent self-interest than with conspiracy, (2) their immunity under the doctrine of sovereign compulsion, (3) the admissibility of expert testimony that the district court found to be based on false and unsupported assumptions (fig. 9.1).[1] The Court granted certiorari on the first two questions, and, having reversed the Third Circuit on the first question, it did not reach the second.

Since the Third Circuit had said that the direct evidence presented a genuine issue of the existence of a conspiracy, the defendants emphasized the immunity argument. The issue of whether the defendants' conduct was consistent with their independent self-interest was raised only by the circumstantial evidence. The defendants sought to avoid having to confront the direct evidence and the possibility of a trial and a jury's huge award of damages by claiming immunity from the U.S. antitrust laws. Offering the Japanese government's letter, saying that they had acted under MITI's directions, the defendants tried to circumvent the Sherman Act.

MITI's role was also a defense against the conspiracy charge. Only free actors could conspire, and the defendants were merely MITI's agents. The other direct evidence pertained to the alleged home market conspiracy, and the home market was outside the purview of the U.S. courts.[2]

The main question raised by the circumstantial evidence was whether the conspiracy theory was plausible. The defendants maintained that the alternative hypothesis that they had acted independently was more plausible. *Cities Service* required the plaintiffs to show conduct contrary to the defendants' self-interest, which they had failed to do. Nor had they met the *Monsanto* test that the evidence had to exclude the possibility of independent action.[3] In

---

1. Petition for a Writ of Certiorari to the U.S. Court of Appeals, 3d Cir., Matsushita Electric Industrial Co. et al., v. Zenith Radio Corp. and National Union Electric Corp., in the Supreme Court, June 7, 1984, 11 (hereafter referred to as Petition).

2. Petition, 12–13.

3. Petition, 11, n. 9.

Questions Presented:
1. Appropriateness of summary judgment when the evidence is more consistent with defendants' economic self-interest than with inference of conspiracy.
2. Defendants' immunity to prosecution under sovereign-compulsion doctrine.
3. Appropriateness of exclusion of expert testimony that district court found to be based on false or unsupported assumptions.

A. The Direct Evidence Case
   i. Direct evidence referred to home market and not to alleged conspiracy to destroy U.S. competitors.
   ii. Minimum-price arrangements and Five-company Rule, which were mandated by MITI, were not direct evidence of conspiracy.
B. The Circumstantial Evidence Case
   i. Plaintiffs must show that the conduct was contrary to defendants' independent self-interest and therefore was more consistent with inference of conspiracy than with inference of independent behavior.
   ii. A firm will not deliberately accept predatory losses in a market because it earns profits in another market.
   iii. Domestic-export price difference consistent with defendants' independent self-interest.
   iv. Defendants could not rationally hope to recoup predatory losses. In general, predatory behavior is unlikely.
   v. There was no "low-price" agreement. Export controls set minimum prices and allocated customers. These controls raised prices in U.S. market.
   vi. Affirmation of appeals court decision would result in suppressing competition.
C. On Sovereign Compulsion
   i. Japanese government mandated minimum-price agreements and Five-company Rule.
D. On the Expert Testimony
   i. District court found that critical portions of plaintiffs' expert testimony were based on false or unsupported testimony.

Fig. 9.1. The defendants' petition to the Supreme Court

particular, the plaintiffs had not shown a motive to conspire. They had pointed to the home market profits, but these were not an incentive to lose money in another market.[4]

Further, the domestic-export price differences did not imply a conspiracy, for, as the district court said, in a new market a firm would ask a lower price than in one in which it was already well established.

Citing Bork, Areeda and Turner, McGee, and Easterbrook, who said that

---

4. Petition, 13–14.

predatory pricing is unlikely, the defendants contended that it would have been irrational for them to conspire to attain a monopoly by predatory pricing. A scheme to raise prices makes sense—but not one to engage in a costly predatory campaign.[5] Moreover, in view of RCA's and Zenith's dominant market position, which made it difficult for the defendants to gain a monopoly, the defendants could not have expected to recoup their losses. Also, it was unreasonable for the defendants to expect a monopoly where import barriers easily could be set up. And, if they did gain a monopoly, high prices would have allowed other companies to increase their sales.[6] Thus, the appeals court broke with *Cities Service* by allowing a fact finder to speculate that the Japanese manufacturers had conspired.[7]

The petition also warned the Court that affirming the Third Circuit would invite antitrust suits against foreign companies based on claims that the export prices were less than the home market prices.[8]

Concerning the expert testimony, the district court had excluded the parts based on false or unsupported factual assumptions. The Third Circuit had held that, if an expert claimed to have used data of a type other experts relied on without being challenged by another expert, then the district court could not exclude the testimony.[9] However, after the district court had found that the defendants' conduct was more consistent with competition than with conspiracy, expert testimony based on false and unsupported factual assumptions should not have defeated a summary judgment.[10]

The Plaintiffs' Reply

The plaintiffs emphasized the direct evidence (fig. 9.2), which enabled the appeals court to avoid questionable inferences from circumstantial evidence. Denying the relevance of *Cities Service,* the plaintiffs said that the only direct evidence in that case, the defendants' failure to deal with the plaintiff, did not prove a conspiracy. Also, the Third Circuit's decision did not contravene *Monsanto,* in which the Supreme Court agreed that the direct evidence supported the finding of conspiracy.[11] In addition, in the present case an abundance of circumstantial evidence showed a common scheme to conceal dumping prices and to eliminate U.S. competitors. Moreover, concealing the prices and attempting to eliminate U.S. competitors was inconsistent with the defen-

---

5. Petition, 16.
6. Petition, 16.
7. Petition, 15.
8. Petition, 16.
9. Petition, 25.
10. Petition, 28.
11. Respondents' Brief, 12–13, 17.

1. The Argument Concerning the Conspiracy
   A. Record contains direct evidence of price-fixing agreements.
   B. Common scheme to conceal actual dumping prices from Japanese government and from U.S. Customs Service and common scheme to eliminate U.S. competition contradicted defendants' independent self-interest.
2. On Sovereign Compulsion
   A. Defendants did not present a statement by a Japanese legal officer about the legal effect of MITI's "direction."
   B. Defendants presented no record evidence that the Japanese government determined export prices or ordered the Five-company Rule. Defendants departed from the price agreement.
3. On Expert Opinion
   A. Defendants presented no evidence that the factual data on which plaintiffs' experts relied was not of the type customarily relied upon by experts in the field or that it lacked a foundation for admissibility.

Fig. 9.2. The plaintiffs' reply

dants' independent self-interest. Further, by raising home market prices, the conspirators could maintain an acceptable overall rate of return while cutting their export prices sharply.[12]

The reply to the sovereign-compulsion defense was that the defendants would not have suffered penalties by not conforming to MITI's direction. This was shown by a provision in the Manufacturers' Agreements allowing a participant to withdraw after giving thirty days notice. Also, since the defendants conducted business in the U.S., they were subject to its laws. In addition, MITI did not direct the defendants to fix prices in Japan, to dump, or to conceal their prices from MITI and the U.S. Customs Service.[13]

Turning to the experts' reports, the plaintiffs said that the defendants did not deny that the data in the reports were consistent with accepted standards. Moreover, the experts determined that collusion was the best economic explanation of defendants' conduct, as revealed by data from the defendants' own discovery responses.[14]

I will not repeat the criticisms in chapter 8, but some discussion is in order. The plaintiffs continued to neglect the theory of the case, despite the district court's plaudits for the defendants' conduct and the Supreme Court's demand for a strong motivational argument in previous conspiracy cases. *Cities Service* and *Monsanto* demanded a stronger refutation of the alternative interpretation. The plaintiffs should not have ignored the cost-price compari-

---

12. Respondents' Brief, 19–20.
13. Respondents' Brief, 24–25.
14. Respondents' Brief, 28–29.

sons, which, as we shall see, the Court said, might have changed its mind. The brief also ignored the evidence of capacity expansion, which dramatically indicated how far the companies were prepared to go to take a large share of the U.S. market. In addition, the plaintiffs could not show that the market-sharing agreements cut the costs of predation without an extended economic analysis. Moreover, a complete economic analysis might have persuaded the Court that the package of the agreements, below-cost pricing, and capacity expansion was incompatible with the competition theory. Only the conspiracy theory offered a complete explanation. An analysis would also have shown the illogic of the Japanese manufacturers' defense by establishing that independent competition was inconsistent with the low export prices. An economic analysis also was necessary to show that the agreements injured the plaintiffs by lowering the costs of predation, thus enabling the defendants to take a large share of the market.

The Department of Justice Brief

Before discussing the brief by the Department of Justice, I will review some of the department's earlier statements on foreign-based predation. In 1977 Donald I. Baker, the Assistant Attorney General in Charge of the Antitrust Division, said that the department had avoided suing members of a foreign export association for conduct permitted by the Webb-Pomerene Act.[15] The act allows registered export associations to fix prices, allocate quotas, and allocate customers. The Antitrust Division investigated whether U.S. exporters would have violated the Webb-Pomerene Act by engaging in practices similar to those of the foreign exporters. It also investigated what other governments authorized their exporters to do. The division believed that it was helpless when a foreign government controlled exports. Baker said:

> It has seemed likely to us that if a foreign government is committed to the idea of controlled exports, it could probably achieve such control through direct state involvement, a liberal merger or joint venture policy, or some form of mandatory system. In light of this, it seems quite probable that if we were to sue a foreign export association, arguing that governmental authorization was an insufficient defense, the ultimate result of such a suit might well be continuation of the same conduct in even a more rigid form, as well as foreign policy controversy.[16]

---

15. Letter from Donald I. Baker, assistant attorney general, Antitrust Division, Department of Justice, to Senator Edward M. Kennedy, February 16, 1977.

16. Letter, Baker to Kennedy.

Baker's successor, John H. Shenefield, said:

> While our Webb-Pomerene Act exemption from antitrust laws is occasionally embarrassing to us when we talk tough about foreign cartels, we will not tolerate or ignore evidence of anticompetitive activities by foreign export cartels in United States markets. Where we find such a cartel, even if organized and supervised with the approval of a foreign government, imposing anticompetitive restraints in United States markets, we will investigate and, if warranted, prosecute. [17]

Evidently, the department did not want to disturb relations with Japan, and it had no ready way of reconciling the Webb-Pomerene Act with a strong defense against foreign cartels.

In 1977 the division decided that the *Matsushita* case was not good enough for its own full-scale investigation. In April 1978 Shenefield said that the division "found no evidence of on-going concerted activity by Japanese enterprises aimed at the U.S. market." [18] In his view there was neither evidence of the check price agreements continuing beyond 1973, nor of any concerted predatory activity even prior to 1973. In any case, the Orderly Marketing Agreement (OMA) would reduce Japanese color TV sales in 1978 to approximately 16 percent of the U.S. market.

The Department of Justice's brief (fig. 9.3) emphasized policy rather than legal arguments. The threat of treble damage liabilities would inhibit foreign-based competition, and district courts would be reluctant to resolve antitrust cases on motions for summary judgment. Foreign relations also were a concern. Rejecting the sovereign-compulsion defense would offend the governments of other countries as well as that of Japan. Most disturbing was the possibility that the Court would deprive the administration of the tool of voluntary restraint agreements for resolving trade disputes, for the agreements require the exporting country's government to limit exports by assigning quotas to individual companies. The agreements might expose the exporters to treble damages liability.

On the direct evidence the legal arguments were close to those of the defendants, but not identical. The brief avoided arguing that MITI's direction implied that there was no conspiracy. Instead, it dismissed the home market evidence as irrelevant, and it argued that the export agreements did not prove a conspiracy to set predatory prices.

On the circumstantial evidence the department said that one could as

---

17. Letter, Baker to Kennedy.
18. Statement by John H. Shenefield, assistant attorney general, Antitrust Division, before the U.S. Senate Committee on the Judiciary, April 12, 1978.

1. Policy Considerations
   A. Prospect of incurring treble damages liability will discourage vigorous competition by foreign companies.
   B. Affirmation will discourage district courts from resolving antitrust cases on motions for summary judgment.
   C. Third Circuit's rejection of sovereign-compulsion defense threatens adversely to affect U.S. foreign relations.
   D. Affirmation would threaten to deprive the United States of the tool of VRAs for resolving trade disputes.
2. The Direct Evidence Case
   A. Direct evidence related to resale prices in Japan, check prices, and Five-company Rule, which did not prove agreement to charge low predatory prices in the United States.
3. The Circumstantial Evidence Case
   A. Under *Cities Service* plaintiff can survive motion for summary judgment only by showing that evidence is more consistent with inference of conspiracy than with inference of independent action.
   B. Conduct of defendants at least as consistent with independent conduct as with conspiracy. Secret rebates and sales at dumping prices consistent with independent efforts to penetrate a new market.
   C. To reveal secret rebates would have exposed defendants to liability for violation of antidumping laws.
   D. Defendants may have sold at profitable prices. Third Circuit did not analyze evidence of below-cost pricing.

Fig. 9.3. The Department of Justice Brief

validly conclude that the individual defendants had dumped independently to penetrate a new market as that they had conspired. Also, the defendants' refusal to divulge each other's secret rebates to the U.S. Customs Service did not imply a conspiracy, since by doing so they would have admitted violating the antidumping laws. Finally, the appeals court should have analyzed the evidence to determine whether the export prices were in fact below costs.

The Majority Opinion

By a vote of five to four the Supreme Court reversed the Third Circuit. The majority consisted of Chief Justice Burger and Justices Marshall, Rehnquist, O'Connor, and Powell, and Justices White, Brennan, Blackmun, and Stevens made up the minority.

The majority's critical argument for rejecting the direct evidence case was that the agreements, in and of themselves, could not have injured the plaintiffs (fig. 9.4). Concerning the alleged home market cartel, a footnote said that, while the Sherman Act reaches foreign conduct affecting commerce in this country, such a cartel could not depress U.S. prices. If the defendants raised home market prices, they could either reduce total output or sell more

Court granted certiorari on first two questions presented. Reversed the court of appeals on the first question and did not reach the second. Case remanded for further proceedings.

1. The Direct Evidence Case
   A. Plaintiffs cannot recover damages for conspiracy to raise prices in U.S. market or to impose restraints that have the effect of raising prices.
2. The Circumstantial Evidence Case
   A. Asserted conspiracy is to price "predatorily," which means pricing below some appropriate measure of cost.
   B. The requirements to survive summary judgment:
      i. Must show injury, which entails showing a conspiracy to monopolize through predatory pricing.
      ii. Plaintiffs' claim must make economic sense. Plaintiffs must exclude the possibility of independent conduct in individual defendants' self-interest. Plaintiffs also must show that the inference of conspiracy is reasonable in light of the competing inference of collusion that could not harm plaintiffs.
   C. Inference of conspiracy not reasonable. Lack of a motive to engage in predatory pricing.
      i. Defendants could not reasonably have expected to recoup predatory losses and earn monopoly profits.
      ii. Consensus among commentators on predatory pricing that it is rarely tried.
      iii. A predatory conspiracy is less likely than a predatory attempt by a single firm.
      iv. Prospects of achieving a U.S. monopoly were poor.
      v. Home market monopoly may provide means for a predatory attempt, but it does not supply a motive.
      vi. Plaintiffs' evidence of predatory losses has less probative value than economic factors.
   D. On remand appeals court may consider new evidence, which must exclude possibility that defendants were competing for business.

Fig. 9.4. The Supreme Court opinion

goods in other markets. The latter choice was the more profitable and therefore the more plausible one. As the Court said:

> That choice does not flow from the cartelization of the Japanese market. On the contrary, were the Japanese market perfectly competitive petitioners would still have to choose whether to sell goods overseas, and would still presumably make that choice based on their profit expectations. For this reason, respondents' theory of recovery depends on proof of the asserted price-cutting conspiracy in this country.[19]

---

19. 475 U.S. 574, at 582–83 n. 6.

Nor did the export agreements injure the plaintiffs, since they tended to raise prices. According to the Court: "Such restrictions, though harmful to competition, actually *benefit* competitors by making supra-competitive pricing more attractive."[20]

Although the Court agreed with the Third Circuit that the Five-company Rule limited competition, it doubted that the Rule prevented the defendants from underpricing one another. Their prices already were low enough to sell their goods. Despite its relegation to a footnote, the statement is important:

> The Court of Appeals correctly reasoned that the Five Company Rule might tend to insulate petitioners from competition from each other. 723 F.2d, at 306. But this effect is irrelevant to a conspiracy to price predatorily. Petitioners have no incentive to underprice each other if they already are pricing *below* the level at which they could sell their goods. The far more plausible inference from a customer allocation agreement such as the Five Company Rule is that petitioners were conspiring to *raise* prices, by limiting their ability to take sales away from each other.[21]

The footnote went on to agree with Judge Becker that, inasmuch as the manufacturers' sales subsidiaries resold to other customers, the Five-company Rule probably had no significant effect.

The bulk of the opinion focused on the circumstantial evidence case. Underlining the importance of the plausibility test, the Court said that not only did the conspiracy theory have to be plausible but it had to be more so than the competition theory. Applying McGee's analysis of predatory pricing in general, the Court decided that the conspiracy theory failed the test. Since predatory pricing was rare, the defendants were not likely to have preyed, and the summary judgment was valid. Although the Court affirmed the district court, its reasoning was different. Neither the defendants nor the lower courts had paid much attention to the general proposition that predatory pricing is rare. The defendants had referred to writings on the subject, but the independence issue took most of their attention, as it did that of the district court. McGee's general proposition achieved prominence only in the Supreme Court majority opinion, which leaned heavily on his writings and on those by Robert Bork, Frank Easterbrook, and Roland Koller.[22] The argument so dazzled the Court that the facts were virtually ignored.

---

20. 475 U.S. 574, at 583.
21. 475 U.S. 574, at 596 n. 20.
22. 475 U.S. 574, at 1357–58.

As in the direct evidence case, the primary issues in the circumstantial evidence case were the existence of a conspiracy and injury. The Court distinguished three alleged conspiracies in the export market, the check price agreement, the Five-company Rule, and the conspiracy to monopolize the U.S. market through predatory pricing. It said that only the last one could have caused injury. The check price agreement and the Five-company Rule tended to benefit the plaintiffs.[23]

A long footnote discussed the issue of what would have constituted predatory pricing in this case:

> This term has been used chiefly in cases in which a single firm, having a dominant share of the relevant market, cuts its prices in order to force competitors out of the market, or perhaps to deter potential entrants from coming in. In such cases, "predatory pricing" means pricing below some appropriate measure of cost.
>
> There is a good deal of debate, both in the cases and in the law reviews, about what "cost" is relevant in such cases. We need not resolve this debate here, because unlike the cases cited above, this is a Sherman Act § 1 case. For purposes of this case, it is enough to note that respondents have not suffered an antitrust injury unless petitioners conspired to drive respondents out of the relevant market by (i) pricing below the level necessary to sell their products, or (ii) pricing below some appropriate measure of cost. An agreement without these features would either leave respondents in the same position as would market forces or would actually benefit respondents by raising market prices.[24]

The statement that "predatory pricing" usually referred to pricing by a dominant firm is notable, inasmuch as even collectively the defendants did not acquire a major share of the U.S. market. Also, the Court was willing to consider costs. Since this was a Section 1 case, it did not have to decide the appropriate cost measure for Section 2 cases, which involve attempts to monopolize. Apparently, a case concerning a conspiracy to restrict competition did not require the selection of a cost measure. We note that the Court defined "predatory" as pricing below the level necessary to sell their products.

Citing *Cities Service*, the Court required a persuasive economic argument. According to the Court:

> To survive a motion for summary judgment or for a directed verdict, a plaintiff seeking damages for a violation of § 1 must present evidence

---

23. 475 U.S. 574, at 584 n. 7.
24. 475 U.S. 574, at 584–85 n. 8.

"that tends to exclude the possibility" that the alleged conspirators acted independently. Respondents in this case, in other words, must show that the inference of conspiracy is reasonable in light of the competing inferences of independent action or collusive action that could not have harmed respondents.[25]

Although "to exclude the possibility" is a more severe requirement than "reasonable in light of the competing inferences," Justice Powell evidently regarded them as equivalent.

Justice Powell held that the plaintiffs' claim was not sensible, since the goal of destroying competitors was implausible. Too, a long-run predatory gain was uncertain, and entry was possible. The Court added this view concerning the experts' conclusions: "there is a consensus among commentators that predatory pricing schemes are rarely tried, and even more rarely succeed."[26]

The agreements themselves were not proof, because they raised prices. The plaintiffs had to show a predatory motive. If the Japanese manufacturers had no such motive and other explanations of their behavior were equally plausible, then one could not infer a conspiracy. The defendants' prices had taken business away from Zenith and NUE, and they had limited competition among themselves. The opinion said: "This conduct suggests either that petitioners behaved competitively, or that petitioners conspired to *raise* prices."[27] Neither was consistent with an agreement to price below the level necessary to sell their products, which is to say, with a predatory conspiracy.

Elaborating, Justice Powell wrote that a rational firm will only prey on the expectation of later monopoly profits exceeding the forgone profits plus the interest on the forgone profits. Here the Court moved toward an opportunity cost definition of losses. The forgone profits were the difference between what the defendants might have earned had they not preyed and what they actually earned. The forgone profits were the predatory losses. To gain such monopoly profits a firm has to drive its rivals out of business, and it will not prey unless it has this expectation. The long footnote referred to earlier suggested a definition of predatory losses based on the ordinary concept of costs, which included expenditures for wages, raw materials, and so on. But the main text of the opinion shifted to the view that predatory losses were forgone profits. Thus, according to Justice Powell, the forgone profits were those that free competition would offer the alleged conspirators.[28] Further, the

---

25. 475 U.S. 574, at 587–88.
26. 475 U.S. 574, at 589.
27. 475 U.S. 574, at 597.
28. 475 U.S. 574, at 588.

Court said that the plaintiffs alleged that the defendants had conspired over a period of many years to charge below-market prices in order to stifle competition. Apparently accepting this definition of predatory pricing based on market prices, the Court said that such a conspiracy was difficult to carry out. According to the Court, the alleged conspiracy's failure to achieve its ends in the two decades of its alleged operation was strong evidence that the conspiracy did not exist.[29]

The Court then went on to show that the defendants had not achieved a monopoly. Zenith's and RCA's market shares had persisted. Although the defendants' collective market share rose rapidly to nearly 50 percent, it never was large enough for monopoly power. Accordingly, the expectation of long-range net profits was unrealistic. Evidently in the Court's view, if the defendants did not win a monopoly, they had not expected one. Moreover, monopoly prices would attract new competitors, unless they were barred by high capital requirements or strong brand names. Another reason the defendants were unlikely to have preyed was that the long-run profits were uncertain. Further, because the conspirators would fight over the division of the immediate losses and of the later profits and some conspirators might cheat, a conspiracy was even less likely than predation by a single firm. The Court believed that the anticipation of such problems would have stopped the Japanese TV manufacturers from undertaking a predatory scheme.[30]

Moreover, a home market monopoly may have enriched the defendants, but it did not provide a motive and so did not increase the probability of a predatory conspiracy.[31] Unless the defendants expected to capture a U.S. monopoly, with which to recoup their losses, they would not conspire to prey. To recoup the losses accrued over a period of two decades with interest the resulting monopoly profits had to last a long time. The defendants could not have expected the other conspirators to cooperate over so long a period, new firms not to enter the market, and to escape antitrust liability.[32]

The Court was influenced by a comment on the case by Judge Frank Easterbrook. A footnote quoted the comment in full:

> The plaintiffs maintain that for the last fifteen years or more at least ten Japanese manufacturers have sold TV sets at less than cost in order to drive United States firms out of business. Such conduct cannot possibly produce profits by harming competition, however. If the Japanese firms drive some United States firms out of business, they could not recoup. Fifteen years of losses could be made up only by very high prices for the

---

29. 475 U.S. 574, at 590.
30. 475 U.S. 574, at 590–93.
31. 475 U.S. 574, at 590–93.
32. 475 U.S. 574, at 592.

indefinite future. (The losses are like investments, which must be recovered with compound interest.) If the defendants should try to raise prices to such a level they would attract new competition. There are no barriers to entry into electronics, as the proliferation of computer and audio firms shows. The competition would come from resurgent United States firms, from other foreign firms (Korea and many other nations make TV sets), and from defendants themselves. In order to recoup, the Japanese firms would need to suppress competition among themselves. On plaintiffs' theory, the cartel would need to last at least thirty years, far longer than any in history, even when cartels were not illegal. None should be sanguine about the prospects of such a cartel, given each firm's incentive to shave price and expand its share of sales. The predation-recoupment story therefore does not make sense, and we are left with the more plausible inference that the Japanese firms did not sell below cost in the first place. They were just engaged in hard competition.[33]

Thus, for the Court, the chief question was the probability rather than the fact of predatory pricing. It was, however, interested in the evidence of below-cost pricing. Another footnote reported that the Court agreed with the district court's analysis of this evidence. According to Justice Powell, the appeals court had reversed the inadmissibility ruling, but it did not "disturb" the district court's analysis. The Court decided that the evidence had little probative value in comparison with the economic factors suggesting that such conduct was irrational.[34]

A third footnote explored the significance of the Five-company Rule, which the appeals court had reasoned might insulate the defendants from competition with one another. I quote:

But this effect is irrelevant to a conspiracy to price predatorily. Petitioners have no incentive to underprice each other if they already are pricing *below* the level at which they could sell their goods. The far more plausible inference from a customer allocation agreement such as the five company rule is that petitioners were conspiring to *raise* prices by limiting their ability to take sales away from each other. Respondents—petitioners' competitors—suffer no harm from a conspiracy to raise prices. Moreover, it seems very unlikely that the five company rule had any significant effect of any kind, since the "rule" permitted petitioners to sell to their American subsidiaries, and did not limit the number of distributors to which the subsidiaries could resell.[35]

---

33. Frank H. Easterbrook, "The Limits of Antitrust," *Texas Law Review* 63 (August 1964): 26–27. Quoted in 475 U.S. 574, at 591–92 n. 15.

34. 475 U.S. 574, at 594 n. 19.

35. 475 U.S. 574, at 596 n. 20.

The Court decided that without a plausible motive there was no genuine issue for trial.

Although the Court suggested that on remand the appeals court consider other evidence, it indicated that a finding of a predatory conspiracy was unlikely:

> On remand, the Court of Appeals is free to consider whether there is other evidence that is sufficiently unambiguous to permit a trier of fact to find that petitioners conspired to price predatorily for two decades, despite the absence of any apparent motive to do so. The evidence must "tend to exclude the possibility" that petitioners underpriced respondents to compete for business rather than to implement an economically senseless conspiracy. In the absence of such evidence, there is no "genuine issue for trial" under Rule 56(e), and petitioners are entitled to have summary judgment reinstated.[36]

On remand the Third Circuit found that Zenith and NUE did not present any evidence of a predatory conspiracy that the Supreme Court had not already seen. The Supreme Court's reversal was final.[37] Further, the Third Circuit held that the effect of the reversal on the charge of conspiracy under Section 1 also applied to the charge under the 1916 Antidumping Act.

The Minority Opinion

The minority would have affirmed the Third Circuit's judgment and allowed a trial. Justice White's dissenting opinion held that the Court's decision gave antitrust trial judges more discretion in deciding motions for summary judgment than *Cities Service* and *Monsanto* did and that the evidence raised genuine issues of material fact (fig. 9.5). The majority went too far in requiring antitrust plaintiffs to persuade judges before a trial of the plausibility of their allegations.

Justice White reasoned that in both *Cities Service* and *Monsanto* the Court had held that a piece of evidence standing alone was insufficient for a plaintiff to withstand summary judgment. These cases did not undermine the doctrine that in deciding motions for summary judgment the courts must give the plaintiff the benefit of the doubt. Justice White's sharp comment was:

> If the Court intends to give every judge hearing a motion for summary judgment in an antitrust case the job of determining if the evidence

---

36. 475 U.S. 574, at 597–98.
37. In re Japanese Electronic Products Antitrust Litigation, 807 F.2d 44 (3d Cir. 1986).

Minority would affirm Third Circuit judgment and remand case for trial.

1. *Cities Service* and *Monsanto* did not undermine doctrine giving plaintiffs benefit of doubt.
2. Genuine factual issue concerning harm to plaintiffs raised by experts' analysis of conspiracy in home and U.S. markets and of below-cost sales.
3. There was direct evidence of collusion.
4. Fact finder could reasonably conclude that the Five-company Rule was not a price-raising device.
5. Fact finder should decide whether defendants valued profit maximization over growth in light of evidence that defendants exported at losses over a long period. Court should not decide issue.
6. Evidence of collusive dumping and long-term below-cost sales may lead to reasonable conclusion that Five-company Rule caused plaintiffs to lose business that they would not have lost had defendants competed with one another.

Fig. 9.5. The dissenting opinion

makes the inference of conspiracy more probable than not, it is overturning settled law. If the Court does not intend such a pronouncement, it should refrain from using unnecessarily broad and confusing language.[38]

The dissenting opinion argued that the Court had ignored genuine material issues. According to the Court, recovery under Section 1 required proof that the defendants had conspired to drive the plaintiffs out of the market by pricing below either the level necessary to sell their products or some appropriate cost measure. The Court assumed that otherwise an agreement was harmless: it would either leave the plaintiffs in the same position as under market forces, or it would benefit them by raising prices. The plaintiffs, however, may have been harmed in other ways. Citing the DePodwin Report, the dissenting opinion suggested that the price-raising scheme in Japan reduced consumption of the defendants' products there and resulted in raising exports, which depressed prices in the U.S. The report also indicated that the Five-company Rule harmed the plaintiffs by restraining competition among the defendants in the U.S. market. The Court's preference for its own "economic theorizing" was no reason to prevent a trial at which the fact finder could evaluate these views on how the defendants' alleged collusion harmed the plaintiffs.[39]

Justice White disagreed with the Court's statement that the direct evidence had little, if any, relevance to the alleged conspiracy. The minority saw nothing wrong with the Third Circuit's reasoning that there was direct evi-

---

38. 475 U.S. 574, at 601.
39. 475 U.S. 574, at 601–3.

dence of collusion. It also agreed that, after reviewing the evidence of cartel activity in Japan, collusive establishment of dumping prices, and long-term below-cost sales, a fact finder might reasonably conclude that the Five-company Rule injured the plaintiffs.

The motivation for a conspiracy was plausible. Justice White agreed with the Third Circuit that a reasonable fact finder might conclude that the allocation of U.S. customers combined with price-fixing in Japan was intended to concentrate the effects of dumping on U.S. competitors while eliminating competition among the defendants in either market.[40]

The minority held that the Third Circuit was not required to inquire into the likelihood of predation. All that it was required to do was to decide that the defendants' long-term, below-cost sales created a factual issue, which it did. The issue was not whether the judge's analysis was better than the plaintiffs' experts' but only whether a reasonable jury could conclude that the defendants had sold at below cost over a long period.[41]

Justice White also criticized the Court's theory for consistently assuming that the defendants maximized profits rather than growth. The Court should have allowed this assumption to be argued before a fact finder, particularly in view of the evidence of substantial export losses over a long period.[42]

Comments

The Department of Justice Brief

The Japanese government's approval of the export agreements had an undue influence on the Department of Justice. Authorization by a government should not permit export cartels to destroy U.S. industries, and the foreign location of their home office should not exempt companies from U.S. laws. If the Webb-Pomerene Act is an embarrassment, then it should be repealed. It is a mistake to believe that the act gives U.S. companies parity with foreign companies in their ability to prey. Since U.S. antitrust laws prohibit establishing home market monopolies and independent, competitive firms will not prey on competitors in foreign markets, the act does not enable American companies to conduct foreign predatory attacks. Moreover, the U.S. government has never encouraged predation abroad. By contrast, the Japanese antitrust laws are much less effective, and MITI may actively champion predatory campaigns. Unless the U.S. decides to abandon its antitrust laws and promote its own exporters' predatory campaigns, why tolerate those waged by Japanese cartels?

---

40. 475 U.S. 574, at 604–5.
41. 475 U.S. 574, at 606.
42. 475 U.S. 574, at 604.

Also, U.S. companies have not taken advantage of the Webb-Pomerene exemption. Currently, only nineteen export associations are registered with the FTC. The members export cinema films, cotton, soda ash, phosphate, poultry, sulfur, wood chips, dried fruit, cordage, pulp and paper, tallow, produce, peanut oil, uan solutions, and cigarettes.[43] Since most of the products are sold in competitive markets, it is unlikely that the companies take advantage of the act to fix prices and divide markets.[44]

The evidence of collusion in the home market plus the export agreements, the large domestic-export price differences, and the defendants' large capacity to supply the U.S. market were enough to warrant prosecution by the Department of Justice. Unlike the plaintiffs in *Matsushita*, the Department did not have to prove injury to prevail in an antitrust case, and a victory in court would have resulted in an award of treble damages. The threat of a treble-damage award plus that of civil suits by injured U.S. competitors following such a decision would have deterred other foreign cartels from destroying U.S. industries. Moreover, it is highly unlikely that the Department of Justice would have tolerated similar behavior by American companies. Much of the Department's defense of its refusal to prosecute the Japanese television manufacturers was grounded on their nationality and the likely reaction of the Japanese government. However worthy good foreign relations are, this goal should not override the purpose of protecting U.S. industries against foreign monopolists. MITI should not decide the fate of U.S. industries.

The Majority Opinion

The direct evidence alone warranted a trial. The Court did not challenge the evidence of the existence of a conspiracy, and a complete and correct economic analysis would have shown that the market-sharing agreements had injured the plaintiffs.

Concerning the home market conspiracy, the Court did not take into consideration the likelihood of independent competitors setting export prices as much below the home market prices as the defendants did. It did not recognize that the defendants had to collude in the home market to enable them to set large domestic-export price differences. Independent competitors

---

43. Federal Trade Commission, *Export Trade Associations and Their Members Registered Pursuant to the Webb-Pomerene Act,* May 9, 1991.

44. The associations include the U.S. affiliates of foreign-based companies. The Japanese trading companies, Nichimen America, Inc., Sumitomo Corporation of America, and C. Itoh Cotton, Inc., are members of the American Cotton Exporters' Association. The French company Rhone-Poulenc Basic Chemicals Company is a member of the American Natural Soda Ash Corp. Three of the associations include numerous members. The American Cotton Exporters Association has sixty-two members, the American Poultry U.S.A., Inc., has fourteen members, and the California Dried Fruit Export Association has forty-one members.

with home market shares equal to those of the defendants might have discriminated in price between the home and export markets, but the margins would have been much smaller than those estimated by the Brugliera report. The home market collusion thus was a necessary condition for the size of the domestic-export price differences. Since the TV manufacturers only agreed to as low export prices as they did because higher prices would not have gained them the export sales, the home market conspiracy injured the plaintiffs.

The premise that all sellers receive the same price for an identical good, which refers to a moment in time, did not imply that the agreements raised the plaintiffs' prices over time. The plaintiffs may have received the same price as the defendants, but their prices fell over time. Since the agreements enabled the defendants to underprice the plaintiffs, they injured the plaintiffs. Moreover, the Court ignored the plaintiffs' loss of sales.

The single-price argument implicitly assumed that without the restrictions prices would have dropped farther and the defendants would have gained the same market share. But the prospect of unacceptable losses would have made the defendants loath to bear the costs of a campaign in the U.S. Exclusive rights to a U.S. distributor's purchases from Japanese suppliers made the attempt worth the costs. An unprotected manufacturer, contending with compatriot competitors and with the distributor playing them off against it, would have been pressed to cut its prices to marginal costs, which were well below average costs because of debt financing and the guarantee of permanent employment to workers, to say nothing of the buildup of capacity to supply the U.S. With agreements limiting their losses, the defendants were willing to undertake a campaign. The Court denied that the agreements had this effect, but the statement that the defendants had no incentive to underprice one another if they already were pricing below the level at which they could make sales assumed that they were behaving as a single firm. It was the agreements, however, that merged the firms for the purpose of selling in the U.S., and independent firms would not have undertaken a predatory campaign. For the Court the assessment of the direct evidence required no complex economic analysis. But the economic analysis was not as simple as the Court assumed.

The heart of the Court's rejection of the circumstantial case was that the alleged predatory losses were incredible. Here the Court did undertake what it understood to be a complex economic analysis of the defendants' conduct to ascertain the motivation. The principal issue for the Court, the plausibility of the conspiracy theory, hinged on the likelihood of a conspiracy.

The main ground for the Court's rejection of the plaintiffs' case was that the Japanese manufacturers would not deliberately have lost money over a long period to gain a U.S. monopoly. Easterbrook's comment on the case greatly influenced the Court. The opinion raised the issues of what was meant by losses and whether the goal was monopoly. The Section 1 charge alleged only that the goal was to destroy some competitors, not that it was to gain a monopoly. The Court interpreted the charge to imply the monopoly goal, for otherwise it made no sense for the defendants deliberately to take losses over a long period. Thus, what was meant by losses was critical.

On the issue of what constituted losses, Easterbrook's comment misled the Court. Although the opinion referred to costs in the usual sense, which it said were relevant to the issue of predatory pricing, its ruling was based on opportunity costs, which it evidently equated with home market prices. The opinion suggested opportunity costs as the criterion for predatory pricing by referring to competitive prices as a standard. It also cited the plaintiffs' assertion that the export prices were below the market. The market the plaintiffs obviously referred to was the home market. In addition, the Court, evidently following Easterbrook, said that the plaintiffs alleged that the losses accrued over the course of two decades. But the plaintiffs had said only that the export prices were below the home market prices over a long period. Easterbrook and the Court evidently interpreted the home market prices to be "costs." The plaintiffs' experts had said that the export prices were below costs in the ordinary sense for four years, so the Court was not referring to the experts' estimates. Justice Powell was referring to the allegation of persistent dumping. Moreover, the Court thus denied that the defendants had practiced dumping over some long period without challenging the plaintiffs' evidence. The Court broke with the traditional avoidance of fact finding. Here it became an active fact finder.

Although the Court cited McGee to support its position that persistent predatory pricing was rare because it was unprofitable, he had not adopted the opportunity cost definition of predatory losses. Clearly, the Court was confused on this issue. McGee did not define predatory losses as the difference between the but-for-predation price and the actual price. He defined it as the difference between average costs and the actual price. To apply the opportunity cost concept McGee would have had to define the predatory loss as the difference between the profit-maximizing price and the predatory price. Since the dominant firm's profit-maximizing price presumably yields monopoly profits, the predatory loss so defined exceeds that based on the average cost. McGee, however, used the average cost definition.

Easterbrook said, as we have seen: "The plaintiffs maintain that for the last fifteen years or more at least ten Japanese manufacturers have sold TV sets at less than cost." True, the reference to fifteen years or more suggested that the losses were the difference between the home market price and the export price. The plaintiffs had not maintained that the defendants had deliberately borne losses on exports over this long a period, only that they had been dumping that long. The Court may have adopted Easterbrook's mistaken interpretation of the plaintiffs' claim. In any case, unintentionally perhaps, the

Court based its rejection of the plaintiffs' case on an opportunity cost definition of predatory losses.

What is more, the opportunity costs were not the prices actually received in the home market. If the defendants had sold the exported receivers in the home market, they would not have received the then prevalent prices. The home market prices would have been depressed far below the current level. Indeed, the home market prices then would have been below average costs. We can get some idea of how much shifting the receivers exported to the U.S. to the home market would have affected home market prices by assuming that the long-run elasticity in Japan was the same in 1970, when NUE filed suit, as H. S. Houthakker and Lester Taylor estimated for the U.S. at about the same time. The long-run elasticity was the appropriate one, since the TV manufacturers added capacity to supply the U.S. market. The proportion of total output exported to the U.S. was too large for it to come from excess capacity built for the home market. Houthakker and Taylor's estimate of the long-run elasticity was 1.3. [45] That year Japan exported 40 percent of the monochrome sets manufactured in Japan to the U.S., and 20 percent went to other countries, leaving 40 percent for domestic consumption (table 6.6, p. 113). Thus, shifting the exports that went to the U.S. to the home market would have doubled the quantity of monochrome receivers supplied to domestic consumers. If the elasticity was 1.3 over the relevant range of the demand curve, the price would have fallen by 77 percent. [46] In the lower part of the range the elasticity would be less than in the upper part, so the estimate probably errs on the low side. Similar calculations for color receivers result in an estimated drop in the home market price of 13 percent. Since the overall average profit rate was a little more than 5 percent of sales, even the drop in the price of color receivers would have produced a loss. Thus, the manufacturers did not acquire the capacity for the home market, and the charge did not imply losses per receiver equal to the domestic-export price difference.

The true opportunity cost of an exported receiver was the average cost, including the cost of plant and equipment. As was already noted, the exports to the U.S. were too large a proportion of total output to be supplied by increasing the utilization of capacity built to supply the home market. Plant capacity had to be added to produce for the U.S. market. The opportunity cost of an exported receiver thus was what could be produced by the resources employed in its production, which is measured by average cost. The plaintiffs' experts estimated the losses on this basis for the limited period 1967–70. No

---

45. See chapter 3.

46. $e = \dfrac{\Delta q/q}{\Delta p/p} = 1.3$ and $\Delta q/q = 100$. Hence, $\Delta p/p = 77$.

estimate was made for losses either before or after this period. The estimated losses were not incredible. They were much less than the losses estimated on the basis of the domestic prices.

Further, the Court accepted McGee's statement that firms would not prey to either win or preserve a monopoly position and applied it in the present case. Here again the Court was confused. McGee's theory applied to dominant firms, not to firms with a small share of the market. The dominant firm's large market share implied immediate losses exceeding those of the victims. Yet the Japanese manufacturers, whose initial market share was small, could inflict large losses on the U.S. manufacturers at small cost to themselves.

The question of the probability of the defendants accepting losses arose only in connection with the issue of motivation. According to the Court, only the prospect of monopoly could motivate a firm to take losses over a long period, and, since that prospect was nil, there was no motivation to do so, and therefore the defendants had not borne losses over a long period.

This complex statement raises several issues. First, the preceding discussion of the definition of losses shows that the Court exaggerated the size of the losses by adopting the home market price as the measure of opportunity costs. As we have said, this issue was the central one for the Court's decision, and its choice of the current home market price as the measure was in error.

Second, it was the TV manufacturers' expectations that were at issue, not the actual costs or the actual prospect of monopoly. Without the benefit of hindsight the defendants may have been optimistic on both scores.

Third, with a small share of the market they may have anticipated eliminating their competitors at small immediate cost to themselves.

Fourth, the prospect of monopoly may not have been as unrealistic as the Court believed. Zenith's and RCA's large market shares could not prevent a tight oligopoly willing to take losses from taking over the market. The defendants' failure to monopolize the market was not evidence of an unrealistic goal, since the failure was due to the U.S. government's intervention through an OMA limiting Japan's exports of color receivers to the U.S., not to the cost or other advantages of the U.S. large manufacturers over their Japanese competitors. The Japanese TV manufacturers were able to underprice Zenith and RCA, despite the advantages of the U.S. firms, because they were willing to take immediate losses.

Fifth, the defendants' goal need not have been a complete monopoly to gain monopoly profits. A complete monopoly was not necessary to gain some monopoly power, and, as their market share grew, the defendants could raise their prices. They could keep prices low enough to discourage entry but high enough to earn what they considered to be a reasonable return. Such manipulation would have been difficult if entry was easy and rapid when the price was slightly above the competitive level. But entry may have been moderately difficult, and potential entrants would have been aware of the threat posed by the Japanese industry's capacity to supply the U.S.

Sixth, the defendants' conduct was evidence of motivation to eliminate competitors and acquire a large share of the U.S. market, if not of a monopoly. They added capacity to supply the U.S., they entered into agreements limiting competition among themselves, and they sold at prices below their average costs.

The Court also said that conspiratorial predation was even less likely than single-firm predation. This statement implicitly assumed the mathematical impossibility of a single firm's market share equaling that of the group of which it was part. In addition, collusion eliminated the enormous costs that individual manufacturers would have borne by competing with one another. Also, the combined capacity was necessary to supply a large part of the U.S. market. Moreover, dividing losses and later gains was not impossibly difficult. The market-sharing rules automatically settled the division.

The Court deemed the alleged low pricing to be inconsistent with the alleged market-sharing agreements. But the Court reached this conclusion only because it could not explain the behavior. There was nothing inconsistent between the acts themselves. The Court's competition theory could not account for them, but the conspiracy theory explains them quite simply. The low export prices were intended to eliminate U.S. competitors, and the market-sharing agreements limited the losses.

The Court neglected to consider in detail the evidence of the conduct supporting the allegation of a conspiracy. It did not consider the cost evidence. As the Court said, sales below cost might indicate a violation of Section 1. Corrections for the errors, alleged by Yamagishi, in the estimates of costs probably would not have eliminated the differences. The Yamagishi affidavit did not indicate how large the errors were. The plaintiffs would have had an opportunity at trial to examine defendants' employees and experts about Japanese accounting practices. The examination would have concerned the companies' accounting practices and the magnitude of the cost difference between selling TV receivers in Japan and exporting them.

The Court also neglected the capacity built up by the Japanese manufacturers for export to the U.S. The capacity was too large to have been intended for the home market. It is unlikely that competition for a large share of the domestic market led each of them to add so much capacity. The manufacturers agreed to output quotas, and during the 1960s, when the capacity was added, MITI's Industrial Finance Committee, which included manufacturers' representatives, regulated investment in new capacity.[47] Nevertheless, in the 1960s the TV manufacturers added greatly to their capacity, much

---

47. See chapter 2.

more than the domestic market could absorb, even at lower prices than those actually set.

The Court's analysis of the purpose and effects of the market-sharing agreements was incomplete. The discussion in the context of the evaluation of the circumstantial evidence did not go beyond what it had said in the part of the opinion dealing with the direct evidence. The Court said that it could not make sense of these agreements in conjunction with the reduction of prices because it adopted the competition theory. Instead of rejecting the theory, the Court refused to believe the evidence of market-sharing agreements and prices below costs. The conspiracy theory did explain the behavior. Thus, since the competition theory is incomplete, the conspiracy theory is more plausible.

The Court may have decided as it did because it was ignorant of Japanese attitudes toward cartels and monopoly power. It said that predatory prices were rare, but this rarity is partly due in the U.S. to a vigorously enforced law that deters companies from organizing cartels. Also, despite its inappropriateness, the McGee analysis carried a great deal of weight. McGee's analysis of predatory pricing concluded that it is rare. Accordingly, the Court concluded that the plaintiffs' allegations were implausible. This conclusion did not emerge from a careful examination of the plaintiffs' case—from the discovery of inconsistencies or conclusions without factual basis. It was not based on the particular facts of the case but was, rather, the offspring of a theory of predatory pricing. Treating the theory as though it were conclusive record evidence, the Court would not permit a trial. A close inquiry at trial into the details of the defendants' agreements and their effects was prohibited.

Moreover, the McGee analysis does not apply to Japanese cartels exporting to the U.S. The probability of their preying on U.S. firms is greater than that of U.S. dominant firms preying on their competitors in the U.S. Further, even if the probability is low, the Court should have allowed a trial. There was enough evidence in this particular case to indicate the goal of eliminating some U.S. companies. And, in any case, a low probability does not exclude the possibility of predatory behavior. To say that it does is equivalent to arguing that the fact that the vast majority of the population are not criminals excludes the possibility of criminal behavior. It is especially inappropriate for the courts to decide not to review the facts of a case on the basis of such a theory. Unlawful behavior, which presumably is rare, is the business of the courts.

While the Court said that it might have considered costs, it rejected the plaintiffs' study of costs and export prices on the same ground as the district court had. This is the kind of issue, however, that is best resolved in a trial in which experts present their testimony. The Court may have refused to accept the evidence, because it did not want to commit itself to a standard of predatory pricing, which it believed to be rare. It may have been influenced by the advice of one of the authors, then Judge Bork, to adopt no standard, because any such standard may do more harm than good.[48] Despite its statement that it was willing to consider costs in a Section 1 case, the Court may have feared setting a standard for Section 2 cases. Whatever the reason, it did not consider the cost evidence.

The theory that predatory pricing is unlikely contributed to the rejection of the evidence of losses on exports. The Court would not allow fact finders to reach implausible inferences of conspiracies. So important was the theory that the Court required plaintiffs to provide strong support for the evidence before accepting it, even for the purpose of evaluating the summary judgment. The theory was so persuasive that it overturned the law on summary judgments, which gave plaintiffs the benefit of the doubt. An economic theory, which rested on narrow assumptions of profit maximization, rationality, and foresight about the state of the U.S. TV market, and, which to boot was inappropriate to the facts of the case, overrode the evidence.

The Court would not have permitted similar cartel arrangements among U.S. firms. The reasons given by the Court for tolerating the defendants' agreements did not refer to their nationality; they were based on analysis of the economic effects. But suppose a group of American firms were to have behaved like the Japanese manufacturers did and increased its share of the market over time by underpricing excluded competitors. Initially the group would have had a small share of the total market so that its losses would have been small compared to those of the excluded competitors. But the members of the group would have built enough capacity to supply a much larger part of the total market. Surely, then, nonmember competitors could sue. The damage to the nonparticipants would consist of the lost sales at the prices that they would otherwise have received. If this was not a strong enough case, then perhaps the additional evidence that the participants in the agreements set prices below average cost would clinch the argument.

The Minority Opinion

The minority sagely argued that the direct evidence of a home market cartel, collusive setting of dumping prices, and below-cost pricing over a long period may have been sufficient to persuade a reasonable fact finder that the Five-company Rule was not merely for the purpose of raising prices. Justice White agreed with the Third Circuit on the key point that the rule may have harmed U.S. manufacturers, including the plaintiffs, by concentrating the effects of dumping on them while eliminating competition in both the home and export markets. The evidence warranted a trial.

---

48. Robert H. Bork, *The Antitrust Paradox: A Policy at War with Itself* (New York: Basic Books, 1978), 154.

CHAPTER 10

Conclusion

The Antitrust Case

The direct evidence amply demonstrated that the conspiracy had injured the plaintiffs. Clearly, the restrictions on competition in the home and export markets had enabled the defendants to take a large share of the U.S. market for TV receivers and to depress prices in that market. Collusion in the home market was a necessary condition for the large differences between home market and export prices, and the Five-company and Antiraiding Rules effectively combined the Japanese manufacturers into the equivalent of a single firm for exporting to the U.S. The rules enhanced their bargaining power with U.S. mass distributors and thus their competitive power against U.S. manufacturers.

The Supreme Court's rejection of the direct evidence was based on an incomplete analysis of the effects of the restrictions on competition in the home and export markets. The statement that collusion in the home market to raise prices could not affect the plaintiffs failed to recognize that independent competitors would not have accepted export prices as much lower than the home market prices, as the defendants did. The conclusion that the market-sharing agreements, which tended to raise defendants' prices, did not harm the plaintiffs failed to recognize that by limiting the defendants' predatory losses the agreements enabled them to carry out a predatory campaign. The direct evidence was sufficient to warrant a trial on the Section 1 complaint.

The Court also rejected what it deemed was the circumstantial evidence on the ground that the predatory losses alleged by the plaintiffs were improbable. The Court characterized the plaintiffs' estimates of the differences between the home market and export prices as alleged losses. It then proceeded to say that such large losses could only be motivated by the goal of monopoly. Because such behavior was improbable, the Court decided that it had not occurred. The majority opinion supported this conclusion by citing authorities, including McGee, Easterbrook, and Bork, who had deemed predatory pricing generally to be improbable, as well as with the arguments that the alleged losses were too large to be offset by prospective monopoly profits and that efforts to achieve a monopoly would have been in vain.

The basic flaw in this reasoning was to deem the differences between the home market and export prices as losses. The plaintiffs did not describe the differences as losses. Moreover, the plaintiffs' experts' estimates of losses referred to differences between the average costs and export prices, not to those between home market and export prices. And these estimates were for a much shorter period than the Court's two decades. The Court evidently adopted the view that the home market prices were the but-for-predation prices, which is to say, the opportunity costs of the exports. It was this view that led the Court to describe the alleged domestic-export price differences as losses. But the home market prices were not the opportunity costs, inasmuch as the manufacturers would not have been able to maintain these prices had they sold the exported goods in the home market. The prices would have fallen to a much lower level. Clearly, the capacity employed to produce the exported TV receivers was built for that purpose. Accordingly, the opportunity cost was the average cost, including the cost of plant and equipment, which was the cost of the resources used to manufacture the exported receivers. These resources might have been used to produce other goods.

The other errors followed. If the losses were large, as the Court deemed that the plaintiffs alleged, then they were predatory losses in the narrow sense, meaning that they were deliberately undertaken to achieve the goal of monopoly. If the Court had correctly viewed the losses to be smaller, then it might have concluded that the goal was, as the plaintiffs maintained, the more realistic one of gaining a large share of the U.S. market. The Court would not have had to invoke the generalization that predatory pricing—which is to say, pricing with a view to achieving monopoly—was rare, as asserted by various theoretical articles on the subject. In short, it might have attended to the facts of the case.

The theoretical articles evidently carried great weight. They were, however, not appropriate, since they did not deal with a market in which the predator had a small share. What is more, the Court misapplied the McGee analysis by using the home market price as the standard for defining losses rather than average cost. Also, the statement that the consensus among commentators was that predatory pricing was rare ignored the fact that the articles referred to dominant firms and not to predators with a small market share. And there was no consensus.

Most important, the Court denied the plaintiffs the opportunity of a trial, in which reasonable jurors might have found in their favor. What is astonishing is that the Court decided that the plaintiffs had not presented an issue of material fact and did so on the basis of a theoretical analysis rather than a review of the facts.

One of the considerations that influenced the Court was the possibility of chilling competition by exposing Japanese manufacturers in other industries to the risk of treble damages. Plaintiffs facing strong Japanese competition might bring antitrust suits. But allowing a trial need not make it easy for plaintiffs to win a predatory case. If, as in this case, plaintiffs show restrictive agreements, a monopoly in the home market, the construction of capacity to supply a large part of the U.S. market, export prices below domestic prices, export prices below average costs, and rapid growth of the defendants' share of the market, they should be allowed a trial. Such a case will not be easy to make. Effective prosecution of predatory cases need not deter exporters' competitive efforts.

As a result of *Matsushita,* the antitrust laws provide no protection for U.S. companies against predatory foreign monopolists. I have argued that the threat of predation by foreign monopolists, especially those based in Japan, warrants safeguards. But to merit a trial U.S. companies must now show that the putative predator sought to monopolize their market and that the probability of success was dangerously high. The evidence of predation presented in this case was not good enough. The Court has set up unwarranted and insuperable barriers to plaintiffs seeking redress against predation under the Sherman Act.

I propose that special procedures be adopted for predatory cases in which the defendants are foreign manufacturers. Following Joskow and Klevorick, I propose that a court take up such a case in two stages. In the first stage the plaintiffs will be required to establish that the defendants have monopoly power in their home market. This is analogous to Joskow and Klevorick's proposal that a domestic predator be shown to have monopoly power in its market.[1] As in antitrust cases dealing with domestic markets, the plaintiffs would have to examine concentration, the condition of entry, collusive arrangements among the leading firms, and profits from domestic sales. The plaintiffs would also be required to show that the defendants had built capacity to supply the U.S. market. Unless the plaintiffs showed monopoly power in the home market and the availability of capacity to supply a large part of the U.S. market, the court would dismiss the case. If a single firm had a home market monopoly, the case then would move on to the second stage. When the monopoly is held by several firms through a cartel the plaintiffs would also have to show that the defendants colluded in the U.S. market.

The second stage would be taken up with the export prices. I have proposed the domestic price as the standard for predatory pricing. If domestic prices persistently exceed the export prices by a substantial margin, then the courts should decide in favor of the plaintiffs. Sporadic price differences would be tolerated. But, if the price difference continued over a period exceeding, say, one year, then the court would rule that predatory pricing had occurred. I have defended the domestic price standard on several grounds: it is

---

1. See chapter 4.

consistent with the optimum allocation of resources worldwide, foreign monopolists would be prevented from destroying efficient U.S. firms, and it would protect U.S. workers against unemployment resulting from foreign companies exploiting their domestic monopoly power. A practical consideration is that the domestic price standard is easier to apply than the alternative standard of the average cost.

If the alternative standard is adopted, and the plaintiffs establish that the domestic prices have exceeded the export prices, then the defendants will be required to show that the export prices exceed average costs. The burden of proof will be on the defendants once the plaintiffs have shown that dumping has occurred. The definition of average cost should accord with economic rather than accounting principles. Thus, the average cost should be estimated on the basis of the current, best-practice technology and current wages, materials prices, and costs of building and equipment. Low book values of old plants should not be allowed to reduce the estimates of average costs when their replacement costs are much higher.

Plaintiffs should not be required to show motivation. They should not be required to show that the defendants were seeking to monopolize the U.S. market. If the plaintiffs show that the domestic prices substantially exceeded the export prices over a long period, this should be sufficient, once it is established that the exporters have domestic monopoly power and have built the capacity to supply the U.S. market and, in multidefendant cases, that they have colluded in the U.S. To require a demonstration of motivation would entail evaluating the probability of achieving monopoly power, which is difficult. Moreover, the defendants may have wrongly estimated the probability of reaching this goal, or they may have sought only to expand their market share. In any case, foreign monopolists should not be allowed to exploit their domestic power to prey on U.S. industry.

Nor should the plaintiffs be required to show that the defendants have succeeded in capturing a large share of the U.S. market. To impose this requirement would allow plaintiffs to bring suit only after a predator has destroyed a large part of an industry. Moreover, the failure to gain a large share may be due, as in *Matsushita*, to an OMA or other policy measures. Also, the predator may be more optimistic than it should be. In any case, the predator need not attain its objective to inflict damage on its U.S. competitors.

Implementation of this proposal would require legislation. As the law now stands, especially following *Matsushita*, the plaintiffs must show intent. In addition, the proposal calls for the special treatment of foreign predators. Also, it would specify the conditions that a plaintiff must meet to prosecute a case successfully.

Cases could be brought by the Antitrust Division or by private parties. The legislation would specify remedies that the courts could impose in cases brought by the government. The courts might impose fines that would be estimated on the same basis as antidumping duties. The fine would equal the difference between the domestic and the export price, after appropriate adjustments for circumstances of sales, multiplied by the number of units exported.

To ensure enforcement the law would also provide that, as in antitrust cases, private parties could collect treble damages. The possibility of such awards would induce plaintiffs to come forward.

The critical element in the proposal is the adoption of a price standard in predatory cases involving foreign defendants. To adopt such a standard Congress would have to be persuaded of the seriousness of the threat of predation by foreign monopolists, particularly those in Japan. The evidence of widespread collusion in Japanese industry, the numerous antidumping orders against Japanese manufacturers, MITI's support of export drives, and the ministry's tolerance and encouragement of restrictions on competition indicate that the threat is serious.

Economics and Law

The district court and the Supreme Court made it excessively difficult to establish that the defendants had sought to destroy competitors. The evidence of below-cost pricing, while not conclusive, should have been sufficient to allow a trial. The defendants' objections and Japanese accounting practices could have been evaluated, and the plaintiffs would have had the opportunity to estimate any errors resulting from the failure to include an allowance for selling costs. The district court was too quick to accept the defendants' objections and exclude the comparisons of export prices and costs.

The district court was unwilling to accept comparisons of prices that erred, even when the errors could be shown to be small. The court insisted on more direct estimates of prices than those based on the commodity tax formula, despite the formula's defensibility. Nor would it accept the comparisons of home market and export prices based on defendants' answers to interrogatories. Errors due to differences in selling costs provided the ground for the dismissal of these comparisons. The district court should have allowed a trial in which the evidence could be closely examined, since the estimates of the price differences were sufficiently large to withstand the defendants' objections.

An independent economist evaluating the evidence on prices and costs would have concluded that it warranted further investigation. This was particularly true for the comparisons of export prices and costs, since these might have played a crucial role in the assessment of motives. The independent economist would have recognized that correct estimates would have supported the plaintiffs.

More generally, neither the district court nor the Supreme Court carefully analyzed the facts. What was most astonishing was the characterization of the defendants' behavior as competitive. I have commented on the courts' analyses leading to the conclusion that the agreements in the export market did not harm the plaintiffs and that the home market collusion was immaterial. On both questions the analyses were incomplete. We have also seen that the analysis leading to the conclusion that the defendants did not prey on the plaintiffs was flawed.

Further, the district court and the Supreme Court were unwilling to permit a trial on the basis of the accumulation of all the evidence, preferring to interpret each piece of evidence independently for its significance. The home market monopoly was declared irrelevant, the agreements were declared not to injure the plaintiffs, and the cost-export price comparisons were dismissed because of errors. Unlike the competition theory, the conspiracy theory tied the pieces together in a coherent story that made sense. An independent economist would have tried to provide a complete explanation of the behavior. He or she would have seen that the competition theory was incomplete and might have recognized that the conspiracy theory made more sense. In any case, an independent economist would have concluded that the plaintiffs had presented a genuine issue of fact.

It is also evident that the Supreme Court did not read the cited literature on predatory pricing with care to determine whether the authors' models were appropriate for the facts in the case. The Court did not recognize that the defendants did not constitute the dominant firm, the subject of the literature. Nor did the Court pay close attention to the authors' definition of predatory losses. Moreover, it was careless of the Court to invoke the authors' conclusion that predatory pricing is rare to support its own conclusion that the defendants' alleged conduct was incredible.

It may be unreasonable to expect the courts to make correct economic analyses in antitrust cases. *Matsushita* demanded a complex analysis, and it probably was not unique. The courts may have to do their own analyses. No journal articles may have anticipated and analyzed the defendants' behavior. And the courts may mistakenly apply the conclusions of articles that appear to bear on a case but which, in fact, do not. In *Matsushita* the Supreme Court was mistaken in believing that its decision was consistent with what it called a consensus of commentators on predatory pricing. The problems raised by the courts' lack of competence in economics are particularly severe in relation to motions for summary judgment. The clash of rival views in a trial may result in an adequate exploration of the central economic issues. But a court does not have the benefit of such an exploration before a trial.

The weaknesses of the district court's and Supreme Court's economic analyses in *Matsushita* suggest that in complex antitrust cases the courts need the assistance of their own economists. The economic issues frequently are central even in cases based only on direct evidence. As we have seen, the Supreme Court rejected the direct evidence on grounds having to do with the effects of the defendants' conduct, which only an economic analysis could assess. The Supreme Court majority's decision was based on such an analysis, but it was incomplete. Moreover, it based its rejection of the circumstantial case on an economic theory of predatory pricing, which it misapplied. Also, we have seen that district court Judge Becker fancied himself an economic theorist. Not only is the assistance of an economist likely to improve the courts' decisions in antitrust cases, but also the knowledge that they have to confront an economist as well as a judge will improve the quality of the parties' economic presentations.

This is not to say that a court-appointed economic consultant is a guarantee of a correct decision. A case may present new problems that are difficult to analyze, especially when they concern motivation, and the existing literature may be of little help. There is the risk that an economist would be more prone to be swayed by a theoretical analysis and pay less attention to the actual conduct. The theoretical tools are the economists' stock in trade. In addition, the usual assumption of profit maximization may not be valid in a particular case. As Justice White pointed out, the Japanese manufacturers may have given priority to the goal of growth rather than that of high profits. Giving economists more influence is not without risk. But the significance of restrictive agreements and other behavior cannot be assessed without a theoretical analysis, which is what economists are trained to provide. The tools of economics were unnecessary to recognize that the market-sharing rules in *Matsushita* restricted competition, but they were necessary to determine the effects on plaintiffs' prices. The district court's and Supreme Court's analyses erred, and the risk of an overemphasis on economic theory appears worth taking. The courts usually pay close attention to the facts, and the assistance of an economist should improve the quality of the courts' economic analyses.

The Antidumping Law

The 1921 Antidumping Law did not prevent the predatory dumping of TV receivers, because the Nixon, Ford, and Carter administrations did not enforce it. The law itself appears to be adequate, especially after the change in 1974. If the Customs Service were allowed and had the resources to conduct the necessary investigations and to implement the law, predatory dumping would be deterred. The implementation of the law would be facilitated by easing the requirements for the proof of dumping. To a large extent the delays in the assessment of the antidumping duties in the TV receiver case were due to conflicts over the comparability of domestic and export models and to the determination of the domestic prices. The Customs Service should be able to determine antidumping duties on the basis of approximate estimates. Haggles over small differences only create delays, which render the law ineffective. In the case of goods from Japan the commodity tax method provides adequate estimates of the domestic prices. An administration that supports the law would be able to enforce it effectively.

The Reagan and Bush administrations and the Department of Commerce, which took over the administration of the antidumping law in 1980, appear to have enforced it more vigorously. As chapter 3 reports, the department has issued a large number of antidumping orders, and in many cases the anti-dumping duties have been large. Despite the more vigorous enforcement, however, Japanese manufacturers continue to dump. This suggests that the antidumping law alone is inadequate. It may be necessary for Congress to pass an amendment to the Sherman Act along the lines suggested here.

Elzinga and Fisher on *Matsushita*

The comments on the Supreme Court's decision by Kenneth Elzinga, one of the defendants' experts, also primarily concerned the profitability of predation.[1] Elzinga said that, according to the plaintiffs, during the period from 1968 to 1975, the average price charged by the Japanese manufacturers for color receivers was 62 percent of the "but-for-predation price."[2] The plaintiffs compared the export prices with the home market prices, so the 62 percent figure represents the export prices as a percentage of the home market prices. According to Elzinga's estimates, the manufacturers would not have been able to recoup their losses even over an infinite time period. His analysis of the predatory pricing in the monochrome market was similar.

As chapter 9 shows, however, the defendants would have been unable to sell the exported TV receivers in the home market and maintain the home market price. So, the home market price was not the but-for-predation price. Since capacity was added to supply exports, the appropriate measure of cost was long-run average cost. As chapter 6 reports, the plaintiffs' experts provided estimates showing that between 1966 and 1970 the defendants' export prices were below average cost, including the cost of plant and equipment. Elzinga did not comment on these estimates. His analysis spelled out the Supreme Court's profitability argument for reversing the decision of the Third Circuit. The criticism of the Court's reasoning on this issue in chapter 9 applies to Elzinga's argument.

Elzinga referred approvingly to the district court's conclusions that: (1) the evidence did not establish that the home market prices exceeded the export prices; (2) competitive, profit-maximizing firms may charge lower export than home market prices;[3] (3) the Five-company Rule did not always hold;[4] (4) the Rule was easily circumvented through the sales subsidiaries; (5) limiting competition among the Japanese manufacturers benefited Zenith and NUE by

---

1. Kenneth L. Elzinga, "The New International Economics Applied: Japanese Televisions and U.S. Consumers," *Chicago-Kent Law Review* 64 (1988): 941–67.

2. Elzinga, "New International Economics Applied," 952.

3. Elzinga, "New International Economics Applied," 959.

4. Elzinga, "New International Economics Applied," 960.

making it easier for them to sell to buyers who could not obtain supplies from more than one Japanese supplier; and (6) the Five-company Rule was inconsistent with the hypothesis of a low-price conspiracy.[5]

Elzinga also agreed with Judge Becker's conclusions with respect to the home market that: (1) the evidence of a conspiracy was untrustworthy; (2) it was not the work of economists to evaluate the evidence of meetings and documents bearing on the issue of a conspiracy; and (3) a home market monopoly did not supply a motive for foreign predation,[6] I have commented on these arguments.

Another of the defendants' experts, Franklin Fisher, also commented on the case.[7] Like the Supreme Court and Elzinga, Fisher was taken up with whether it was reasonable to expect the defendants to prey on U.S. competitors rather than with the evidence that they did. According to Fisher, it is not enough to show pricing below cost to prove predation. We quote: "One must also show that the price was reasonably expected to bring the supra-normal profits that would make it profitable. If not, then someone—possibly the defendant in its business decisions, but more likely the plaintiff's attorneys and experts in their analysis—has made a mistake."[8] Fisher referred to Elzinga's analysis of the likelihood of the defendants recouping the losses alleged by the defendants. He also said that predation cannot be at work when the pricing does not drive out competition. The large remaining shares of U.S. firms indicated that the Japanese were not engaged in predation.

I have commented on Elzinga's estimates. Chapter 9 discusses the persistence of the U.S. companies' market shares.

Fisher went on to summarize the Supreme Court's description of the difficulties that a cartel would have in maintaining discipline: (1) cartel members were unlikely to expect their predatory losses to be compensated, particularly since the market would not be "rigorously" divided;[9] (2) the participants would have an incentive to cheat, the defendants could not expect the market shares gained by predation to persist in the recoupment period when entry was likely; (3) the Five-company Rule did not protect the Japanese manufacturers against one another; (4) it did not ensure that each alleged predator would take its share of the losses; and (5) U.S. distributors could buy from the sales subsidiaries. We have discussed these arguments.

Fisher conceded that the customer allocation may have been necessary

---

5. Elzinga, "New International Economics Applied," 961.

6. Elzinga, "New International Economics Applied," 963–64.

7. Franklin M. Fisher, *"Matsushita:* Myth v. Analysis in the Economics of Predation," *Chicago-Kent Law Review* 64 (1988): 969–77.

8. Fisher, *"Matsushita,"* 970.

9. Fisher, *"Matsushita,"* 971.

for the operation of the predatory conspiracy and to that extent contributed to the plaintiffs' losses.[10] But, since the predatory conduct did not make sense even for a single, unified predator, he did not accept the argument.

Apparently, Fisher felt it was necessary to explain why the defendants had entered into the minimum-price agreement and the Five-company Rule. He ascribed them to MITI and its efforts to avoid friction with the United States.[11] To ascribe the agreements to MITI suggests, however, that the ministry expected the agreements to restrict competition, even if Fisher does not. If MITI expected the agreements to be effective, it is likely that the TV manufacturers did as well. Further, there was no evidence that MITI mandated the Five-company Rule. Also, the Supreme Court based its decision on the economic argument that a predatory conspiracy was unlikely, not on the sovereign-compulsion defense. Thus, to defend the Supreme Court decision the argument should explain why the defendants, under no compulsion, entered into the market-sharing agreements.

Fisher also discussed whether different prices in different markets implies below-cost pricing in the low-price market. It is not clear why Fisher addressed this question, since the plaintiffs did not claim that price discrimination implied below-cost pricing in one market. The plaintiffs supported the contention that the export prices were below cost with estimates of costs and of export prices, not with an analysis of the economics of price discrimination.

In support of his argument that price discrimination does not imply below-cost pricing, Fisher said that a monopolist gives up the marginal revenue from the sale of a television set in Japan by selling it in the U.S., not the price. The marginal revenue is less than the price. He also said that the same analysis applied to a cartelized market. The argument so far is unobjectionable, but it does not invalidate the plaintiffs' case. Indeed, as chapter 9 shows, the defendants would not have built as large a capacity as they did if they did not dump in the United States. The marginal revenue from shifting exported TV receivers to the home market would have been less than the average cost.

Fisher proceeded to the argument that price discrimination is consistent with a competitive home market. According to Fisher, "In the first place, if the two markets were separate, then there would be no reason to expect the two competitive prices to be the same."[12] I have no objection to this statement. There is no reason to expect prices to be the same in two separate,

---

10. Fisher, *"Matsushita,"* 973.
11. Fisher, *"Matsushita,"* 973.
12. Fisher, *"Matsushita,"* 976.

competitive markets. If, however, the Japanese market were competitive and the export prices were lower than the home market prices, then the Japanese manufacturers would not export. The two markets were not separate, inasmuch as the Japanese TV manufacturers exported to the U.S. They were only separate insofar as the Japanese market was closed.

Fisher also said that the two markets were not separate, since the same plants produced TV receivers for both. He argued that in that case the marginal cost to produce TV receivers for the export market should be the same as that for the home market. Accordingly, the competitive equilibrium of price equal to marginal cost should have produced the same price in each market. Fisher then said:

> The problem here is that one cannot conclude from this argument and the (alleged) fact of lower prices in the U.S. than in Japan that below-cost selling was taking place in the U.S. market. All that one can say is that it cannot be true that both markets were in competitive equilibrium. Since the appealing hypothesis (and the one urged by the plaintiffs) is the usual inference that the highprice market (Japan) was not competitive, it is hard to make much of this argument in an American antitrust action about predatory prices.[13]

Agreed, the Japanese market was not in competitive equilibrium. The appeal of the plaintiffs' hypothesis that the Japanese market was monopolized is heightened by the fact that the home market prices exceeded the export prices over a long period. The difference was not due to a temporary disequilibrium in the competitive Japanese market. That the home market was not competitive is also supported by the factual record. This conclusion, however, was relevant to the antitrust case, and it was also important for the plaintiffs' argument that the Japanese manufacturers preyed on their U.S. competitors. Independent, competitive firms would not have preyed.

The plaintiffs also said that the export prices were below costs. But this statement was not an inference from the difference between home market and export prices or from this difference plus the evidence showing a collusive oligopoly dominating the home market. The conclusion was based on estimates of export prices and costs. Fisher did not comment on the estimates.

Without saying so, Fisher appears to have equated predatory pricing with below-cost prices. I have argued that persistent dumping should be deemed predatory. Even accepting Fisher's view, however, the evidence indicates predatory pricing.

Fisher concluded with the following "moral":

---

13. Fisher, *"Matsushita,"* 976.

Below-cost pricing is an oft-repeated fear. Especially when foreign competition is involved, competitors are likely to complain when market prices are below their own costs, or even if prices are below what they would like them to be. While the story of predation is analytically sound, in the sense that it provides a consistent theory in which below-cost pricing takes place, the special nature of the story makes its applicability narrower than legend would suggest. Many economists find the predatory story hard (although not impossible) to believe. Fortunately, in *Matsushita*, where the story was truly incredible, the Supreme Court also refused to believe it.[14]

I do not dispute that the applicability of the theory of predatory pricing is narrow. The practice is unlikely to be widespread, especially by U.S. companies. The facts of the case, however, warranted a trial. The home market was monopolized, the defendants entered into agreements, which restricted competition among themselves and facilitated their predatory campaign, they built capacity to supply the U.S. market, their home market prices exceeded their export prices, and the evidence indicates that they exported at below cost. This story is somewhat more credible than Fisher said. Indeed, he conceded parts of the story, if not the conclusion. Apparently, the only item missing to make the story credible for Fisher was conclusive evidence that the export prices were below costs. Yet he did not attempt to evaluate the evidence. A definitive conclusion on the issue of the price-cost differences would have required a trial, which, unfortunately, the Supreme Court refused to allow.

---

14. Fisher, *"Matsushita,"* 976–77.

INDEX

AC. *See* Average costs
Adachi, Kaoru, 83, 84
Addyston Pipe and Steel Co. v. U.S., 54
Advice cartels, 25
Agriculture, in Japan, 12
Alcoa case, 146
Alexander's, Inc., 118
All-Japan Federation of the Associations of Radio and Electric Appliance Dealers, 77–78
Antidumping Act of 1916, 48, 53, 129, 132, 148–50, 164
Antidumping Law of 1921: court proceedings about, 117–28; enforcement of, 5, 7, 37, 49, 50–51, 125–28, 181–82; Japanese violations of, 4–5, 31–35, 117; scope of, 53
Antimonopoly Law, U.S.. *See* Sherman Act
Antimonopoly Law of 1947, Japanese, 23–28, 30, 36, 76, 80
Antiraiding Rule, 3, 97, 98, 100, 130, 135, 137–38, 175
Antitrust laws. *See* Sherman Act
Application for Confirmation of Shipment, 98
Application for the Validation of Shipment, 130
Areeda, Phillip, 62–66, 72, 149, 152
Association News (JMEA), 92
Association of Radio and Electric Appliance Dealers of Hiroshima, 80
AVC. *See* Average variable costs
Average costs (AC), 16–17, 63, 65–69, 71, 74, 104–9, 170, 185

Average variable costs (AVC), 16–17, 63–67, 69, 71, 72

Babcock, Barbara A., 124
Baker, Donald I., 155
Baldwin, Robert, 31
Bank of Japan (BOJ), 14
Bank of Mitsui, 20
Baumol, William, 67
Becker, Edward R., 2, 53, 82, 83, 96, 100, 102, 106–8, 132, 134–43, 145, 148–50, 159, 181, 184
Best information available (BIA) estimates, 36, 118
BIA. *See* Best information available estimates
Blackmun, Harry, 157
Bork, Robert, 152, 159, 173, 175
Brennan, William J., 157
Brugliera, Vito, 101, 130, 131, 149, 168
Brunswick case, 56
Bureau of Labor Statistics, 13
Burger, Warren E., 157
Bush, George, 182

C. Itoh trading company, 19
Cartelization campaign, in Japan, 24, 29, 73, 76–77, 158
Cartels: dumping by, 2, 31–36; market-sharing agreements in, 2, 3, 5, 29–30, 91–99; monopoly power of, 2
Carter, Jimmy, 4, 117, 127, 181
Case against Home Electric Appliance Market Stabilization Council, 28, 76, 133, 145